TWENTIETH CENTURY VIEWS

The aim of this series is to present the best in contemporary critical opinion on major authors, providing a twentieth century perspective on their changing status in an era of profound revaluation.

Maynard Mack, *Series Editor*
Yale University

BERNARD MALAMUD

A COLLECTION OF CRITICAL ESSAYS

Edited by
Leslie A. Field
and
Joyce W. Field

Prentice-Hall, Inc. *Englewood Cliffs, N. J.*

A SPECTRUM BOOK

Library of Congress Cataloging in Publication Data

FIELD, LESLIE A   comp.
  Bernard Malamud.

  (A Spectrum Book)
  Bibliography: p.
  1. Malamud, Bernard—Criticism and interpretation—
Addresses, essays, lectures. I. Field, Joyce W., joint
comp.
PS3563.A4Z64   813'.5'4   74–23353
ISBN 0-13-548032-9
ISBN 0-13-548024-8 pbk.

We are grateful to Farrar, Straus and Giroux, Inc., and Russell and Volkening, Inc., as agents for the author, for permission to reprint selections from the following works by Bernard Malamud:

The Assistant, Copyright © 1957 by Bernard Malamud

The Fixer, Copyright © 1966 by Bernard Malamud

The Magic Barrel, Copyright © 1950, 1951, 1952, 1953, 1954, 1955, 1956, 1958 by Bernard Malamud

A New Life, Copyright © 1961 by Bernard Malamud

Pictures of Fidelman, Copyright © 1958, 1962, 1963, 1968, 1969 by Bernard Malamud

The Tenants, Copyright © 1971 by Bernard Malamud

10 9 8 7 6 5 4 3 2 1

PRENTICE-HALL INTERNATIONAL, INC. (*London*)
PRENTICE-HALL OF AUSTRALIA, PTY. LTD. (*Sydney*)
PRENTICE-HALL OF CANADA, LTD. (*Toronto*)
PRENTICE-HALL OF INDIA PRIVATE LIMITED (*New Delhi*)
PRENTICE-HALL OF JAPAN, INC. (*Tokyo*)

Acknowledgments

We would like to thank the authors and publishers who have granted us permission to reprint their copyrighted works in this volume, and the authors who have contributed original essays. Our very special thanks go to Bernard Malamud for granting us an interview for use in this book.

J. F.
L. F.

Contents

From Bernard Malamud, with Discipline and with Love
   (*The Assistant* and *The Natural*)
   by William Freedman

Introduction

Malamud, Mercy, and Menschlechkeit

by Leslie and Joyce Field

I

By 1966 Bernard Malamud was already the author of four novels and two collections of short stories. International recognition for his literary achievements took a number of forms, not the least of which were a number of scholarly-critical articles, and a full-length critical book, to be followed in 1970 by a book of essays on his writings up to that time.

In many ways an evaluation of Malamud at that time was presumptuous: in the next few years he would add to his bibliography another novel and two collections of short stories, one of which could also be viewed as a picaresque novel. Malamud, of course, continues to write; evaluations of his writing are still premature. However, an ongoing dialogue about the direction of Malamud's work is worthwhile, especially in the light of his most recent fiction.

In *The Fixer*, all the themes which Malamud had introduced in his earlier works were refined and brilliantly reworked into their most powerful, controlled, and effective statement. In a recent interview Malamud himself reaffirms his current concern with a number of these interrelated themes. In our view, some of the most significant are a search for a new life in the manner of the *Bildungsroman*, i.e., a focus on growth and development from boyhood to manhood; the prison motif; the necessity for moral involvement, or freedom vs. responsibility; the value of suffering; the ritualistic and mythic elements in life; the search for a father or a son's displacing of a "father," or the scapegoat or orphan motifs; and a consuming concern with Love, Mercy (*Rachmones*), *Menschlechkeit*.

Although it may be difficult to sharply separate these themes because they are so closely interwoven, we believe that through an examination of these elements which permeate the works before and after *The Fixer*, one can see the continuity and development of Malamud's essential con-

cerns, as a writer and perhaps as a man. The critics in this book (and
in our earlier collection) do address themselves to these matters in one
way or another, as Malamud does also briefly in his own words. Thus
this collection complements the earlier one which appeared in 1970.*

II

The theme of a new life involves the protagonist's leaving his home
in search of change, a second chance, new opportunities. Sometimes
the change brings good, sometimes not.

On the surface, the change may involve only different surroundings.
But the change should—if it is going to be a good one—involve a
growth in the person from boyhood to manhood, that is, a giving up
of the selfish concerns of youth for an involvement in the problems of
mankind, an acceptance of life's responsibilities.

In *The Assistant*, Frank Alpine's conversion to Judaism becomes
such a change. But for Roy Hobbs, the failed hero of *The Natural*, the
change in his physical surroundings does not include this necessary
interior growth, and thus he is a failure.

S. Levin, in the novel *A New Life* (1961), goes West to a new career
in new surroundings and freedom. What he finds, eventually, is a third
new life when he gives up the Greek dream of freedom for the Jewish
acceptance of responsibility and moral entanglement.

When Henry Levin, in "The Lady of the Lake," changes his name to
Henry Freeman to escape his Jewishness, this denial of his past leads to
the loss of his beloved, a concentration camp survivor, who says she
has suffered too much for her heritage to betray it. Because Levin-
Freeman refuses to accept his Jewishness, his "change" brings him no
good.

In his search for the increased opportunities outside of the prison-
like confines of the *shtetl*, Yakov Bok shaves off his beard and changes
his name. This change brings disaster. Ironically, however, inside the
actual prison, Yakov learns that the purpose of freedom is to create it
for others. His change brings moral growth. By refusing to confess and
betray Russian Jewry, he accepts responsibility for the Jewish community and becomes actively involved in the fate of his people. This
novel, among other things, shows the growth of the hero.

III

In Malamud's fictional world, there is always a prison. It can lie in
the physical environment—a grocery store, a tenement, an artist's gar-

---

* Leslie A. Field and Joyce W. Field, eds. *Bernard Malamud and the Critics* (New
York: New York University Press, 1970).

ret, a bordello, a *shtetl*, or a real prison cell in a dungeon. But it can also lie in being imprisoned by one's own self and within one's self, being confined by one's ineptitudes and thus becoming a victim of one's own self.

Furthermore, some critics have said, Malamud's central metaphor of Jewishness *is* the prison, a perfect symbol for the human and most particularly the Jewish condition. Metaphorically, the prison becomes an acceptance of life's limitations and responsibilities in this sense. Thus, ironically, in imprisonment there can be freedom.

Robert Alter says that the prison "is Malamud's way of suggesting that to be fully a man is to accept the most painful limitations; those who escape [them] . . . achieve only an illusory self-negating kind of freedom, for they become less than responsible humans." * And Malamud himself has said recently that the prison is "a metaphor for the dilemma of all men throughout history. Necessity is the primary prison, though the bars are not visible to all. Then there are the man-made prisons of social injustice, apathy, ignorance. . . . Our most extraordinary invention is human freedom." **

IV

When Malamud was asked for his reaction to the many recent commentaries on the use of the *schlemiel* in his fiction, he replied "with many apologies" that he did not "much care for the *schlemiel* treatment of fictional characters." Of course he has a point if one uses the *schlemiel* as a reductive approach.

But just as there must be built-in tension between the president and the press, so there must often be a like tension between an author and the community of critics.

Many have recognized that from Roy Hobbs of *The Natural* and Frankie Alpine of *The Assistant* through S. Levin of *A New Life,* Yakov Bok of *The Fixer,* and Harry Lesser of *The Tenants,* and on through many of the short story characters—especially Arthur Fidelman who came to rest in *Pictures of Fidelman*—the Malamud *schlemiel* appears to realize a variety of themes and motifs. And the *schlemiel* operates powerfully in the recent stories collected in *Rembrandt's Hat.*

Whether the *schlemiel* epitomizes the born loser, the hard-luck guy, the poignant misfit, or, collectively, world Jewry, he has a long and honorable history. One can trace him back to the nineteenth-century Yiddish writers who gave us types like Tevye the milkman, and extend

* In *Bernard Malamud and the Critics,* p. 35.
** See "Interview" in this book.

it to the New-World Herzogs and Fidelmans. The *schlemiel* is a composite of history, legend, myth, and folklore. And underlying all is the comic element. More often than not the comic figure of the *schlemiel* seems to be a victim, but because he and his creators redefine his world, in the end he achieves the moral victory often denied to others.

V

Malamud's work presents us with the necessity for moral involvement vs. the seductions of freedom (disengagement) and examines the value of suffering. One becomes immersed in this area in much that is elusive and overlapping, not the least in the enigmatic statement that "all men are Jews." Recently Malamud recalled that he had said "all men are Jews except they don't know it." To be sure, he did not actually expect people to take his words literally. But he does believe that it is "an understandable statement and a metaphoric way of indicating how history, sooner or later, treats all men." * Though it is possible that Malamud has now said his last word on this matter, we doubt it. We believe that his definition of Jewishness includes such universal human virtues as moral obligation to one's fellow man and the community; acceptance of responsibility; being involved in the suffering of others; and learning from one's own suffering. Thus we have an expanded definition or a metaphoric elaboration. In Malamud this metaphor seems to find its most comprehensive use in the gallery of Jewish characters—Bober, Bok, Levin, Fidelman, and Lesser. Let us take Bok as our paradigm. Bok becomes the father-hero if one focuses on his last "vision." Here he symbolically kills the Tsar, the Little Father of Russia, and one assumes, as in ritual, thus displaces and replaces the Father. He reminds the Tsar that as leader of his people, he has failed to rule with justice and mercy and has thus failed in his charge. According to Yakov's view of Spinoza, if the State "acts in ways . . . abhorrent to human nature it's the lesser evil to destroy it." And, "better him [the Tsar] than us." One should remember that "us."

Yakov learns to accept his Jewishness, too. "We're all in history . . . but some more than others, Jews more than some." As Yakov concludes, "One thing I've learned . . . there's no such thing as an unpolitical man, especially a Jew." Truly "he had stepped into history."

As for the value of suffering, Yakov says while in prison, contemplating death because he thinks he can endure no more, "What have I earned if a single Jew dies because I did . . . if I must suffer let it be for something." Here, of course, he is echoing Morris Bober as he defines his role of suffering Jew to Frank Alpine. When his lawyer says

* See "Interview" in this book.

to him, "You suffer for us all," Yakov answers "It's without honor."
Nevertheless, by this time he has accepted his fate. How far he has
come in seventy pages! Earlier, "His fate nauseated him. Escaping from
the Pale he had at once been entrapped in prison. From birth a black
horse had followed him, a Jewish nightmare. What was being a Jew
but an everlasting curse? He was sick of their history, destiny, blood
guilt." In the last pages, however, *they* becomes *we*. Earlier he had said
that "he suffers for no one but himself." At the end he acknowledges
that he has suffered for all Jews. He notes that he has learned from
and been changed by his experiences: "I'm not the same man I once
was." Before the trial Yakov decides to fast "for God's world." The
guard says, "I thought you didn't believe in God." Bok answers, "I
don't."

Despite the complexities and nuances, we believe that the Bobers,
Boks, Lessers, and many other Malamud characters are ultimately revealed as people who become involved in one way or another, but
always positively, and always with the Jewish milieu.

VI

A great deal of Malamud criticism has been devoted to discovering
and analyzing his use of myth, ritual, and symbolism: vegetation rituals, seasonal patterns, fertility myths, Grail quests, The Fisher King,
the orphaned hero, the scapegoat, Christian symbols, and symbolism
of names. Much of this complex analysis is dependent upon a close
examination of the texts; unfortunately, popular commentary on Malamud's fiction often ignores the intricate symbolism and the patterns
of meaning which Malamud so painstakingly weaves into his work.

If one works for a moment with Yakov's name and the idea of the
scapegoat, some of the complexities and nuances become apparent. We
are all familiar with the old Hebraic use of scapegoat—literally a live
goat; the meaning is extended to a person or group bearing the guilt
for a larger group. The name Bok means goat, and Shepsovich means
son of a sheep. The charge of ritual murder against Yakov is really an
indictment against the entire Jewish nation, Yakov simply being the
"accidental" victim standing for all Jewry.

Seasonal patterns of myth are also apparent in *The Fixer* and are
quite important in *The Natural, The Assistant,* and *A New Life.* Certain events occur appropriately at specific seasons, thus leading the
reader to tie the present to the sweep of history and to ancient myths
and rituals.

We believe that one of the most important of the mythic elements
involves the search for a father—either real or spiritual, within or outside of oneself. Although the theme is found frequently in Greek lit-

erature and in the folklore of all peoples, historically the search for a
father is central to Jewish writings. Beginning with the Jewish pa-
triarchs—Abraham, Isaac, Jacob—it finds a further expression in the
story of Moses and the Exodus, and runs through the great history of
biblical kings where, between the ambivalent Davids and Solomons, we
have hostility and acceptance, hate and love. Overarching all is the
tension between the acceptance and the rejection of the Father of us
all—the One God. In this sense Malamud is a very Judaic writer, who
tends, ironically, to undercut the Christian themes that appear in his
work. Most of his heroes or anti-heroes or *schlemiels* are still young,
and are either orphans or have a vague, ineffectual father somewhere
in their backgrounds.

In almost all cases we have men who are free spirits, who insist upon
freedom—but at the same time are destroying themselves because of
that freedom. They have no purpose, no goal. And there is no one to
guide them; there is no authority. So, even though Frank Alpine and
S. Levin and Yakov Bok don't realize it, they are really looking for
that authority or guide which is represented by a real or substitute
Father and/or God. Frank Alpine accepts and then becomes Morris
Bober. S. Levin accepts responsibility as a father. Yakov Bok accepts
Raizl's child as his own. Even Harry Lesser accepts Willie Spearmint
as a brother-son. Perhaps one of the most important elements in Malamud's handling of this theme is that the Yakov Boks accept themselves,
their families, their communities; they step out of a nebulous history
in limbo into the Judaic tradition of Abraham, Isaac, Jacob—and the
covenant with God. Whether or not they would approve this formal
Judaic tradition, they have indeed become *mentschen*.

VII

This brings us to the humanity or *menschlechkeit* in Malamud—
love, mercy (*rachmones*). It is more than a coincidence that Malamud's
latest novel, *The Tenants* (1971), ends with a struggle to the death by
two writers—Harry Lesser (a Jew) and Willie Spearmint (a black man).
The final thoughts in the novel are given to the Jew—Harry Lesser:
as both men die, Harry is convinced that "each . . . feels the anguish
of the other." Then Malamud writes "THE END." After this formal
ending, we have the chorus of the Jewish landlord:
"Mercy, the both of you, for Christ's sake . . . *Hab
Rachmones*, I beg you . . . Mercy Mercy Mercy. . . ."
Mercy is then repeated more than 100 times.

We should recall too the final scenes in *The Fixer*: Yakov, as he
rides in the carriage from prison to the Russian Hall of Judgment,
imagines his confrontation with the Tsar—the so-called father of Rus-

sia. *"Rachmones,* we say in Hebrew—mercy, one oughtn't to forget it," Yakov says to the Tsar. Because the Tsar had no *rachmones,* he was destroying the Jewish people; therefore, Yakov, who in his imagination destroyed the Czar, was leaving the way open for the reappearance of the true father of the Jews and all people—the God of Mercy, the God who has *Rachmones.*

VIII

In 1958—when Malamud was just achieving recognition, he said in an interview that "The purpose of the writer . . . is to keep civilization from destroying itself." "My premise," he said, "is that we will not destroy each other. My premise is that we will live on. We will seek a better life. We may not become better, but at least we will seek betterment." "My premise," he continued, "is for humanism—and against nihilism. And that is what I try to put in my writings." In the following year—1959—in his address when he won the National Book Award —Malamud once again emphasized the important role of humanism in his writing.

In April 1968, with the Six-Day War not yet a year old, Malamud, now famous, was in Israel on a brief lecture tour. When asked about his role as a Jewish-American writer, he said: "What has made the Jewish writers conspicuous in American literature is their sensitivity to the value of man." "Personally," he concluded, "I handle the Jew as a symbol of the tragic experience of man existentially. I try to see the Jew as universal man. Every man is a Jew though he may not know it. The Jewish drama is a . . . symbol of the fight for existence in the highest possible human terms. Jewish history is God's gift of drama." *

In 1973, a few months before Israel's fourth major war broke out, Malamud may have inadvertently uttered a prophetic warning to mankind when he reiterated these sentiments, adding that to call every man a Jew is a way of "indicating how history, sooner or later, treats all men." **

West Lafayette, Indiana
November 9, 1973

* See *Jerusalem Post* (Weekly overseas Edition), April 1, 1968, p. 13.
** See "Interview" in this book.

An Interview with Bernard Malamud

by Leslie and Joyce Field

The following commentary and summary from an exchange of letters between Mr. Malamud and the interviewers from May 11, 1973 to August 2, 1973 reveal the nature and scope of this interview.

We wrote Mr. Malamud asking him to agree to an interview because even though his fiction is the important thing, we felt that a full-scale interview could contribute a great deal also. His response to a variety of questions would, we believed, be most helpful to readers, students, critics, and scholars.

Ours was a simple plan. We would spend a few hours with Mr. Malamud taping questions and answers. We would then send him transcripts of the tape and he would modify as he saw fit—to best reflect what he wanted to say at any given point. Our object was simply to get a straightforward series of responses to questions often asked about his fiction. But we left other options open. For example, perhaps he would choose to do all of this by mail rather than through a personal interview.

Mr. Malamud chose the mail interview route. He pointed out that in the past he had avoided most interviews, "especially when tape recorders are relentlessly present," because he was often unhappy with his own responses. He added that he dislikes explaining his fiction because by describing his "intent" he may in effect "betray" his work. He fears that people may substitute what he says about his writing for their own imaginative reading of his fiction. Thus a certain kind of interview could be self-defeating.

Mr. Malamud went on to say that he doesn't "like to say where stories originated, from what incident, real or imagined, from my life or anyone else's." He felt strongly that one shouldn't confuse the author's life with his fiction or even devote much effort to relating the two—"That's a critic's pleasure and not mine."

When the questions were sent to Mr. Malamud, we emphasized that we had tried to follow certain guidelines, some of which he himself had proposed. We would use only those questions which had been

"An Interview with Bernard Malamud," by Leslie and Joyce Field. An original interview-essay prepared for this collection.

asked in one way or another by readers, critics, students. We would try to avoid questions addressed to specific interpretations of his works, his characters. We would also try to avoid belaboring him with queries about sources. And, finally, we would try to eliminate personal matters.

We realized that we hadn't succeeded on all counts. However, we asked him to answer those questions he felt he could answer as completely as possible. He had the choice of answering part of a question rather than the whole. Or he could modify certain questions before he answered. In a word, we wanted him to be comfortable in his approach and to feel free to tailor the whole to suit his needs.

For the most part, the questions appear here as they were originally presented to Mr. Malamud. One question was eliminated. The one on baseball was recast by him, and he revised one of his answers. At his suggestion, a summary of our correspondence was used rather than a verbatim transcript of the letters. Finally, we believe we exercised our best editorial judgment in shortening a few questions when the answers were received.

The Fields. It has been reported that you once said: "A Malamud character is someone who fears his fate, is caught up in it, yet manages to outrun it. He's the subject and object of laughter and pity." Could you elaborate on this statement? Do you still consider that it capsulizes recent important Malamud characters—for example, Fidelman, Yakov Bok, and Harry Lesser?

Malamud. I can't work up any great enthusiasm for the statement but what I imagine it means is that my characters often outwit their predictable fates. I'd say that holds for Fidelman, Yakov Bok, and even Harry Lesser.

The Fields. How did you happen to write a baseball novel?

Malamud. Baseball players were the "heroes" of my American childhood. I wrote *The Natural* as a tale of a mythological hero because, between childhood and the beginning of a writing career, I'd been to college. I became interested in myth and tried to use it, among other things, to symbolize and explicate an ethical dilemma of American life. Roy Hobbs is as American as the White House lawyers involved in Watergate.

The Fields. As you know, the "academic novel" has been a subject of critical commentary. It used to be said, for example, that every professor of English had at least one academic novel within him that was crying to get out. Would it be accurate to say that a novel such as *A New Life* (although it obviously does much more than depict academic life) could not be written today because the campus is now a composite of a drastically altered set of symbols?

Malamud. This is an involved query concerning what to me was the simple act of writing a novel out of my experience. The "academic novel," as such, simply doesn't interest me.

The Fields. One fairly popular view has it that the *schlemiel* as metaphor or character in fiction is an uneasy transplant from East European Yiddish fiction to modern American fiction. As a matter of fact, two recent full-length books on the *schlemiel* conclude that the *schlemiel* as fictional character was able to work quite effectively for a Malamud and a Bellow up through the sixties. At that point these critics sound the death knell for the *schlemiel.* They say, for example, that an America which is going through (or has just gone through) Vietnam and civil strife, a country which is no longer considered a "winner," cannot accept with equanimity a fictional depiction of a "loser." How do you react to this commentary on the use of the *schlemiel* in fiction?

Malamud. With many apologies, I don't much care for the *schlemiel* treatment of fictional characters. Willy-nilly, it reduces to stereotypes people of complex motivations and fates—not to mention possibilities. The literary critic who wants to measure the quality and depth of a fictional character has better terms to use.

The Fields. When you received the National Book Award for *The Fixer* you said the novel was not simply a fictional retelling of the Beilis case of Czarist Russia, that it involved much more, that in some way it also owed much to a later horrible event in history—the Nazi Holocaust. Could you elaborate on this? Moreover, do you believe you could have used the Dreyfus case or the Sacco-Vanzetti case to express equally well what it was you had to say in *The Fixer*?

Malamud. My original desire was to write a novel based on the Sacco-Vanzetti case, but when I began to read on the subject I had the feeling that I couldn't invent a more dramatic story than the original. Since I was interested in how some men grow as men in prison I turned to the Beilis case, which my father had told me about when I was a boy. *The Fixer* is largely an invention. That is, I've tried to bring it as close to a folk tale as I could. However, in it I was able to relate feelingfully to the situation of the Jews in Czarist Russia partly because of what I knew about the fate of the Jews in Hitler's Germany.

The Fields. I. B. Singer has said he writes about devils, sprites, and evil spirits—about the supernatural in general—because he believes in the supernatural. Much earlier, Hawthorne explained that he wanted to find some "neutral ground" for his fiction. Your use of the supernatural has been compared to that of Singer and Hawthorne. Do you believe in the supernatural? Do you look for a "neutral ground" in your fiction as you order your supernatural or fantastic worlds? Or do some other explanations apply to this world of your fiction?

Malamud. I don't believe in the supernatural except as I can invent it.

Nor do I look for a "neutral ground" for my fiction. I write fantasy because when I do I am imaginative and funny and having a good time.

The Fields. In one of your early, infrequent interviews, we believe you said that Kafka was one of the modern authors who had influenced you. How?

Malamud. He writes well. He moves me. He makes me want to write well and move my readers. Other writers have had a similar effect. I guess what I'm trying to say is that I am influenced by literature.

The Fields. There has been much critical commentary concerning a statement you are alleged to have made: "All men are Jews." Did you ever actually make this statement? Do you believe it is true? It is, of course, a view one cannot take literally. In any event, would you elaborate on the "All men are Jews" statement?

Malamud. I think I said "All men are Jews except they don't know it." I doubt I expected anyone to take the statement literally. But I think it's an understandable statement and a metaphoric way of indicating how history, sooner or later, treats all men.

The Fields. Some have seen parallels between your work and painting, especially the spiral, mystical works of Chagall. This has been observed, for instance, in your short story "The Magic Barrel." Elsewhere readers have remarked on your concern with the plastic arts in general—in *Pictures of Fidelman,* for example. What influence has painting had on your fiction? Have you consciously tried to fuse one art form with another?

Malamud. It's true that I did make use of what might be called Chagallean imagery in "The Magic Barrel." I did so intentionally in that story, but I've not done it again in any other piece of fiction, and I feel that some critics make too much af Chagall as an image maker in my work. Chagall, as a painter, doesn't mean as much to me as Matisse, for instance. Painting helps me to see with greater clarity the multifarious world and to depict it simply.

The Fields. Saul Bellow, Philip Roth, Bruce J. Friedman, and other contemporary American novelists have rejected the label "Jewish-American Writer." In one way or another you have also. Nevertheless, you, the other writers mentioned—and one could bring in additional writers such as Chaim Potok and Herbert Gold—are still being classified as Jewish-American writers by many scholars, critics, and readers. It is our impression that the responsible people who place you and others in this category do not intend to reduce your stature or disregard the universalism they see in your work. They have simply categorized or schematicized as scholars are prone to do, much as one labels Faulkner a Southern-American writer because the spirit of place (the South) imbues his work or Graham Greene an Anglo-Catholic writer because a certain spirit of a specific religion permeates much of his significant work. How do you respond to this categorizing of you and your work? Would you reject the term Jewish-American writer categorically?

Malamud. The term is schematic and reductive. If the scholar needs the term he can have it, but it won't be doing him any good if he limits his interpretation of a writer to fit a label he applies.

Bellow pokes fun at this sort of thing by calling "Bellow-Malamud-Roth" the Hart, Schaffner and Marx of Jewish-American literature.

The Fields. Whether or not you accept the label of Jewish-American writer, would you not agree that your writing reveals a special sense of a people's destiny that more often than not cannot be fully grasped in all its nuances and vibrations by those who are not fully sensitized to that people or its destiny? On one level, for example, it has been said that one must be a Russian in order to respond completely to the nineteenth-century notion of salvation through suffering that is dramatized so well by Dostoevsky. Or that only blacks can truly appreciate the plight of black America. Could one not also say that only those who understand the *Yiddishkeit* of the characters or the Yiddish milieu are able to respond fully to the silent communication between a Morris Bober and a Brietbart or between a Yakov Bok and his father-in-law, and so on?

Malamud. I'm sensitive to Jews and Jewish life but so far as literature is concerned I can't say that I approve of your thesis: that one has to be of a certain nationality or color to "fully grasp" the "nuances and vibrations" of its fiction. I write on the assumption that any one sensitive to fiction can understand my work and *feel* it.

The Fields. Much has been made of the prison motif in your work. Do you see the prison metaphor as one that aptly describes the dilemma of modern man? If so, could you elaborate on this?

Malamud. It's a metaphor for the dilemma of all men throughout history. Necessity is the primary prison, though the bars are not visible to all. Then there are the man-made prisons of social injustice, apathy, ignorance. There are others, tight or loose, visible or invisible, according to one's predilection or vulnerability. Therefore our most extraordinary invention is human freedom.

The Fields. It has been noted that if one is to interpret your work correctly, one must not weigh Judaic interpretations too heavily. One must rather look to the Christian symbolism or perhaps the Judaic-Christian. How do you respond to this?

Malamud. I don't know whether there is a "correct" interpretation of my work. I hope not.

The Fields. You yourself have said that in your fiction you are concerned with humanity, man's humanism. Could you explore this notion somewhat?

Malamud. I don't think I ought to. People can read; they can read what I say. That's a lot more interesting than reading what I say I say.

— *The Fields.* Some have remarked that you are not interested in a novel of ideas as such, but in a depiction of human nature. Henry James, for example, was quite vocal in explaining his fictional approach (which he attributed to Turgenev's influence). That is, he would start out with a clearly defined character thrust into a specific situation. How that character responded to the situation became all-important. Do you believe your own fictional approach follows this Jamesian-Turgenev method?

Malamud. Basically, that's it, but I don't think I would limit my "fictional approach" to the "Jamesian-Turgenev method." One learns from Shakespeare as well. My novels are close to plays. I had once, as a young writer, wanted to be a playwright.

The Fields. The tension between life and art seems to be a major concern in your fiction. One could see it in some of your early work. And as recently as *The Tenants* and *Rembrandt's Hat* it is obvious that this tension is still a significant part of your fiction. Of course *Pictures of Fidelman* is introduced by the epigraphs taken from Rilke and Yeats, and is followed by A. Fidelman's terse conclusion. Many would agree that life versus art is central to the Fidelman stories. Do you concur? Can you perhaps now probe in a bit more detail the life versus art theme as you see it?

Malamud. It isn't life versus art necessarily; it's life *and* art. On Fidelman's tombstone read: "I kept my finger in art." The point is I don't have large thoughts of life versus art; I try to deepen any given situation.

The Fields. As one reads through your work one is tempted to continue pairing concepts, terms such as the life and art mentioned earlier. Another pair—love and redemption—comes to mind. The Frank Alpines and Yakov Boks, for example, apparently do redeem themselves. But terms such as love, humanity, belonging, compassion or *rachmones* or *menschlechkeit* (and other terms as well) seem to slip in and out of one's consciousness in this context. In a variety of ways, you seem to demonstrate that love brings redemption to an individual. But both of these terms—love and redemption—are endowed by you with a multiplicity of meanings. Would this be a fair estimation? Or would you prefer one to place love and redemption into a narrower, perhaps more religious context?

Malamud. Yes, there are various ways. I wouldn't want to place love and redemption in a religious context, although acting out love and redemption may be a religious deed.

The Fields. Characters in your fiction from time to time wrestle with their Jewishness. In response to a question, Morris Bober defines Jewishness.

Bok ultimately feels he must rejoin his people. But these characters and others seem to adapt as minority people to the pluralistic societies they find themselves in—whether it be the United States, Russia, or Italy. One of our students recently noted that the current writers who frequently people their work with Jews—Bellow, Roth, I. B. Singer, etc. —and who explore serious matters concerning Jewishness, probe or suggest a variety of possible identities. These may involve religion, assimilation, acculturation, bundism, social action, etc. But Zionism (specifically seeking one's Jewish identity in Israel) is quite conspicuous by its absence. As a matter of fact, this student further observed that the real (in-depth) American Zionist novel has not only *not* been written, but probably will never be undertaken by a major American writer. Do you agree? Why has Zionism played such a minor role for the Jewish characters who have populated so much of our fiction during the last two decades?

Malamud. I agree. Writing about Zionism wouldn't interest me. I'd rather write about Israel if I knew the country. I don't, so I leave it to the Israeli writers.

The Fields. Not too long ago Robert Alter noted the black-white confrontations in *Rabbit Redux, Mr. Sammler's Planet,* and *The Tenants.* In the latter two books, of course, the whites assumed another dimension because they were Jews. It is perhaps no coincidence that these books emerged at a time of great conflict between blacks and whites in this country and in certain pockets of the country between blacks and Jews. Do you yourself see a new relationship developing in the United States between blacks and Jews? If so, how do you define this relationship?

Malamud. It's impossible to predict—it may go one way; it may go another. A good deal depends on the efficacy of American democracy. If that works as it ought—guaranteeing blacks what they deserve as human beings—a larger share of our national wealth, equal opportunity under the law, their rights as men, the relationship of blacks and Jews and other minorities are bound to improve.

The Fields. At one time you mentioned that even though a number of years separate your first Fidelman story from the last one, when you initially created Arthur Fidelman you had plans that went beyond "The Last Mohican." Can you explain why it was that they became a series of separate stories ultimately woven into a novel rather than a novel more in the form of *The Assistant* or *The Tenants?* Also, the name Fidelman. Some critics have played around with the name as symbol. Few, however, have noted that it is also your mother's maiden name. Was this choice significant or incidental?

Malamud. Right after I wrote "The Last Mohican" in Rome in 1957, I worked out an outline of other Fidelman stories, the whole to develop one theme in the form of a picaresque novel. Why do it the same way all the time?

I used my mother's maiden name because I needed a name I liked.

The Fields. Has your wife's Italian background contributed to your "Italian" stories in the same way that your Jewish background has contributed to your "Jewish" stories? We are talking here more of an Italian and Jewish context, characterization, and rhythm of place rather than simply settings and people that happen to be Italian and Jewish.

Malamud. Yes. I met Italians in America through my wife before and after we were married, and because she had been to Italy and could speak Italian like a native, we decided to live in Rome with our children in 1956–7. Through her relatives and acquaintances I was almost at once *into* Italian life and got the feel of their speech, modes of behavior, style. When I go abroad I like to stay in one place as long as possible until I can define its quality.

The Fields. Do you read much of the criticism of your fiction? How do you respond to literary criticism in general?

Malamud. I read here and there in criticism about my work when it hits the eye. I don't go looking for it. I like imaginative interpretations of my books, whether I agree with them or not. I enjoy criticism that views the work in ways I haven't anticipated—that surprises me. I dislike crap —criticism, favorable or unfavorable, that really doesn't understand what the books are about. I do take seriously insightful criticism of individual works that affirm judgments, negative or positive, of my own.

The Fields. Does teaching interfere with your writing of fiction or does it help and complement in some ways?

Malamud. I devote little time to teaching now—a quarter of a program, one class in the spring. Teaching "interferes" only in cutting down writing time. On a day I teach I can't write. But teaching helps more than it hinders. It gets me out of my study and puts me in touch with people. And I like reading, and talking about books.

I'm not arguing that the academic life is the life for a writer—often it restricts experience and homogenizes it; but I am grateful that when I was earning little or nothing as a writer, because of teaching, when I wrote I wrote only what I wanted to write.

The Fields. In *The Assistant* your characters are frequently referred to as *the Poilesheh, the Swede, the Italyener, the Norwegian, the Greek,* and even *the Jew.* In one sense it reminds one of Stephen Crane's use of *the youthful soldier, the cheerful soldier, the loud soldier, the spectral soldier,* etc. Were you attempting an ethnic view of twentieth-century urban America much as Crane may have tried to depict the world of the Civil War Soldier through a set of humors?

Malamud. No, I don't play those games. That's the way the Bobers talk.

The Fields. Another reference to Stephen Crane, a variation. Are you very concerned with drawing prototypes and archetypes in your fiction as opposed to depicting realistic human beings? In other words, do you find yourself deliberately flattening out some of your characters much as a Stephen Crane would do or as a Cézanne would do in painting because you are at times much more interested in something beyond the depiction of a recognizable three-dimensional character?

Malamud. I would never deliberately flatten a character to create a stereotype. Again—I'm not much one for preconceptions, theories—even E. M. Forster's "flats and rounds." Most of all I'm out to create real and passionate human beings. I do as much as I can with a character. I may not show him in full blast every moment, but before the end of a fiction he has had a chance to dance his dance.

The Fields. It appears that you rarely develop children or young characters in your fiction, especially in your longer fiction. Children are in the background often in novels such as *The Natural* and *A New Life,* but are almost nonexistent in other works. Have you been conscious of this characteristic of your fiction? Do you have any thoughts on this matter?

Malamud. I've got to leave something for my old age.

The Fields. Would you agree that yours is basically a comic vision of life?

Malamud. There is comedy in my vision of life. To live sanely one must discover—or invent it. Consider the lilies of the field; consider the Jewish lily that toils and spins.

The Fields. Do you see a major shift in the point of view of your recent short stories collected in *Rembrandt's Hat* as opposed to views you may have held when you wrote *The Magic Barrel* and *Idiots First*? There is still, of course, the concern with humanity or *menschlechkeit*. Is there more stoic acceptance in these stories?

Malamud. They're the stories of an older man than the one who wrote *The Magic Barrel* and *Idiots First,* possibly a man who knows more than he did ten or fifteen years ago.

The Fields. Do you read more fiction or nonfiction these days? At any rate, could you give us some notion of your current reading?

Malamud. I read a good deal of biography. I like some of the Latin American novelists I've been reading lately. I read too much half-ass American fiction and not enough good poetry. At the moment I'm rereading *Walden.* I'm also reading Jane Goodall's study of chimps, *In the Shadow of Man.* More than half of my reading centers around what I may need to know for my own writing.

The Fields. Would you say something about your writing habits, the physical setting for your writing, and perhaps along the way give a few clues about your earliest writing experiences, etc.?

Malamud. I've answered this question in an interview with Israel Shenker in the *N. Y. Times.** It's not a question that I love to answer more than once. Young writers have a legitimate but exaggerated interest in the way other writers work. To them I'd say the way to work is the way you write best.

The Fields. You've mentioned another novel you are working on now. Would you care to give us some idea of its direction and scope?

Malamud. I don't believe, as Hemingway seemed to, that you hex a work-in-progress simply by talking about it. I'm writing another novel—a difficult one, just started, which may not see the light of day. If it does, the opening paragraph may read as follows:

"Although it isn't yet end of summer, William Dubin, at one moment of his walk in the country—rural into pastoral—beats his arms vigorously across chest and shoulders as though he had suddenly encountered cold, the clouds have darkened, and a snowstorm threatens. He had, in a way, been thinking of winter."

The Fields. Can you think of other questions which have not been asked or which should be asked or which you would like asked? Perhaps you can supply answers for these unasked questions.

Malamud. No, I've talked too much.

---

* Reprinted as "Bernard Malamud on Writing Fiction: An Interview by Israel Shenker," *Writer's Digest,* 52:7 (July 1972), 22–23. Appeared originally in *The New York Times,* Oct. 3, 1971, pp. 20, 22.

Bernard Malamud and the Jewish Movement*

by Sheldon Norman Grebstein

Only those too perverse or fuzzy-headed to recognize cultural facts now refuse to acknowledge the existence of a Jewish Movement in contemporary American writing, and especially the writing of fiction. Saul Bellow, its brightest luminary, has been at work for more than thirty years. Bernard Malamud, a less spectacular but no less durable writer, began in the early 1950's. Even Philip Roth, just yesterday a child prodigy, has been around for better than ten years. In terms of simple longevity, then, the Jewish-American novel is more than a vogue. And with three such writers as Bellow, Malamud, and Roth, all versatile and consistently productive, it seems unlikely to fizzle out. As yet no signs appear of self-imitation, sure clue of a movement's degeneration. There is also an entire second string of writers of varying ages and abilities, Leslie Fiedler, Herbert Gold, Bruce Jay Friedman, to name but three. Not to speak of the Popular Front: e.g., Herman Wouk, Leon Uris, Jerome Weidman. Even those not aligned with the Movement, Norman Mailer and J. D. Salinger, contribute to it indirectly with an occasional half-Jewish hero and secularized Jewish *schmerz*.

Let's call this coincidence and coexistence of so many able Jewish writers just plain luck. After all, genius exists where you find it. But if luck were the only reason for this curious abundance of Jewish literati, and for the emergence of the Jew as a kind of culture hero, it wouldn't explain why so many of us read their books or why we are so fascinated by the Jew as literary character, or why, after twenty years, the Movement continues to thrive, or why these writers have had so much impact upon our consciousness. We have had Jewish writers before who wrote about Jews: Abraham Cahan, Ludwig Lewisohn, Ben Hecht, Henry Roth, Daniel Fuchs, Michael Gold; but whatever the reception of individual works—and it was sometimes enthusiastic,

"Bernard Malamud and the Jewish Movement," by Sheldon Norman Grebstein. Originally published in *Contemporary American-Jewish Literature*, Irving Malin, ed., pp. 175–212. Copyright © 1973 by Indiana University Press. Reprinted by permission of the author and publisher.

* This study was supported by a Faculty Research Fellowship awarded by the Research Foundation of the State University of New York.

as in the case of Gold's *Jews Without Money*—there was nothing that could be described as a movement. Thus it seems a safe assumption that this particular time and place holds something unusually salubrious to Jewish genius. Whence this phenomenon, then, that we have been witnessing for the past generation?

In part, it was engendered by a void, born to occupy the space left by the decline or demise of other movements. The time was ripe, just after World War II, for the Great War Novel, but that novel was never written. As it turned out, instead of an entire body of writing we were given a few good books, including two by Jews which presented significant and appealing Jewish characters, Mailer's *The Naked and the Dead* and Shaw's *The Young Lions*. Hemingway and Faulkner, great as they were, surrendered their domination of the scene when it became evident that their best work had already been done. The Southern School proved to be puny. And the black writers never have put it all together, their rage and their talent, though their day could still be coming.

But more important, the Jewish Movement responded to an urgent cultural need. In short, and this is now a truism, the Jewish writer was made the beneficiary of Hitler's death camps. We Americans, spared the war's worst horrors, had to know more about those piles of corpses, teeth, shoes, we saw in the newsreels. Whether out of guilt, morbid curiosity, or both, the Jew became important to us. In the Western imagination the Jew had always played a special role as wizard, magician, possessor of secret knowledge, but never before, until Auschwitz and Buchenwald, had such moral authority been conferred upon him. From hated, feared, or ridiculed figure, lurking on the fringes of the culture, he was transformed into the Man Who Suffered, Everyman. To Americans especially, ever respectful of eye-witness reports and ready to listen to the man who was there, the Jew compelled attention. If, as many believed, the annihilation of the Jews signified the end of the liberal ideal for human character, at least by hearkening to the Jew we might participate in the mourning, vicariously share some of the misery he had undergone, and perhaps gain a deeper understanding of what life was all about. Who could better instruct us than the Jews, those most expert and experienced sufferers? Others had taken a beating, yes, but what other group in human memory had been marked out for genocide?

Thus, the dominant and recurrent theme of the Jewish Movement, a theme which unifies its various members however different in method, is the theme of suffering. Furthermore, although such European-Jewish novels as André Schwartz-Bart's *The Last of the Just,* Elie Wiesel's *Night,* and Piotr Rawicz's *Blood from the Sky* treat the same theme with the unsurpassed authority of those who survived the anni-

hilation, their work does not comprise a movement. We cannot bear
their nihilistic suggestion that the suffering produced naught; or worse,
that the European Jews collaborated in their own slaughter. Our writers, just far enough away from the holocaust to feel its heat but not
be scorched, retain a little optimism, a little affirmation. With us, the
suffering is meaningful. It can even be redemptive, stirring up a faint
hope for the goodness of man after all. Jewish heroes may be *shlemiels*
or *shlimazels* but unlike the major trend of much other contemporary
fiction which depicts man as joke, cripple, or cipher, the Jewish-
American writer continues to emphasize the fundamental worth of life
and the possibility of humanity. Yet he does not retreat into the safe
orthodoxy of formal religion. His affirmation is tough, qualified, secular. He is religious in that he portrays man as more than matter, but
he is not pious.

I have been speaking about that abstraction "The Jewish Writer,"
but all along I have really been thinking about Bernard Malamud.
Bellow may be flashier and more intellectually impressive, Roth may
be subtler, shrewder, and funnier, but Malamud is to my taste the most
solid, the most consistently fulfilled, and—I might as well get this
chauvinism right out into the open—the most *Jewish*. What I mean is
that Malamud best represents the phenomenon of the Jewish Movement; not only is he one of its founders and major practitioners, he is
probably its best single exemplar. In Malamud's work we most clearly
perceive just those characteristics which define the entire Movement.

First and foremost, there is the theme of meaningful suffering, which
in Malamud also implies the quest for moral resolution and self-
realization. But the theme of suffering cannot alone sustain either a
movement or a writer's career. We can take just so much bad news.
Malamud's writing, like that of the Movement at large, is also richly
comic. Paradoxically, the comedy is at once a mode of expression of
the suffering and a way of easing it. With the Jew humor is an escape
valve for dangerous pressures, a manner of letting out things too painful to be kept in. (Could it be that one of the reasons we have able
black writers like Ellison and Baldwin but not a Black Movement, is
the prevailing solemnity of these writers?) Finally, the Jewish writer
speaks in a distinctive literary voice. With Bellow and at about the
same time, Malamud invented and perfected a fresh literary idiom, a
"Jewish style." This style consists of much more than the importation
of Yiddish words and phrases into English, or a mere broken Yiddish-
English dialect, long the staple of popular works presenting lovably
silly Jewish stereotypes (*Abie's Irish Rose*). Rather, it is a significant
development and expansion of the American colloquial style, established as a vital literary medium by Mark Twain. The Jewish style is
for the first time in our literary history a voice that conveys ethnic

characteristics, a special sort of sensibility, and the quality of a foreign language, yet remains familiar and eloquent to non-Jews. Although dialects and dialect styles tend to be reductive, rendering their speakers either funny or absurd, Malamud's style can evoke either tragic dignity or comic foolishness, or, miraculously, both at once.

These are the points I will stress in the pages to follow: suffering, comedy, style, as typical of Malamud and, by extension, of the Jewish Movement.

I

About suffering it is hard to say anything new because others have said so much. Virtually every critic who has written of Malamud—and there is already a sizable body of criticism—has examined this aspect of his work. In his lucid and intelligent first book on Malamud, *Bernard Malamud* (New York, 1966), Sidney Richman names this theme "redemptive suffering," which implies that the meaning of the suffering is to redeem both sufferer and, to some degree, those for whom he suffers (but not entirely, that's Christianity). Malamud thus follows in the ancient Jewish tradition of the prophets, Amos, Jeremiah, the Second Isaiah, who announce suffering to be the Jew's special destiny, evidence of his unique covenant with God, proof of God's concern in that only those who are loved are chastised, and the means of the Jew's peculiar awareness of his identity. Could Malamud have had this biblical passage in mind when he wrote *The Fixer?* The coincidence seems too close for sheer accident, embodying as it does the novel's fundamental situation and symbolism:

> I have given you . . . as a light to the nations,
>   to open the eyes that are blind,
> To bring out the prisoners from the dungeon,
>   from the prison those who sit in darkness.
>
> (ISAIAH, 42:7)

But this begins to make Malamud sound too holy, to suggest that his writing functions as biblical parable, which is not at all the case. He is a good Jew in his way, but he is not trying to rebuild the temple. As Malamud himself has said, "The purpose of the writer is to keep civilization from destroying itself. But without preachment. Artists cannot be ministers. As soon as they attempt it, they destroy their artistry." His heroes all suffer deeply, but they are also secular men whose suffering is not always voluntary, undertaken wholly for exalted reasons, or blessed by great rewards. Malamud's real concern is for the social and moral aspects of suffering as they impinge upon personality. If his characters expect some recompense for their misery, they would like it in the here and now. In sum, although we have no conclusive biographical evidence to assess Malamud's personal religious commitment, the testimony of his work suggests him to be an agnostic humanist. Some of his own remarks support that deduction: "My premise is that we will not destroy each other. My premise is that we will live on. We will seek a better life. We may not become better, but at least we will seek betterment." [1]

This is Malamud's real toughness, the factor that prevents his treatment of suffering from deteriorating into drippy melodrama or comfortable piety. He has a view of man which perceives the property of conscience, the seeking to be better, not as a divine mystery but as natural to humans as skin, hair, voice. Yet this basically optimistic concept of human nature is checked by an almost equally persistent view of man as greedy, treacherous, lustful, and often vicious. Cheerful idealist and hard-eyed realist peer out through the same bifocals.

Consequently, Malamud's depiction of suffering is ambivalent; in each of his major characters altruism and materialism combine as motives for self-sacrifice. In Malamud's first hero, Roy Hobbs of *The Natural*, materialism overpowers altruism. He has impulses for good but keeps making the wrong choices for the wrong reasons: baseball for glory rather than the joy of the game, a girl for sex not love, winning for prizes and payoffs. He never learns to live by the wise Iris' dictum, "Experience makes good people better. . . . Suffering is what brings us toward happiness. . . . It teaches us to want the right things." [2] Roy's venality is symbolized by two climactic episodes in the novel, in which he is twice stricken in the lower organs, suggestive of his errors in responding to the dictates of his appetites rather than his heart. When at the last minute his conscience does take command, he ruins the chance by giving in to other base instincts, anger and revenge. Again we ponder a coincidence: Malamud's only hero who submits neither to love nor to idealism, and whose sufferings are consequently futile, is his only hero not a Jew.

The Assistant, Malamud's masterpiece, achieves his most complex portrayal of suffering. Morris Bober seems a paragon, a holy man, in his honesty, his tolerance, his compassion. The dingy, starving store is illuminated by his goodness, so that when he instructs Frank Alpine in the meaning of Jewishness, "I suffer for you . . . , you suffer for me,"

---

1 Malamud has been quoted in print rarely and there is little biographical information available about him. The two quotations are taken from one of the few sources, a newspaper interview by Joseph Wershba, "Not Horror But 'Sadness,'" New York *Post*, Sunday, September 14, 1958, p. M2.

2 *The Natural*. Random House (Modern Library Edition), New York, no date, pp. 135-136. The original edition was published in 1952 by Farrar, Straus, and Cudahy.

his words have the force of his example.[3] Yet if the store is his earthly trial and his fate, it also serves as a retreat from the buffets of the world, a tomb and a prison. His daughter's final thought about him, at his grave, may be uncharitable but it contains truth: "He could, with a little more courage, have been more than he was." [4] This weakness in Morris, a flaw in his character, is symbolized throughout the novel by his vulnerability to natural forces, fire, gas, and at last the wind and the cold, which have been his enemies from the start.

Frank Alpine's motives are about equally divided between altruism and materialism. Conscience he has; it brings him back to the store to expiate his part in robbing Morris. He also aspires to a better life than that of drifter and hoodlum. And he has ambitions in love, for Helen. But there is a practical side to it. The store is warmer than the street or cellars. A job there offers food and a few bucks. Even the lowly status of poor shopkeeper or clerk is better than that of bum. And the girl is luscious: "Her body was young, soft, lovely, the breasts like small birds in flight, her ass like a flower." [5] When at the end Frank endures circumcision and becomes, in Malamud's cryptic phrase "a Jew," he has attained not only a moral apogee, the height implicit in his name, but has executed a deft romantic strategy as well. Helen can never again call him "uncircumcised dog."

The very title of *A New Life* repeats one of Malamud's basic ideas and the motive driving his heroes to their quests. Levin arrives in Cascadia on the run from his past as derelict drunk, his only conscious aim to make good out West. He wants only to please, to pick up experience, and then to win tenure as a college teacher. But all sorts of messes get dumped into his lap, literally in the opening episodes, figuratively thereafter. From private man he is transformed, willy-nilly, into a champion of the liberal arts, departmental reformer, and tender lover of another man's wife. To settle for merely making good means to collaborate in the fractured state of things, a dilemma symbolized by the cracked pane of glass in his office window looking out upon the campus. Should he sit there in comfort and security, mouth shut, and earn success, or should he try to right wrongs, thus breaking his chances for advancement? For a Malamudian hero it's a foregone conclusion. Thus, although he arrives empty-handed, he leaves with his hands full: the other man's wife, whom he has loved but no longer wants, her children, and a child of his own growing inside her. Why does he accept the responsibility? Out of some nutty Jewish compulsion for self-sacrifice, a mystery, wonderfully dramatized in a culminating scene

[3] *The Assistant*. Farrar, Straus, and Giroux, New York, 1957, p. 125.
[4] Ibid., p. 230.
[5] Ibid., p. 75.

between Levin and Gilley, the novel's bad guy, who has just offered to let him off the hook:

> "An older woman than yourself and not dependable, plus two adopted kids, no choice of yours, no job or promise of one, and other assorted headaches. Why take that load on yourself?"
> "Because I can, you son of a bitch." [6]

The same motivation must apply to Yakov Bok, hero of *The Fixer*. He endures the dreadful misery of his imprisonment not because of any lofty ideals but because he *must* do it. Even when he is made aware that his case has become a national concern and that his fate will affect the destiny of all Russian Jews, he refuses to surrender to his captors' threats or be seduced by their deals, not because he is a saintly martyr or idealist but because he is too stubborn to give in. Hate for his tormentors sustains him much more than love for mankind. Where idealism does enter into the novel, it appears only in glimmers. The most splendid example of it is Bibikov, the magistrate, whose attempt to get Yakov fair treatment under law results in his own death—although it should be noted that Bibikov acts perhaps less out of charity for Yakov than out of his own strict sense of duty and legality. Nevertheless, in standing by the law, Bibikov becomes, in Malamud's definition, a true Jew. Another case is the guard Kogin, who intercedes to save Yakov's life at the cost of his own. And then there is Yakov himself, who gives his name to his unfaithful and runaway wife's bastard child.

But despite these occasional miracles of character refined by suffering, the book more often than not stresses how suffering brutalizes, and man's brutishness in general. If *The Fixer* teaches a lesson, I read that lesson to be how the death camps were possible. By simple tabulation there are far more demented, stupid, ruthless, or sadistic people in *The Fixer* than decent men. Grubeshov, Father Anastasy, Berezhinsky, Marfa Golov—these seem to be the norm for human character. Ultimately only two affirmations rescue the book from bleakest despair: Yakov has been physically bent and weakened by his imprisonment but he has not been broken; and he will, finally, have his day in court. The persecuted and despised Jew will at last be heard.

Contrary to his name, Fidelman, the hero of Malamud's recent work *Pictures of Fidelman* is not so faithful. Innocent abroad in crafty, depraved Italy, he races around with his heart in his pants and his eye on Michelangelo's ceilings. Between his ambitions in art and his hot pants, he falls into much suffering. The sex complications are nothing

---

[6] *A New Life.* Dell, New York, 1963, p. 330. The original edition was published in 1961 by Farrar, Straus, and Cudahy.

new in Malamud, though never before rendered in such quantity or gusto; Malamud's men are always wanting women who are not good for them, having them, and then paying more than they can afford in emotional or moral currency. Throughout his work Malamud intimates that a Jew can't have sex just for fun, that it always gets complicated; and if we adduce the testimony of such other works as *Herzog* and *Portnoy's Complaint*, there seems to be a concurrence of Jewish opinion on the subject.

But sex and its problems is not the real subject of *Pictures of Fidelman*; it only shapes the plot. The novel's real subject is art, and the questions the book poses under its comic breath are about art: What is the relation of art to life? Which is more important in the making of good art, the artist's vision (i.e., character) or talent? Or, in terms of the subject of suffering: How is the artist's experience (suffering) transformed into art? If I interpret the book rightly, the answers it seems to give back are essentially anti-formalistic. To translate the concluding episode into a paradigm, a translation it demands, it says that before one can become a craftsman one must submit oneself in love to another, and be taught craft by him and the experience of love. Malamud makes the point with a startling sexual metaphor: that the love which leads to craft begins with the actual penetration by another. Fidelman finally abandons bad art and becomes a good craftsman, just as he becomes a good lover—instructed in both craft and love not by a woman but by a man. The novel's concluding sentence is at once absolutely clear as a culmination to Fidelman's saga and tantalizingly ambiguous as a general suggestion for conduct: "In America he worked as a craftsman in glass and loved men and women." [7]

The same emphasis on loving and its costs that we have seen in Malamud's novels is reiterated in his stories, from the first tale in *The Magic Barrel*, which ends with a man undergoing an unjust trial to prove a worthiness already proven, to the last story in *Idiots First*, wherein a man kills himself to share the fate of the wife he has abandoned, herself a martyr to their vows. But as suggested in this story, "The German Refugee," and in such others as "Take Pity" and "The Death of Me," suffering for love can cost almost too much. If there are gains for Malamud's characters, they can usually be measured only in moral inches. Not always is man's capacity to suffer for his loving enough to fend off the angel of death, as it does momentarily in the fable "Idiots First." Malamud's affirmation burns too much to be everyone's dish of tea. It is a sweeter brew than the *goyische* wormwood and gall served by the likes of Burroughs and Beckett, but it is hardly

---

[7] *Pictures of Fidelman.* Farrar, Straus, and Giroux, New York, 1969, p. 208.

bland. As Malamud himself admitted, he writes not with horror but

II

Much of the sweetening, or more accurately bittersweetening, comes
from the comedy, almost as typical of Malamud's work as its concern
with suffering. Characteristic of Jewish humor, Malamud generally
avoids such generally common sources of wit as pun, word-play, intellectual humor (although one finds some of this in Bellow). Traditionally, Jewish humor is stark, edged, cynical. It communicates the double
view of the man who is supposedly superior to the common run of
humanity because he has been chosen, but finds in actuality that he has
really been singled out for extra knocks on the head, dealt by those to
whom he is presumably superior. Consequently, Jewish humor mocks,
sneers at human foibles and pretensions, and delivers ironic observa-
tions about itself and its practitioners, the chosen people. Frequently
it verges on self-hatred ("An anti-semite is a man who hates Jews more
than he should"), or conveys the desperation of a wisdom about moral
conduct which is impossible to practice. While scholars of Jewish
culture tend to minimize or overlook it, there is also a coarse and
bawdy strain of Yiddish humor, as I know from the jokes I heard as I
was growing up, a humor of natural functions: eating, evacuation,
sexuality. Perhaps this latter humor was adapted from the peasantry
who surrounded the Jewish enclaves in Eastern Europe, sustained and
enlarged in America by what it took from the urban streets. Finally,
there is that rich vein of Jewish humor which deals with the fantastic,
the incredible, the bizarre, treating them as though they were commonplace.

Although, as I will demonstrate, Malamud draws upon all these varieties of humor, I find the mode of fantastic comedy particularly interesting and successful. In this mode Malamud implies the imma-
nence of a spiritual dimension or realm of human experience without
committing himself to a specific faith, doctrine, or theology. In short,
the fantastic and the metaphysical enter into Malamud's world as
though they were fact, and he solidifies them and ties them to earth by
depicting them in the same voice and with the same solidity of specifi-
cation that he uses for grocery stores and Czarist prisons. One might
say that this is Malamud's version of the quasi-religious folklore and
superstition permeating *shtetl* life, and as much a fact of that life as
its food and drink. Until recently this entire mode of writing and the
cultural experience it connoted was limited to Yiddish readers familiar
with the work of such writers as Mendele Mocher Sforim and Sholom
Aleichem. But in the past decade Isaac Bashevis Singer's fiction has

become widely known in translation, and Singer himself a distinguished member of the Jewish Movement. Malamud is thus the heir to rich Jewish traditions, and worthy heir that he is, he remakes them his way and reinvigorates them.

Fantastic comedy recurs throughout Malamud's writing, in various forms. It can be the central plot of a work, as in such stories as "The Jewbird" and "Angel Levine." In the first, a bird with a Yiddish accent flies through the window of a New York apartment, and availing himself of the Jewish custom of granting lodging to vagrants and strangers who ask it, takes up residence with the family. But the father, a Jewish antisemite, resents the bird's influence with wife and son, harasses the creature, and finally, we deduce, murders it. The bird, dying, identifies his assassins only as "Anti-Semeets." This story-joke is funny to the end, but not too funny. It sends up disquieting reverberations. In "Angel Levine," another story-joke, a black Jewish angel arrives to solace a poor man and his sick wife, but is repelled and deprived of his angelic power to heal by the man's skepticism. It takes searching and an act of faith before Angel Levine can be restored and do his job. In a little parable of race relations the Angel for a time descends to the kind of debauched behavior the skeptical Jew imagines as proper to Negroes. Again the goofiness turns into sobriety just as the tale ends. The humor in these fables derives from the credulous and matter-of-fact rendition of the absurd: a talking bird? a black Jewish angel? Why not? Too, Malamud's homey colloquial style (more of this later) strengthens the effect. Were the style more elaborate, the language itself fantastic, the whole thing would be only a gag. But the writer's manner of narration makes these events seem as ordinary as bread. In this way Malamud employs an archetypal principle of comic technique: incongruous juxtaposition. He also communicates the idea of Jewish transcendence, the indissoluble and simultaneous merger of the spiritual and the real.

The novels also contain a strong element of fantasy, which has a double function, especially in such primarily realistic works as *The Assistant* and *The Fixer*. The fantasy could be described as the leavening in Malamud's realistic bread, making it rise a little toward heaven; it can be thus interpreted as an extrapolation of that something in man which insists he is more than animal. It also functions to modulate, making the bread easier to get down by alleviating the dry taste of misery with some fun. And, of course, there is an aspect of Malamud's work which depends largely upon fantastic comedy for its substance.

Malamud's first novel *The Natural* is largely a work of fantastic comedy, and though a flawed book, there is such verve in it and such an abundance of talent, one might have predicted that this was to be Malamud's *métier*. In brief, Malamud transforms the national game of baseball, familiar to all and in which all are experts, into a contest among demigods and conducted as though it were a sacred ritual in a cosmic arena. This placing together of unlike pairs, baseball and the universe, already inspires a comic response. For the literary reader Malamud provides an extra dimension of incongruity by juxtaposing a sports story, rendered with the appropriate data and terminology, against a mythic context which draws upon the myths of the Quest Hero, the Fisher King, and, to some degree, the White Goddess.

All sorts of highjinks go on. The hero has superhuman powers as an athlete and rewrites the record book with his magical bat, Wonderboy, but, Malamudian man, is afflicted with an uncontrollable yen for the wrong woman. Though a wizard who, at one point in the narrative, inexplicably produces out of thin air a dead herring, a salami, a rabbit, and streams of silver dollars, he is no magician at coming through in the clutch. Roy's exploits at the plate sometimes invoke celestial responses: at his first hit for the New York Knights a little rain falls upon the parched wasteland of a field; when he has agreed to throw a crucial game, heaven sends down thunder, lightning, and darkness, and Wonderboy shatters in his hands. Too, there is an entire supporting cast of evil spirits: two dark and beautiful temptresses, a one-eyed gambler, a sinister judge who occupies a dark room at the top of a tower, and a malicious dwarf named Otto Zipp.

The pervasive dreariness of *The Assistant,* with its central locale of the dark store, is relieved and modulated by occasional but effective comic moments, notably one brief yet vivid episode of fantasy in which Morris Bober receives a visit from the devil and succumbs to his temptation. However, in keeping with the general method of the book, the agent of evil appears not in a spectacular scene but in a muted little encounter so close to credibility it can almost be taken as actual. I quote part of it here:

> At the counter stood a skinny man in an old hat and a dark overcoat down to his ankles. His nose was long, throat gaunt, and he wore a wisp of red beard on his bony chin.
> "A gut shabos," said the scarecrow.
> "A gut shabos," Morris answered, though shabos was a day away.
> "It smells here," said the skinny stranger, his small eyes shrewd, "like a open grave."
> "Business is bad."
> The man wet his lips and whispered, "Insurinks you got—fire insurinks?"
> Morris was frightened. "What is your business?" . . .
> "A smart man hears one word but he understand two. How much you got insurinks?"

"Two thousand for the store."

"Feh."

"Five thousand for the house."

"A shame. Should be ten."

"Who needs ten for this house?"

"Nobody knows."

"What do you want here?" Morris asked, irritated.

The man rubbed his skinny, red-haired hands. "What does a macher want?"

"What kind of a macher? What do you make?"

He shrugged slyly. "I make a living." The macher spoke soundlessly. "I make fires." [8]

In this scene we can discover how Malamud blends the fantastic with the realistic, for in such a novel as *The Assistant* the wholly bizarre and surrealistic would be an intrusion.

First, there is a basis of probability in the visit of a stranger whose profession it is to set fires, because among small businessmen facing bankruptcy, the fortuitous blaze—covered by insurance—is hardly an unknown phenomenon. Too, the macher's method, the strip of celluloid, is exactly that used by professionals. Furthermore, his argument, the guiltlessness of an act by a poor little man against the vast, rich, impersonal insurance company, consists of just the right logic for such a situation. Finally, a "macher" is, by definition, a man of affairs, an entrepreneur, one who knows what success is and how to get it. In this sense the macher appears as a familiar figure to all men.

But then Malamud cues us into the stranger's true nature with cunning, seriocomic hints. Harmless, even ludicrous, in appearance, he disarms by the way he looks. In his age he suggests the longevity of evil. The old hat and dark overcoat lend him the necessary cover of poverty and inconspicuousness, for machers who make fires should not call attention to themselves. The devil is all the more persuasive for looking ordinary. Yet we wonder about the costume. Does it also cover horns and a tail? The greeting of the good sabbath on the wrong day leads to the sure conclusion that the stranger is not a true Jew; or, to stretch the point a little, that the devil keeps his own holidays. The references to the stranger's gauntness, close by the mention of open graves, seem to portend man's mordant destiny—both the physical death and, if one participates in the exchange of "success" for an evil deed, the soul's death as well. Then, the tiny red beard and the red-haired hands suggest little tongues of flame. At last, the scene is completed when Morris descends (note that) to set the fire, only to be rescued by Frank. By this time, in Malamud's magical way, the interlude is neither so fantastic

[8] *The Assistant*, p. 241.

nor so funny. However, it has functioned both to underscore the novel's themes and to lighten its mood. In the same way the slapstick episode at Morris's funeral, when Frank falls into the grocer's grave at precisely the moment when the bereaved are overwhelmed by sorrow and burst into tears and lamentation, counterpoints the scene's sentiment by turning it for an instant grimly funny. Like the macher episode Frank's pratfall has moral significance, but in this case the downward movement signals an upward trend.

The fantastic component in *The Fixer,* to some degree anticipated by the characters' dreams and visions in *The Assistant,* consists entirely of Yakov's dreams, fevers, and hallucinations during his long and dreadful confinement. But these, however farfetched, are often too painful to be comic, even when they stage such improbable scenes as Yakov's imagined confrontations with the Czar. Indeed, the bitterness of Jewish humor is nowhere better exemplified than in *The Fixer.* A prevailing source of comedy comprises examples of the incredible misconceptions and superstitions about the Jews held by the Russians, misconceptions for which the Jews, not the Russians, suffer. I doubt if a more horrendous humor exists in any culture than this sort, frequent in *The Fixer*:

> The days were passing and the Russian officials were waiting impatiently for his menstrual period to begin. Grubeshov and the army general often consulted the calendar. If it didn't start soon they threatened to pump blood out of his penis with a machine they had for that purpose. The machine was a pump made of iron with a red indicator to show how much blood was being drained out. The danger of it was that it didn't always work right and sometimes sucked every drop of blood out of the body. It was used exclusively on Jews; only their penises fitted it.[9]

This is the double view of Jewish humor, with a vengeance, wherein the absurd stupidity of the Gentile—always good for a laugh—turns fearfully against the possessor of the superior intellect. Perhaps the only form of "comedy" more terrifying would be jokes about the gas ovens at Dachau, but we have yet to hear them. Another example of the inferior mentality of the Gentile, demonstrating that the persecutor is worse than those he despises, can be seen in a prison guard's recommendation of the New Testament to Yakov, all the more funny because of the grain of rough-and-ready logic in it. "The Old won't do you any good at all," Zhitnyak said. "It's long been used out and full of old graybeard Jews crawling around from one mess to another. Also there's a lot of fucking in the Old Testament, so how is that religious? If you want to read the true word of God, read the gospels." [10]

9 *The Fixer.* Farrar, Straus, and Giroux, New York, 1966, p. 139.
10 Ibid., p. 231.

The comedy of *A New Life* and *Pictures of Fidelman* abandons fantasy almost entirely. Rather, these novels depend upon zany and often bawdy situations and employ the earthy humor, burlesque, and slapstick which derive from human lusts, mistakes, and misconduct.

Two typical and hilarious examples of burlesque in *A New Life*, really two variations on the same joke, involve the condition of undress. In the first Levin disrobes to crawl into the hay, literally, with a waitress, only to have his clothes stolen *in medias res* by a Syrian rival. Perhaps Malamud means to comment on the way things are between the Arabs and the Jews, with the Arabs spoiling not only the Jew's pleasure at just the moment he is to take it, but also his relations, so to speak, with the Gentile world. In the second episode Levin faces his freshman class at the opening of the semester and, enthralled by the class's close attention to his every murmur and what he assumes to be their rapt sympathy with his lofty pedagogical ambitions, builds himself up to an almost ecstatic fervor for his mission:

> In his heart he thanked them, sensing he had created their welcome of him. They represented the America he had so often heard of, the fabulous friendly West. So what if he spoke with flat a's and they with rocky r's? Or he was dark and nervously animated, they blond, tending to impassive? Or if he had come from a vast metropolis of many-countried immigrants, they from towns and small cities where anyone was much like everyone? In Levin's classroom they shared the ideals of seeking knowledge, one and indivisible. "This is the life for me," he admitted, and they broke into cheers, whistles, loud laughter.[11]

Only he discovers, a minute later, that what he had mistaken for empathy and intellectual comradeship was, in fact, his students' bemusement with the open front of his trousers. This is another instance of the prevailing motif in Malamud, sometimes painful, sometimes funny, most often both at once, that Jews without their pants on are particularly likely to get into trouble. Indeed, these episodes presage the novel's major action, Levin's maladroit love affair with Pauline Gilley, wife of his department chairman.

Quite aside from the burlesque sexuality of *A New Life*, a matter which Malamud treats with decreasing emphasis and increased seriousness as the novel proceeds—and sex becomes love, and love becomes commitment—*A New Life* demands comment as the only instance to date of Malamud as satirist. Although the satire finally collapses under the weight of too much academic detail and too much debate, for a time Malamud's fantastic gift exhilarates his depiction of Cascadia College and its English department. In this respect the novel's scene temporarily partakes in the great tradition of satire as fable: Gulliver's Lilliput, Martin Chuzzlewit's America, Sinclair Lewis's Zenith, all of

---

11 *A New Life*, pp. 85–86.

them peopled not by *homo sapiens* but by goblins in human costume. The problem in *A New Life* is that the satire turns too grittily truthful, too near the quality of a *roman à clef*, and Levin, lovable and interesting as *shlemiel*-cum-lover, becomes something of a bore as academic crusader. Consequently, the novel is too playful to persuade entirely as realism and not playful enough to persuade as satire.

Pictures of Fidelman avoids that mistake. Although hardly Malamud's largest achievement, it is surely his most accomplished as a comic work. The humor arises from the antic misadventures in Italy of a would-be art student and painter. Perhaps the richest comedy is that of deliciously bawdy sexual farce, as when Fidelman can gain the favors of his landlady, for whom he has lusted in vain, only by masquerading as a priest. Surely this scene, which concludes an early episode, must be among the strangest absolutions depicted in a literary work:

> She grabbed his knees. "Help me, Father, for Christ's sake."
>
> Fidelman, after a short tormented time, said in a quavering voice, "I forgive you, my child."
>
> "The penance," she wailed, "first the penance."
>
> After reflecting, he replied, "Say one hundred times each, Our Father and Hail Mary."
>
> "More," Annamaria wept. "More, more. Much more."
>
> Gripping his knees so hard they shook, she burrowed her head into his black-buttoned lap. He felt the surprised beginnings of an erection. "In that case," Fidelman said, shuddering a little, "better undress."
>
> "Only," Annamaria said, "if you keep your vestments on."
>
> "Not the cassock, too clumsy."
>
> "At least the biretta."
>
> He agreed to that.
>
> Annamaria undressed in a swoop. Her body was extraordinarily lovely, the flesh glowing. In her bed they tightly embraced. She clasped his buttocks, he cupped hers. Pumping slowly he nailed her to her cross.[12]

But as hilarious as such scenes are, Malamud grounds them upon certain hard actualities which keep the book from dissipating into mere ribald spoofing. There is the authentic context of the Italian locale: of cold, poverty, venality, a people scrabbling for the next meal, including Fidelman himself. Simultaneously, there is the presence of great art, part of the air breathed in Italy, and the irresistible appeal to attempt it oneself. Thus Fidelman's wild sexual encounters are played off against his increasingly desperate and futile attempts to become an artist. The incongruous juxtaposition in *Pictures of Fidel-*

[12] *Pictures of Fidelman*, pp. 67–68.

man is, then, that between the coarsely sexual and the sublimely aesthetic.

Too, the novel may be viewed as a kind of comic *bildungsroman,* intermixed with the International Theme and structured as a picaresque story cycle. Fidelman arrives in Italy respectably dressed and with the worthy ambition to become an art critic. Then, just as in the first episode he is robbed of his attaché case containing the initial chapter of his projected book, and swindled out of his extra suit of clothes, the layers of his superficial identity are stripped away episode by episode in a series of comic but also bitter encounters, until he is no longer definable as a middle-class American Jew. Instead, he gains a more basic identity: craftsman and lover. Furthermore, he has travelled there the hard way, through privation, failure, humiliation, abuse, crime, and fakery—an experience which brings him in the book's surrealistic penultimate episode face to face with the devil. In Fidelman Malamud has created his own version of an enduring Jewish comic prototype, the *luftmensch* with feet of clay. We have known worse people.

III

So far in this essay nothing has been said about Malamud's style, a subject the critics have largely avoided, as Leslie and Joyce Field point out in the introduction to their recent collection of Malamud criticism.[13] Yet, as indicated earlier, among Malamud's chief distinctions as an artist is his command of a particular literary idiom. This idiom not only bears Malamud's own signature, it has so permeated Jewish-American writing that the Movement itself is in some measure distinguished by it. Furthermore, the style is integral to those very themes and motifs we have been discussing. In a fundamental sense the suffering and the comedy are embedded in the language, and their peculiar simultaneity or proximity, the sweetly tragic and the bitterly comic, must to a significant degree be attributed to the style. In his own way Malamud captures in English what has been called an untranslatable quality of Yiddish, the admixture of the jocular and the solemn, "the fusion of the sacred and the profane."

But style cannot be studied in isolation from the writer's method at large. Before proceeding to a discussion of it, two important points must be made about Malamud's technique.

First, he avails himself of what is perhaps the most versatile and fluent of narrative modes, selective omniscience. In this mode the writer retains the objectivity, the freedom to move through time and

[13] Leslie A. and Joyce W. Field, editors. *Bernard Malamud and the Critics.* New York University Press, 1970.

space, and the power to know all, which are the great advantages of the traditional third-person outside narrator; yet by refraining from editorial intrusions and maintaining the focus on a single character or a few characters, the writer can shift into interior monologue or take a stance which allows him to perceive as through the character's eyes without any obvious break in the narrative seam or detection by the reader. This is, of course, a modern technique, and one at the service of many resourceful writers. It is the narrative perspective Malamud has employed in all his novels and, with rare exceptions, his stories as well. *Pictures of Fidelman,* though in part experimental, generally follows this narrative mode. Consider this passage, illustrative of selective omniscience, which recounts one of Fidelman's earlier, failed attempts at union with his landlady:

> She embraced him, her hairy armpits perfumed. He responded with postponed passion.
> "Enough of antipasto," Annamarie said. She reached for his member.
> Overwrought, Fidelman, though fighting himself not to, spent himself in her hand. Although he mightily willed resurrection, his wilted flower bit the dust.
> She furiously shoved him out of bed, into the studio, flinging his clothes after him.
> "Pig, beast, onanist!"

> At least she lets me love her. Daily Fidelman shopped, cooked, and cleaned for her. Every morning he took her shopping sack off the hook, went down to the street market and returned with the bag stuffed full of greens, pasta, eggs, meat, cheese, wine, bread. Annamaria insisted on three hearty meals a day although she had once told him she no longer enjoyed eating. Twice he had seen her throw up her supper. What she enjoyed he didn't know except it wasn't Fidelman.[14]

By writing this entirely as dramatic scene and in the objective mode, except for the one direct interior monologue statement "At least she lets me love her," Malamud achieves the immediacy and vividness of the I-narrative without paying the heavy price of limitation in time, place, and knowledge.

Another example, from *A New Life,* demonstrates how Malamud employs this particular narrative voice to inform us of the character's thoughts without seeming to tell us directly:

> Levin was moved to discover he cherished what he had best cherished. For the first time since he had parted from Pauline the world seemed home, welcome. He had, as men must, given birth to it; he was himself reborn. Proof: leafy trees stippling green of earth on sky. Flowers casting bright color everywhere. Vast fires in cosmic space—all nature flowing in

---

14 *Pictures of Fidelman,* p. 58.

Levin's veins. He felt tender to the grass. "God's handkerchief," Whitman called it. He watched with pleasure a flat-footed bluejay hopping up and down branches in the blooming cherry tree. He was amiable even to Mrs. Beaty's cat, licking herself on the lawn at night, her whiteness, light. And Levin wanted, still, to be closer to men than he had been. The good you did for one you did for all; it wasn't a bad way to love.[15]

Here we begin outside Levin's head but move inside with a perception which can be either the narrator's or the character's ("Proof, leafy trees . . . space"); then, before the sentence is completed, we are back to the omniscient perspective with "all nature flowing in Levin's veins." Then, as the paragraph concludes, we move inside again: "The good you did for one you did for all; it wasn't a bad way to love." This is Levin's voice, not Malamud's, but the voices blend so well they cannot be distinguished one from the other.

Examples are legion in Malamud's work but the matter need not be further argued. Perhaps his most accomplished use of selective omniscience may be observed in *The Assistant,* wherein Malamud alternates between objective narration and the private minds of his three major characters, Morris, Frank, and Helen, though with swift incursions into the perceptions of even such minor figures as Julius Karp and Ward Minogue. In contrast, Malamud's most deliberately limited and intensive use of the selective omniscient is in *The Fixer,* in which the concentration entirely upon Yakov Bok and the total immersion in his perspective, undistracted and unmodulated by side glances into any other character, reinforces the claustrophobic atmosphere in the novel. This is the formal equivalent to the action, which consists largely of Yakov's experiences in solitary confinement. In a sense, by using this narrative mode, Malamud makes the reader undergo solitary confinement with Yakov.

A second vital point about Malamud's technique, preparatory to a discussion of his style but also intrinsically related to style, is the writer's symbolism. I have hinted that Malamud's best work is realistic, though it should be clear from the frequent and important presence of fantastic comedy that it breaks through strict categories. Indeed, although Malamud is a realist, as demonstrated in *The Assistant, The Fixer,* and the major part of *A New Life,* he is of the best sort: a symbolic realist. The Jewish sense of the Transcendent merged with the Actual expresses itself in Malamud's technique in a hard-rock verisimilitude, in which we smell garbage and know exactly how much money lies in the cash register or what a sadistic prison official does with his fingers when he searches a prisoner. At the same time, we are

[15] *A New Life,* pp. 250–251.

ever aware of the play of the human imagination upon experience and the inexhaustible intimations of the protean natural world. Symbols and emblems recur everywhere in Malamud's fiction, obtrusive only in the case of his first book, *The Natural,* and even there not inappropriate to a work with a frame of myth. Elsewhere they are wholly integrated.

So, for example, to develop some suggestions made earlier about *The Assistant,* the characters' movements in that work—quite normal in a building containing a cellar, a first-floor store, and living quarters above—assume symbolic purport. As already implied, these movements constitute a dramatic metaphor for the characters' moral conditions. Frank comes up from the cellar where he has been hiding, to the store, and then to a room on the floor above. This parallels his climb from bummery to decency. Conversely, Morris goes upstairs to sleep and dream, his only escape from his prison—the store. In his one concession to evil, he goes downstairs to set fire to his business but is saved from this by Frank, who has already experienced what things are like in the cellar. In another important scene, Frank's descent into the grocer's grave signifies his inheritance of the grocer's miserable life, but it is also a kind of ascension. Furthermore, Malamud renders the symbolism ironic and thereby more profound (perhaps inspired by Hemingway's practice) by sometimes reversing the usual connotations and associations. Frank climbs up the airshaft to spy on Helen's naked body in the bathroom, just as he aspires to possess Helen, but morally his action is down. In rescuing Helen from Ward Minogue's assault, he lifts her up, but then, overcome by his own desires, he pushes her to earth to take her himself.

This sequence of movements, noted here only in part, comprises but one of several symbolic patterns in *The Assistant.* In that novel as elsewhere Malamud utilizes many others: heat and cold, light and dark, fragrance and stench, the indoors and the outdoors, to mention a few. Too, throughout his work he consistently uses weather, season, climate, as corollary and symbolic context for his characters' actions and moral conditions. He also skillfully employs emblems: mirrors, books, articles of clothing, for example. Thus whether the locale be a run-down grocery somewhere in Brooklyn or a glass works on the island of Murano, and whether the mood be realistic or comic, there is always much more to see in Malamud's stories than what will happen next.

With this cursory treatment of matters deserving separate and detailed study in themselves but necessarily reduced here to a mere preface, we come finally to Malamud's style. I speak of Malamud's style as though it were a single entity. More accurately, there are three styles, or a confluence of styles.

First there is a "straight" or standard belletristic style; that is, a style composed of the same linguistic materials used by other modern writers, with a syntax familiar to all speakers of American English, and a diction drawn from the common vocabulary of standard-informal usage. The passage cited below, from *The Fixer*, exemplifies Malamud's standard belletristic style. Lucid and vigorous, it contains nothing intrinsically alien or exotic and little identifying it as specifically Malamudian if it were taken out of context and seen in isolation.

> At five in the morning the day began and never ended. In the early evening dark he was already lying on his mattress trying to sleep. Sometimes he tried all night. During the day there were the regular checks through the spy hole, and three depressing searches of his body. There was cleaning out ashes, and making and lighting the stove. There was the sweeping of the cell to do, urinating in the can, walking back and forth until one began to count; or sitting at the table with nothing to do. There was the going for, and eating, of his meager meals. There was trying to remember and trying to forget. There was the counting of each day; there was reciting the psalm he had put together. He also watched the light and dark change. The morning dark was different from the night dark. The morning dark had a little freshness, a little anticipation in it, though what he anticipated he could not say. The night dark was heavy with thickened and compounded shadows.[16]

I have named this a standard belletristic style because the informal elements, e.g., "five in the morning," "the psalm he had put together," are balanced against an occasional sonorous and formal literary phrase never heard in the speech of ordinary men: "thickened and compounded shadows." And, of course, the passage has other literary elements, notably the series of sentences beginning with the identical phrase "There was," by whose proximity and similarity Malamud means to convey the repetitiousness and monotony of Yakov's routine, a linguistic replication of what is happening, i.e., imitative form. However, while this passage testifies to Malamud's sophistication and craft, it says nothing of his special function as a Jewish writer.

A second Malamud style, that most unlike the standard belletristic, is a dialect style which deliberately evokes the sound of Yiddish. It demonstrates Malamud's familiarity with the old mother tongue, the common language once spoken by seven million European Jews regardless of their country of habitation. It also demonstrates Malamud's skill at transliterating that tongue into a kind of English. However, Malamud can hardly be credited with inventing the dialect style or being the first to use Yiddish dialect as a literary medium. Dialect styles in America go back well into the nineteenth century, the rustic and Negro dialects especially, and were practiced by such men as Josh

16 *The Fixer*, p. 214.

Billings, James Russell Lowell, Artemus Ward, Joel Chandler Harris, and, of course, Twain. In the twentieth century Yiddish dialect has been a staple of comedy and of comedians for decades, although very rare in serious writing. This is a sample of Malamud's dialect style, from the superb story "The Magic Barrel." The speaker is Salzman, a marriage broker extolling the virtues of one of his clients to a dubious prospective customer:

> Salzman pulled his clasped hands to his breast. Looking at the ceiling he devoutly exclaimed, "Yiddishe kinder, what can I say to somebody that he is not interested in high school teachers? So what then are you interested?"
> Leo flushed but controlled himself.
> "In what else will you be interested," Salzman went on, "if you not interested in this fine girl that she speaks four languages and has personally in the bank ten thousand dollars? Also her father guarantees further twelve thousand. Also she has a new car, wonderful clothes, talks on all subjects, and she will give you a first-class home and children. How near do we come in our life to paradise?"
> "If she's so wonderful, why wasn't she married ten years ago?"
> "Why?" said Salzman with a heavy laugh. "—Why? Because she is *partikiler*. This is why. She wants the *best*." [17]

The dialect elements are obvious: the direct importation of stock phrases ("Yiddishe kinder"), the mangled grammar, the inverted syntax, the emphatic mispronunciation—a kind of Yiddish accent—of ordinary words. Furthermore, as in most dialect styles, the total effect here is reductive in that the passage presents not only an inferior language but also inferior values, presumably "Jewish" values (money, status), as though they were the ultimate goods in marriage. It is another case of self-mockery, although by the time the story ends all its characters attain to a stature impossible for stereotypes.

The third style, the most complex and resonant and that which Malamud has impressed with his own signature, is a mixed or fused style which combines both the belletristic and dialect styles yet is wholly neither. Malamud can be named the co-inventor of this style; he and Bellow began to use it at about the same time, in the early 1950's, though apparently without the conscious indebtedness of either one to the other. The fused style gathers additional force from the juxtaposition or combination of lyric, eloquent, soaring phrases (the belletristic) and homely idiom and vulgate (the dialect). The belletristic exalts the vulgate, infusing it with dignity and seriousness; the vulgate pulls down the belletristic from its literary eminence and makes it speak for ordinary men and coarse experience. The juxtaposition of the two also makes possible that remarkable bitter comedy we observe

[17] *The Magic Barrel,* Farrar, Straus, and Cudahy, New York, 1958, pp. 201–202.

in Malamud, Bellow, and Roth. I cite an example of the fused style from *The Assistant,* a passage notable as well for its synthesis of omniscience and interior monologue:

> Tight-jawed, he opened his book. She returned to hers, hiding her thoughts behind the antics of a madman until memory overthrew him and she found herself ensnared in scenes of summer that she would gladly undo, although she loved the season; but how could you undo what you had done again in the fall, unwillingly willing? Virginity she thought she had parted with without sorrow, yet was surprised by torments of conscience, or was it disappointment at being valued under her expectations? Nat Pearl, handsome, cleft-chinned, gifted, ambitious, had wanted without too much trouble a lay and she, half in love, had obliged and regretted. Not the loving, but that it had taken her so long to realize how little he wanted. Not her, Helen Bober.
>
> Why should he?—magna cum laude, Columbia, now in his second year at law school, she only a high school graduate with a year's evening college credit mostly in lit; he with first-rate prospects, also rich friends he had never bothered to introduce her to; she as poor as her name sounded, with little promise of a better future. She had more than once asked herself if she had meant by her favors to work up a claim on him. Always she denied it. She had wanted, admittedly, satisfaction, but more than that—respect for the giver of what she had to give, had hoped that desire would become more than just that. She wanted, simply, a future in love. Enjoyment she had somehow had, felt very moving the freedom of fundamental intimacy with a man. Though she wished for more of the same, she wanted it without aftermath of conscience, or pride, or sense of waste. So she promised herself next time it would go the other way; first mutual love, then loving, harder maybe on the nerves, but easier in memory.[18]

In this passage literary and Yiddish-colloquial elements are so tightly joined as to be nearly inseparable. The Yiddish voice, here subdued because the character is a thoroughly assimilated second-generation young woman, can nevertheless be heard in the inverted syntax and the odd treatment of verbs: "Virginity she thought she had parted with"; "Nat Pearl . . . had wanted without too much trouble. . . ." Too, the dominant mood, a kind of reflexive neither wholly passive nor active, is typical of Yiddish but scarcely exists in English. Then there are the constant interruptions and interjections of modifying or qualifying phrases and clauses, imparting a faintly alien air of brooding introspection and of constant self-examination. This quality contrasts with the normative briskness and directness of American speech, which depicts actions swiftly completed and thoughts concluded with a minimum of interruption. Malamud further spices this linguistic mixture with colloquialisms, sometimes remotely Yiddish in flavor but

18 *The Assistant,* p. 14.

also those appropriate to the big city: "lay," "lit," "harder maybe on the nerves." In the latter phrase the interposed "maybe" turns a stock expression a little Yiddish. The effect of all this is, of course, to render Helen immediate, human, and accessible to the reader.

Yet we must not overlook the belletristic components in the passage, entirely appropriate to a character who is as bookish as Helen (the book she holds in the scene just quoted is *Don Quixote*). As the colloquial style makes Helen folksily human, the formal and literary elements make her deep and complex. Such phrases as "memory overthrew him," "ensnared in scenes of summer," "torments of conscience," and "the freedom of fundamental intimacy with a man," elevated above common parlance and smacking of her intellectual ambitions and idealism, are not only right for her character, they help define it. Helen herself is constructed of the same mixture of elements as her language: part lusting flesh, part lofty aspiration. Moreover, these elements blend into the larger structure of the paragraph, with its parallel and balanced sentences, thesis/antithesis, reflecting the tensions in Helen's mind as it plays over its experience. These deliberations are reinforced by the strategic repetitions of key words echoed and reechoed, all congruent to the subject of sex, love, morality, and ambition: "undo," "loved," "conscience," "wanted," "love," "loving," "future." The whole thing becomes transformed by this miracle of Malamud's craft, a miracle most modestly performed, from narrative into incantation.

Malamud's artistry proves itself not only in the creation and practice of these styles but also in the diverse narrative functions to which he puts them. In *The Assistant,* to continue our concern with that novel a moment longer, each of the three styles appears in a variety of uses and combinations. The dialect style, for example, functions appropriately in the conversations of those characters for whom Yiddish was the language of their youth, between Morris and Ida, or Morris and Breitbart. We also hear this style in certain interior monologues. Perhaps its most consistent use in the novel is to depict Ida, I suspect as a way to fix her into a kind of narrowness or limitation of vision. Of all the important characters, hers is the meanest worldview. Note this instance, Ida at Morris' funeral:

> Ida, holding a wet handkerchief to her eyes, thought, So what if we had to eat? When you eat you don't want to worry whose money you are eating—yours or the wholesalers'. If he had money he had bills; and when he had more money he had more bills. A person doesn't always want to worry if she will be in the street tomorrow. She wants sometimes a minute's peace. But maybe it's my fault, because I didn't let him be a druggist.[19]

19 Ibid., p. 230.

But what is so artistic about using a dialect style for a dialect character? We have the answer to that in Malamud's treatment of Morris, because, in contrast, Malamud shrewdly avoids the dialect style and renders him, whether by omniscient narration or interior monologue, either in the standard belletristic style or the fused style. This "straight" treatment of Morris reiterates his identity as an Everyman figure and comprises the stylistic equivalent to the novel's thesis that all men are, potentially, Jews. To depict him in the dialect style would be to insist upon his ethnic identity and thus to weaken the characterization. Morris's character gains depth, too, in that Malamud shows him as capable of different levels of speech, depending on the situation. To Ida he speaks strictly in Yiddish dialect, as to Karp and others; to Helen and Frank his speech remains homely but closer to standard and almost purged of its Yiddishisms; to Detective Minogue he speaks in a stilted but "correct" manner which reflects the strain he feels dealing with this man within a formal, official context.

On the other hand, Helen and Frank can be rendered in a style which at times borders on dialect in its loose colloquialism, yet without risk of stereotyping. As Helen's style is slightly more literary because of her aspirations and her education, so Frank's tends to be slangy, appropriate to his background as drifter. However, we perceive a subtle but progressive heightening of Frank's speech and interior monologue, as well as of the omniscient narration describing him, on those occasions when he delves into serious subjects either with Morris or Helen, and as his moral ascension continues. He achieves, in his best moments, a striking combination of literary eloquence and low-down bluntness. A few lines will illustrate: "His goddamned life had pushed him wherever it wanted; he had led it nowhere. He was blown around in any breath that blew, owned nothing, not even experience to show for the years he had lived. If you had experience you knew at least when to start and where to quit; all he knew was how to mangle himself more. The self he had secretly considered valuable was, for all he could make of it, a dead rat. He stank." [20]

The various styles I have remarked in *The Assistant* operate throughout Malamud's work, although, of course, with suitable modification to the needs of each novel. For example, *The Natural* totally lacks Yiddish flavor, rightly so, yet the style is breezy and slangy—accurate to a world of baseball players. At the same time the earthy colloquialism sets up an artistically desirable tension against the novel's heavy mythic and allegorical machinery, with two beneficial effects: it provides an illusion of actuality; it produces a keen humor. *A New Life* is written largely in the fused style, again seemly to the subject and to the novel's hero, an urban Eastern Jew with an M.A. However, just as

[20] Ibid., p. 175.

Levin's Jewishness overtly plays only a small role in the novel, the "Jewish" elements in his thought and speech are suppressed. As is appropriate to the hero's profession as college English teacher, the selective omniscient voice tends to be formal and literary; but it can never be pompous or recondite because it must always remind us of Levin's origins in the urban streets and of the base urgings of his very mortal flesh. In this novel, too, the mixture of colloquial and belletristic materials generates a comic undercurrent.

The same comic potentiality, inherent in any style which employs idiom, helps to enliven *The Fixer* and prevent it from unbearable morbidity. There is nothing at all humorous in the situation of a man falsely accused of ritual murder, nor is there any single episode or passage in the novel that can be described as funny—apart from the galling satire upon Russian ignorance and barbarousness (recall the blood-draining apparatus). Thus, the novel's style must carry most of the task of relieving its gloom. And Malamud does accomplish it, with a doubly ingenious method.

First, he establishes a continual contrast between the language of all the official proceedings, innately formal and bombastic, and the spontaneous simplicity and pungency of Yakov's own speech. Accordingly, there is posed the repeated incongruity between what is uttered by the various magistrates and functionaries, and the pithy, unaffected quality of what Yakov is saying inside his own head. The incongruity becomes even more absurd in that when Yakov replies to his persecutors, he usually does so in the same stilted manner they use. The result is a kind of chorus of voices. Second, the contrast of voices, of what is said and what is thought, communicates an authentic difference of tongues. Yakov thinks and speaks to himself or to other Jews in his native language, Yiddish, whereas he must speak to everyone else in Russian. Although Yakov has learned Russian well, it is not his original language and cannot be used with the fluency and naturalness of Yiddish. Consequently, Yakov's stilted responses to the Russian officials' stilted declarations imitates the truth of the hero's circumstances. The crucial difference is that Yakov always speaks sincerely, while the inflated and artificial mode of the official rhetoric gives it the lie. At the same time Malamud's voice, employing the fused style of an omniscient narrator outside the hero but never very far away, merges with Yakov's. Narrator and hero often become one in that both express themselves in the same way: lucidly, candidly, sometimes earthily, sometimes in short lyric flights. In sum, what Malamud does, linguistically, is to pit the good Jews (Malamud and Yakov) against the bad Russians. You can usually tell the bad guys by their bombast, if they have rank, or if lower class by their nasty, vulgar mouths.

Pictures of Fidelman indicates a further expansion and experimentation in Malamud's technique. Although the narrative is largely rendered in the fused style, Malamud flies higher with the belletristic and dives lower with the vulgate than in any of his other work. He also takes greater chances with narrative perspective, shifting from objective to subjective narration more frequently and swiftly than ever before. He makes other rapid and varied shifts as well: from the conventional narrative past tense to the immediate present, from exposition to dialogue, from interior monologue or selective omniscience to direct impression. Technically the book is as wild and unpredictable as its hero's adventures. Indeed, chapter five is a technical *tour de force,* a packed and dazzling virtuoso demonstration of Malamud's range, a stylistic splurge. One can only describe it as a neo-Joycean, comitragic, surrealistic, stream-of-consciousness, visionary sequence, perhaps a burst of true madness in poor Fidelman but also containing a portion of almost coherent narrative which advances the story line. There is nothing remotely like it in Malamud's earlier writing. I quote a small portion:

12 12 12 12 12 12 12 12 12 12 12 12 12 12 12 12 12 12 12 12
369 369 369 369 369 369 369 369 369 369 369 369 369
veyizmirveyizmirveyizmirveyizmirveyizmirveyizmir
12369123691236912369123691236912369123691236912369
Fidelman painteth three canvases. The Crucifixion he painteth red on red. The Descent from the Cross he painteth white on white. For the Resurrection, on Easter morning, he leaveth the canvas blank.

P

t o tem

L

E

Suss

King

Je vous enmerde. Modigliani.
   Oil on wood? Bottle fucking guitar? Bull impaled on pole? One-eyed carp stuffed in staring green bottle? Clown spooning dog dung out of sawdust? Staircase ascending a nude? Black-stockinged whore reading pornographic book by lamplight? Still life: three apple cores plus one long gray hair? Boy pissing on old man's shoe? The blue disease? Balding woman dyeing her hair? Buggers of Calais? Blood oozing from ceiling on foggy night?

From such writing there seems only one safe conclusion: we cannot tell where Malamud is going next.
   Although for all its virtuosity and comic gusto *Pictures of Fidelman* is a much less estimable work than such solid accomplishments as *The Assistant* and *The Fixer,* this novel does make a number of important affirmations. For one thing, it affirms that despite Malamud's associa-

tion with the Jewish Movement and his importance to it, his material is not restricted to the themes and prototypes characteristic to that Movement. It affirms that he retains the capacity to surprise us, a capacity always beyond the scope of a minor writer. It affirms, moreover, that Malamud continues to be devoted to the subject he believes the writer must treat as his mission: the richness of the development of human personality. Finally, it affirms that whether his treatment be somber or comic, his possibilities as a craftsman are far from exhausted. If it is perhaps too much to expect the Movement to continue its present momentum indefinitely, although it seems far from played out, on the basis of the hard evidence already provided by his talent we can surely look forward to further development on Malamud's part.

I, for one, can hardly wait to see what he will do.

The Tenants appeared after this essay had been written, and too late to be included in it. However, from my first reading of the book I would amend my conclusions here in only one important respect: it seems to indicate that Malamud is capable of unmitigated pessimism, gloomier even than that in *The Fixer*. Or, we could take a little comfort from the ending of *The Tenants* by interpreting it as warning and object lesson to both Jew and Black: learn to get along, *or else*. In any case the novel confirms my belief that Malamud is still growing.

Bernard Malamud's Ironic Heroes

by Sanford Pinsker

If a writer like Isaac Bashevis Singer had to face the agonizing problem of re-creating a ghetto experience that, in some sense, had been all too short-lived, Bernard Malamud and a host of other post-war American Jewish writers had to discover the boundaries of a heritage that, for them, had hardly lived at all. Critic J. C. Levinson has pointed out that "after Buchenwald and Hiroshima, fiction can hardly remain the same, and in the most interesting of our postwar novelists, it has indeed changed." [1] For American Jewish writers, the problem of the Nazi holocausts was particularly acute; the prospect of confronting the six million dead—in either the terms of literary metaphor of the gut response of socio-religious feeling—seemed futile, almost as if the only appropriate reaction was a kind of numbed silence.

Curiously enough, though, the American Jewish writer—traditionally caught in the private difficulty of defining both his "Americaness" and his particular brand of "Jewishness"—now found himself called upon to be a spokesman at exactly the moment when he probably had no desire to speak at all. For a writer like Bernard Malamud, the Jew became a natural symbol for the postwar sensibility, the index of an age questing belief on one hand, but wrenched out of religious contexts on the other. Thus, the Jew emerged as "a type of metaphor . . . both for the tragic dimension of anyone's life and for a code of personal morality." [2]

But while subsequent literary history proved the validity of such statements, they always suggested that something akin to a literary plot had been abrew; the Malamuds and Bellows of the world somehow hatching up the whole thing in a lower East Side delicatessen. Writing in *Commentary* magazine, critic Robert Alter suggests that artistic failures can result

[1] J. C. Levinson, "Bellow's Dangling Men," *Critique,* 3 (Summer 1960), 3.

[2] Theodore Solotaroff, "Bernard Malamud's Fiction: The Old Life and the New," *Commentary,* 33 (March 1962), 198.

when a writer assigns a set of abstract moral values to the representatives of a particular group, the connection thus insisted on may strike the reader as arbitrary, an artistic confusion of actualities and ideals.[3]

To be sure, the statement is provocative enough on its own terms, but even more so when one remembers that it was magazines like *Commentary* which, in effect, created the renaissance of American Jewish writing. Mr. Alter's charge could, of course, be brought to bear against more writers than Bernard Malamud, but it is Malamud whom we tend to think of first. His Jews always appear out of an offstage "nowhere," filled to the brim with suffering as if they had just changed clothes from a four-thousand-year trek across the desert. We are asked to accept—yea, even *believe*—that this is an a priori state of being, part of the author's *donnée* that is beyond question. And slowly what was once the thirties' concern with the "human condition" evolved into a fifties' fascination with a "Jewish" one.

But it is in this confusion between actualities and ideals that Malamud's peculiar tensions are created. The schlemiel may well have been a comic figure whose self-created failures became an index of socioeconomic limitation, but such a character is out of place in arenas of affluence and endless mobility. Marcus Klein sees the change as one from novels of alienation (i.e., works in which characters of sensibility "protect" themselves by systematically moving beyond the boundaries of the hostile society) to those of what he calls "accommodation."[4] Rather than, say, a Stephen Dedalus symbolically flapping his wings in the last lines of Joyce's *Portrait of an Artist as a Young Man* and dreaming about a bohemian life in Paris, the contemporary American writer found himself in the city, in the System, in the affluence—and only vaguely unhappy about the situation.

At the same time that writers were learning how to accommodate, to preserve individuality beneath folds of gray flannel suiting, there was a growing concern about the larger moral issues which were attendant to the times. In some respects, the French Underground had it easier; their existential nausea was the result of a particular time and place. American counterparts, on the other hand, often got a double dose, but delayed some ten years and denied a setting in concrete experience. For American Jewish writers, the figure of the schlemiel became a way of dealing with these realities, although now he was more interested in moral transcendence than economic advancement. For Malamud, especially, the schlemiel was a moral bungler, a character whose estimate of the situation, coupled with an overriding de-

[3] Robert Alter, "Malamud as Jewish Writer," *Commentary*, 42 (September 1966), 71. Subsequent references to Mr. Alter are to this article.

[4] Marcus Klein, *After Alienation* (New York, 1964), pp. 15–17.

sire for "commitment," invariably caused comic defeats of one sort or
another.

The Malamud canon is filled with such schlemiels, from the early
stories of *The Magic Barrel* to his most recent novel, *The Fixer*. I suspect the most damning thing one can say about Malamud's development is that he has done little more than rewrite "The Magic Barrel"
for the past fifteen years. To be sure, a good many modern authors
would welcome such "criticism," especially if they thought a repeat
performance was possible.

For Malamud, the short story is more amenable to ambivalence, and
in "The Magic Barrel" particularly, he achieved a nearly perfect blend
of form and content. Considered as a whole, "The Magic Barrel" is an
initiation story, although the exact dimensions of the "initiation" are
hard to pin down. It opens innocently enough—"Not long ago there
lived in uptown New York, in a small, almost meager room, though
crowded with books, Leo Finkle, a rabbinical student in the Yeshiva
University"—as if to answer the objections of critics who continually
demand that American Jewish literature be more Jewish and less goy-
ish, less like literature. But for all the kosher food and lower East Side
mame-loshen, Jewishness is as much a literary illusion in "The Magic
Barrel" as Negro dialects are in *Huck Finn*. Like most of Malamud's
protagonists, Leo Finkle's problem is an inability to love, a failure to
adequately relate his particular brand of isolation with the isolation
of others. Finkle is initiated into "suffering" almost by accident. He
"had been advised by an acquaintance that he might find it easier to
win himself a congregation if he were married," and so Finkle opens
himself to eros, shadchens (marriage brokers), and his fate as schlemiel.
Initially at least, the rabbinical student is radically different from the
mercuric matchmaker: Finkle represents the force of Law while Salzman stands for the power of Flesh. And yet, Salzman—for all his vul-
garisms—betrays a "depth of sadness" which Finkle uses as a con-
venient mirror for his own.

The progress of the moral schlemiel nearly always involves identification with suffering and some strategy for taking on the burdens of
others. In this sense the schlemiels of Malamud's canon bear a striking
resemblance to the classical folk figure; both desire to change the essential condition of their lives, but each is inadequate to the task. Finkle's
leitmotif is sympathetic suffering in much the same way that Salzman's
is fish. Each of the "much-handled cards" in Salzman's magic barrel
comes to represent a person whose aloneness is a counterpart of his
own. To be sure, Salzman is more pimp than "commercial cupid"—
regardless of Finkle's elaborate rationalizations about the honorable
tradition of the shadchen. In fact, what Finkle really imagines is a
world in which hundreds of cards—each one longing for marriage—

are churned about and finally brought together by this indefatigable matchmaker. Finkle's schlemielhood is a function of his willingness to believe in such highly romantic visions and, moreover, to replace them as quickly as they go sour. Salzman, on the other hand, plays confidence man to the rabbinical student's sensitivity. All his marital candidates sound like used cars, perfectly suited to sales pitches like the following:

> Sophie P. Twenty-four years. Widow one year. No children. Educated high school and two years college. Father promises eight thousand dollars. Has wonderful wholesale business. Also real estate. On the mother's side comes teachers, also one actor. Well known on Second Avenue.[5] [P. 196]

In this way, the juxtaposition of Finkle's hesitation about "buying" and Salzman's aggressive brand of "selling" create what might have been a purely comic situation. However, Finkle gradually begins to see Salzman's portfolio as a microcosm of the world's suffering and his shoulders as the proper place for it to rest. What breaks down, of course, are the very pillars of Finkle's world—the justifications of Tradition, the pragmatic need for a wife, the commonsense arguments for using a matchmaker, etc.

But if the "much-handled cards" of Salzman's portfolio make it clear that others suffer, his traumatic meeting with Lily Hirschorn makes it equally clear that he, too, has vital dimensions that are missing.

> Her probing questions irritated him into revealing—to himself more than her—the true nature of his relationship to God, and from that it had come to him, with shocking force, that apart from his parents, he had never loved anyone. [P. 205]

In some sense, "The Magic Barrel" is a story of love—although the word operates on both the levels of eros and agape. Finkle's "learning," his ability to articulate about his own particular deaths of the heart does not constitute his schlemielhood. Lily Hirschorn—like the other cards in Salzman's magic barrel—was simply another frantic figure yoo-hooing after a life that had already passed her by. But if Finkle had been conned by Salzman, so had Lily. She expected an Old Testament prophet, a man "enamored with God," and instead she got a man incapable of passion in either the physical or spiritual sense of the word. In the Finkle-Salzman-Hirschorn triangle, the end result is initiation; Finkle finds out what he is, and in the context of the story this provides for a certain amount of felt tension.

It is with the introduction of Stella, however, that Finkle moves

---

[5] All page references are included in the text. I have used the Farrar, Straus and Giroux editions of *The Magic Barrel, The Assistant, A New Life,* and *The Fixer.*

from moral initiate to moral bungler. Unlike the portraits of the other women, Stella's dimestore picture revealed that she "had *lived,* or wanted to—more than just wanted, perhaps regretted how she had lived—had somehow deeply suffered" (p. 209). Thus, in a world where "suffering" is the standard for oneupsmanship, Stella emerges as the hands-down winner. Lily Hirschorn may have wanted to live, Finkle himself has the urge to try, but it is Stella who has actually been there. And it is through the figure of Stella (her name suggesting the ironic star which guides Finkle's destiny) that the prospective rabbi hopes to "convert her to goodness, himself to God." In this way, a new triangle is created with Finkle representing a tortured attempt to achieve spiritual resurrection; Salzman (variously characterized as Pan, Cupid, or other fertility figures) emerging as a kind of Yiddishized Creon while Stella vacillates between the scarlet of her prostitution and the whiteness of her purity.

It is the movement toward Stella which makes a schlemiel out of Finkle, at least in the sense that his goal of spiritual regeneration is incommensurate with his activity. In this respect, Finkle's situation is a moral counterpart of traditional Jewish stories in which a character aspires to financial success, only to sow the seeds of his own destruction.

The concluding tableau crystallizes the matter of Finkle's "salvation" and/or "destruction" without providing the luxury of a clear reading direction. On one hand, Finkle runs toward Stella seeking "in her, his own redemption" in ways which make this passionate rabbinical student seem almost akin to the biblical Hosea. On the other hand, however, Salzman is always just "around the corner . . . chanting prayers for the dead." Is the kaddish for Finkle? for Stella? or, perhaps, for Salzman himself? In much of Malamud's early fiction, a kind of ironic affirmation is an integral part of his aesthetic—almost as if movements toward moral change were not enough, but total regeneration was not possible.

The Assistant (1957) seems to be cut from the same bolt of cloth (marked "Judaic suffering") that gave us the moral qualms of a Leo Finkle. In this case, however, the patient suffering of Morris Bober is a more genuine donnée than much of the pain in "The Magic Barrel." I say "more genuine" because Bober is neither the protagonist nor the moral filter of this novel. His "suffering" merely *is* and it is the task of Frankie Alpine, his assistant, to learn what such suffering means and how it can apply to his own situation. To be sure, Frankie has some rather curious notions about Judaism, but then again, Bober may not be the best instructor. At one point in the novel he claims to suffer "for the Law," although it is hard to see exactly how Law—in the sense of *Halakha*—functions in Morris's life. Instead, Bober is more often characterized as a kind of secular *tsaddik,* a man who once "ran two blocks in the snow to give back five cents a customer forgot." His cachet is in his deeds—giving an early morning roll to the gray-haired (and vaguely antisemitic) Poilisheh, extending endless credit to the "drunk women," and even shoveling his sidewalks on Sunday morning because "it don't look so nice for the goyim that go to church."

And yet, the bulk of Bober's suffering was not a matter of economic failure or even the fact that "in a store you were entombed." Rather, it was the unspoken and often elusive failures of fatherhood which continually torment Bober's sensibility. In Malamud's world, people always seem out of breath from carrying too many bundles, both physical and psychological; when they finally do rest for a glass of tea, we tend to believe their "sighs," to feel that such suffering is justified.

> Breitbart, the bulb peddler, laid down his two enormous cartons of light bulbs and diffidently entered the back. "Go in," Morris urged. He boiled up some tea and served it in a thick glass, with a slice of lemon. The peddler eased himself into a chair, derby hat and coat on, and gulped the hot tea, his Adam's apple bobbing.
> "So how goes now?" asked the grocer.
> "Slow," shrugged Breitbart.
> Morris sighed. "How is your boy?"
> Breitbart nodded absently, then picked up the Jewish paper and read. After ten minutes he got up, scratched all over, lifted across his thin shoulders the two large cartons tied together with clothesline and left.
> Morris watched him go.
> The world suffers. *He* felt every schmerz.
> At lunchtime Ida came down. She had cleaned the whole house.
> Morris was standing before the faded couch, looking out of the rear window at the backyards. He had been thinking of Ephraim. [Pp. 6–7]

Jonathan Baumbach characterizes the novel as the intertwining biography of surrogate fathers and surrogate sons. As he puts it,

> *The Assistant* has two central biographies: the life and death of Morris Bober, unwitting saint, and the guilt and retribution of Frank Alpine, saint-elect, the first life creating the pattern and possibility of the second. At the end, as if by metamorphosis, the young Italian thief replaces the old Jewish storekeeper, the reborn son replacing the father.[6]

In some respects, Bober's situation seems to be a variant of Leopold Bloom's, although Ephraim is not Rudy, nor is Frankie Alpine Stephen Dedalus. What seems similar, however, is the manner in which the respective "adoptions" take place. Bober's suffering remains constant; it is a condition of his life and the necessary result of Ephraim's death.

6 Jonathan Baumbach, *The Landscape of Nightmare* (New York, 1965), p. 111.

Frankie, on the other hand, vacillates between visions of absolute goodness and the reality of compulsive evil. What he needs are standards for moral excellence, of which the life of St. Francis is one and the life of Morris Bober is another. About St. Francis, he says: "For instance, he gave everything away that he owned, every cent, all his clothes off his back. He enjoyed to be poor. He said poverty was a queen and he loved her like a beautiful woman" (p. 31). To be sure, he might have well been talking about Bober, and as he grows into his role as "assistant," the distinction between the two figures gradually blurs. However, what Frankie really identifies with is a style of suffering, confusing his own masochism with the martyrs from his Catholic sensibility and the Jewishness of his grocer boss. In this way, he becomes the moral schlemiel, the man whose estimate of the situation is as wrong-headed as his strategies for attaining moral perfection. What he desires, of course, is a kind of sainthood and his movements toward Bober's brand of Jewishness parallel Finkle's attraction to Stella. "Salvation" and/or "destruction" once again becomes the index of Malamud's ironic affirmation, the comic result of schlemielish behavior.

But Frankie does not immediately resemble the sort of schlemiel one remembers from Yiddish jokes nor does Bober's "suffering" seem totally ironic. There is a sense in *The Assistant* that at least a part of Malamud is playing it straight, believing in both Bober's essential goodness and Frankie's ability to learn from it. Things crystallize in the funeral scene, at the point where tensions begin to shift from the father/owner to his assistant/son. The Rabbi—unfamiliar with Bober and called in for the occasion—delivers the following eulogy at his graveside:

> My dear friends, I never had the pleasure to meet the good grocery man that he now lays in his coffin. He lived in a neighborhood where I didn't come in. Still and all I talked this morning to people that knew him and I am now sorry I didn't know him also. . . . all told me the same, that Morris Bober, who passed away so untimely—he caught double pneumonia from shoveling snow in front of his place of business so people could pass by on the sidewalk—was a man who couldn't be more honest. . . . Helen, his dear daughter, remembers from when she was a small girl that her father ran two blocks in the snow to give back to a poor Italian lady a nickel she forgot on the counter. Who runs in wintertime without hat or coat, without rubbers to protect his feet, two blocks in the snow to give back five cents that a customer forgot? . . . He was also a very hard worker, a man that never stopped working. How many mornings he got up in the dark and dressed himself in the cold, I can't count. . . . So besides being honest he was a good provider.
>
> When a Jew dies, who asks if he is a Jew? He is a Jew, we don't ask. There are many ways to be a Jew. So if somebody comes to me and says, "Rabbi, shall we call such a man Jewish who lived and worked

among the gentiles and sold them pig meat, trayfe, that we don't eat, and not once in twenty years comes inside a synagogue, is such a man a Jew, rabbi?" To him I will say, "Yes, Morris Bober was to me a true Jew because he lived in the Jewish experience, which he remembered and with the Jewish heart." [Pp. 228–29]

I suspect that Bober might well be considered a prize schlemiel by those prone to give the passage an ironic reading. The Rabbi asks, "Who runs in wintertime without hat or coat?" and, for the hard-boiled among us, the answer must be "a *schlemiel!*" Bober cares about his customers, but the novel makes it clear that they continually desert him for fancier food and lower prices. At every point in the Rabbi's sermon the facts of the matter ironically undercut his well-meaning sentiment. Bober may have been "honest" (all the details suggest that he is a Hassidic saint, one of the Lamed Vov), but he was hardly a "good provider." His daughter reads *Don Quixote* and dreams of worlds beyond the confines of the grocery store, at the same time blaming Bober for spoiling her chances. His wife simply complains—about business, about Helen's boyfriends, and finally about Bober himself.

And then there is the sticky matter of Bober's "Jewishness." The Rabbi's words of consolation may have cheered a good many American Jews who share such a definition, but it hardly answers the question of Bober's "Jewishness" in the novel itself. For Bober, Jewishness seems to be inextricably bound with suffering, with a common humanity of which Jews—bound by the Law—seem to carry the greatest share. As I have mentioned before, whatever Bober might mean by the Law, it is clearly not talmudic Law that he has in mind. After all, "Nobody will tell me that I am not Jewish because I put in my mouth once in a while, when my tongue is dry, a piece of ham." For Bober, the issue really comes down to who has the "Jewish heart," and when Frankie asks why Jews "suffer so damned much," Bober can only reply:

> "They suffer because they are Jews."
> "That's what I [i.e., Frankie] mean, they suffer more than they have to."
> "If you live, you suffer. Some people suffer more, but not because they want. But I think if a Jew don't suffer for the Law, he will suffer for nothing."
> "What do you suffer for, Morris?" Frank said.
> "I suffer for you," Morris said calmly. [P. 125]

Part of Bober's "mystery"—particularly to a disciple like Frankie—is the ambivalent quality of Bober's instruction. If Bober has the Jewish heart already, how can it be transferred to someone else? For Frankie, the answer seems clear—Bober "suffered," and to be like him, one must also suffer. However, for all his apparent folly, for the personal goodness which he wasted and the unnecessary suffering he endured, Bober's life seems more a tragic commentary on the American Dream and the Traditions of Judaic suffering than an ironic joke about self-destruction. No matter how wrong-headed he might have been about his customers, his family or his friends, Bober's style had a certain amount of dignity, a certain bittersweet quality that made even his sighs seem justified and, more important, profoundly significant.

But the fate of his "assistant" is another matter. In Frankie's first outing after Bober's death, he quite literally makes a schlemiel out of himself.

> Then the diggers began to push in the loose earth around the grave and as it fell on the coffin the mourner wept aloud.
> Helen tossed in a rose.
> Frank, standing close to the edge of the grave, leaned forward to see where the flower fell. He lost his balance, and though flailing his arms, landed feet first on the coffin. [P. 231]

But the incident at the grave is only one of a long series of self-created accidents which spoil Frankie's chances. In an attempt to reverse his luck, to achieve the sort of moral perfection he desires, and most important of all, to emulate his grocer boss, Frankie converts to Judaism. However, it is a Judaism he does not understand and which cannot possibly sustain him. The situation is somewhat akin to Ike McCaslin's brand of learning in William Faulkner's "The Bear." Like Bober, Sam Fathers has intuitive wisdom about the woods that Ike patiently tries to discover. But with Sam Fathers dead and the woods slowly disappearing, the "wisdom" no longer seems to work. Frankie's case is even more complicated because there is a real question as to whether or not he understood Bober—much less his "Jewishness" or the value of his suffering.

For Frankie, conversion to Judaism suggests plot complications that exist beyond the novel itself. We accept the tableau at the conclusion of "The Magic Barrel" and even the multiple possibilities of Salzman's kaddish, as part and parcel of the short story, but it is a bit harder to know what to do with Frankie. Are we to presume that he will emulate Bober by taking over the grocery store and perhaps even marrying Helen? Will he be the one to supply the gray-haired Poilisheh with her six o'clock roll and the "drunken women" with endless credit? The novel concludes with Frankie circumcised and dragging "himself around with a pain between his legs," a pain which both "enraged and inspired him." However, unlike the suffering of his employer, Frankie's is a function of his penchant toward masochism. The old guilts must be punished and what better way than by circumcision? Implicit in the act are the complicated strands of sexual punishment (for his attempted rape of Helen), castration anxiety (for Bober as his Oedipal father), and religious conversion (for a Covenant he does not understand). But in his quest for moral perfection, Frankie Alpine emerges as more schlemiel than authentic Jew, more a victim of his desire for sainthood than actual "saint." At the end, he sees himself as a kind of St. Francis figure reaching into a garbage can to give Helen a wooden rose.

> He [i.e. St. Francis] tossed it into the air and it turned into a real flower that he caught in his hand. With a bow he gave it to Helen, who had just come out of the house. "Little sister, here is your little sister the rose." From him she took it, although it was with the love and best wishes of Frank Alpine. [Pp. 245–46]

Finkle, too, had clutched flowers to his anxious breast and raced after Stella. And, in a similar way, Frank Alpine speeds toward a destiny (or destruction?) he does not fully understand, duping himself with the belief that he is no longer the "assistant" and that Bober's humanity will soon be his.

In *A New Life* (1961), Malamud continued with the progress of a moral schlemiel, but added more of the slapstick complication usually associated with the figure. After all, it is hard to see a novel like *The Assistant* as primarily "comic," at least in the sense that either Bober or Frankie emerge as primarily humorous figures. Perhaps there is something about the nature of grocery stores in Malamud's canon which not only restricts economic possibilities, but comic ones as well. With Pinye Salzman, for example, there was at least endless room to run around, but Bober and Frankie are literally stuck in the store. S. Levin, "formerly a drunkard," hails from the same sort of environment—what Philip Roth calls a "timeless depression and placeless lower East Side"—as the characters of *The Assistant,* until Malamud fairly throws him into both the American West and the groves of academe. That Levin should be a schlemiel is almost as much an a priori assumption in *A New Life* as Bober's suffering was in *The Assistant.* Unfortunately for Malamud, whatever gold may have been in those particular literary hills had already been well panned by the time Levin arrived, the "virgin land" idea having been exploited by one group of scholars while the anti-academic novel was being milked by another.

Although *A New Life* moves Malamud out of the city, its concerns are almost identical to those which provided tension in his earlier fiction. However, this time the focus is split between Levin's role as moral schlemiel and his initial appearance as capital-B Bungler. During the first few scenes of the novel, Levin is the schlemiel out West and newly arrived in academe—the economic scheming of his ghetto ancestors now turned toward the business of departmental tenure and perhaps even an eventual Ph.D. "Bearded, lonely," and looking around for a sign of welcome, Levin is the perfect candidate for the "accidents" which will befall him. In many respects, he is the rabbinical student from "The Magic Barrel" turned upside down, the flip side of Finkle's brand of poignant aloneness. Met by Gerald Gilley, Director of Freshman Composition, Levin spends the evening in a series of outrageous "man who came to dinner" jokes—alternating, as the standard definition of the schlemiel would have it, between the one who "spills the soup" and the one who "gets spilt upon." Levin wastes little time establishing his credentials as that innocent victim of bad luck, the schlimmazzel.

> They sat down at the round table, for which he felt a surprising immediate affection. Pauline had forgotten the salad bowl and went in to get it. When she returned she served the casserole, standing. A child called from the kitchen. Distracted, she missed Levin's plate and dropped a hot gob of tuna fish and potato into his lap. [Pp. 9–10]

But Levin (alas) is denied even the luxuries of being a schlimmazzel. In a post-Freudian world, there are no accidents, or at least nothing is allowed to remain a mere "accident" for very long. And so Malamud begins a long series of pants jokes, each involving Levin as a comic figure and each involved with the element of farce so essential to the fabric of *A New Life*. Levin's trousers are, of course, ruined by the hot tuna and all the elements of a minor scene are present. Pauline suggests that Levin change into her husband's trousers (attention, Freudian critics!) and, after much argument, the situation seems resolved when Levin had "changed into Gilley's trousers in the bathroom."

With the new trousers, however, comes new *tsoriss*. Coaxed into telling the Gilley's youngest son a story,

> Levin, scratching a hot right ear, began: "There was once a fox with a long white beard—"
> Erik chuckled. In a minute he was laughing—to Levin's amazement—in shrieking peals. Levin snickered at his easy success, and as he did, felt something hot on his thigh. He rose in haste, holding the still wildly laughing child at arm's length as a jet of water shot out of the little penis that had slipped through his pajama fly. [P. 13]

Unfortunately, the total effect suffers from a kind of artistic diminishing returns, suggesting that what might work in a Laurel and Hardy movie or on the vaudeville stage may not always work in a novel. Robert Alter has suggested that

> the schlemiel, it should be said, lends himself much more readily to revelation in a short story than to development in a novel, perhaps

because his comic victimhood invites the suddenness and externality of slapstick; when that technique is merely multiplied in being transferred to a novel—where we expect more subtlety and innerness, a more discursive and analytic treatment of character—the comedy becomes a little tedious.

But while Mr. Alter's point is certainly a valid one and helps to explain why *A New Life* is a less satisfactory piece of fiction than, say, a short story like "The Magic Barrel," there is also a sense in which Malamud's schlemiels move from situational humor to moral dilemma, the "comic victimhood" here depending a good deal more upon a frame of mind than the vicissitudes of an external world. In this sense, *A New Life* is an important novel, not because of its limited successes, but, rather, for the varied strands of its failure. To return a moment to Levin's bedraggled trousers, part of the progress of the schlemiel has to do with "great expectations" that are perpetually unfulfilled. For the first hundred pages or so, the prevailing temper of *A New Life* is one of ironic reversal, usually involving either Levin's career as teacher or lover—and always centering, finally, on the comic possibilities of his pants.

His night on the Northwestern town with Sadek is an excellent example. In a way, these two rather bizarre characters complement themselves—Levin, the former drunkard and high school English teacher from the impersonal East, and Sadek, a Syrian graduate student whom Levin describes as a

> fanatic about hygiene. The fumes of Lysol stank up the bathroom for a half hour after he had been in it; he [Sadek] rubbed everything he touched—before, not after—with his personal bottle. He was majoring in sanitary bacteriology and taking courses in rat control and the bacteriology of sewage. [P. 73]

Sadek's concern for the physical paralleled Levin's attention to the moral. To be sure, we see Sadek as excessive, a comic portrait that qualifies him as an actor in the farce of S. Levin's life. When they vie for the "hand" of the fair Laverne—Sadek dividing his time between seduction and frequent urination, while Levin sips his beer and dreams of love—ill luck seems to visit each of them. Sadek is apprehended for indecent exposure ("the toilet facilities of the tavern horrified him and he preferred not to do a major Lysol job there"), leaving the barmaid to Levin by default. Soon the would-be lovers are alone in a barn, each captivated by the uniqueness of their situation; Levin, the irrepressible romantic, observing that this was "my first barn" while Laverne reflects that she had "never done it with a guy with a beard." For Laverne the whole business is standard operating procedure, an effective foil to the ways in which Levin waxes poetic at the possibilities of love, the West and, of course, a new life: "In front of the cows, he thought. Now I belong to the ages" (p. 80).

And, in a sense, Levin does "belong to the ages," although not the ones he had in mind. He is the presumably "sensitive" young man out of an earlier tradition in American literature, the sort of boy who takes sexual initiation seriously because he knows (unconsciously of course) that this is the stuff out of which great literature is made. A more recent writer like James Jones (in, say, *Some Came Running*) might be intrigued by the possibility of unions between Spirit and Flesh. However, Malamud seems more interested in incongruity than resurrecting still another version of "pastoral." Rather than a protagonist plucked out of an American *Bildungsroman,* Levin is really the schlemiel— here in the guise of country bumpkin turned upside down until it is the farmer's daughter who seduces the city salesman.

> *Laverne.* "Why don't you take your pants off?"
> *Levin.* "It's cold here. Have you got a blanket to cover us?"
> *Laverne.* "No, just the one to lay on."
> *Levin.* "In that case I'll keep my jacket on."
> *Laverne.* "But take your pants off or they'll get crinkled. . . ."
> *Levin.* "Your breasts," he murmured, "smell like hay."
> *Laverne.* "I always wash well," she said.
> *Levin.* "I meant it as a compliment." [P. 81]

And if the traditional schlemiel is portrayed as the cuckold, Levin may well be a modern variant, the victim of comic *coitus interruptus*. Just at the moment when "Levin rose to his knees and was about to be in her," Sadek reappears, stealing their clothing and leaving the hapless Levin victimized in the very heart of the great Northwest. The incident may well be the result of ill luck, bad timing or what you will, but for Laverne, the fault is clearly his: " 'You sure are some fine flop,' she said acidly. 'It's what I get for picking you instead of waiting for the one with guts.' " Even when Levin surrenders his trousers to Laverne—this time suggesting more agape than eros—the gesture is lost in a welter of comic complications. Laverne is hit by an empty beer can as they try to hitch a ride, and when they finally arrive at her porch, she "kicked his pants off the porch. 'No, you bastard, don't ever let me see you again in your whole goddam life. Don't think those whiskers on your face hide the fact that you ain't a man' " (p. 85).

But the misfortunes associated with Levin's trousers are not limited to his social life alone; they also play a prominent role in his academic career at Cascadia College. During his first class, "he carefully followed the mimeographed instruction sheet"—only to find that academic hours are longer than he had thought. With the fifteen items already covered, Levin "vaguely considered dismissing the class—what could he teach them the nervous first day—" when he happened to notice the boldface type at the bottom of the page:

N.B. DO *NOT* DISMISS YOUR CLASS BEFORE THE END OF THE HOUR. G.G., DIR. COMP. [P. 89]

The "bold-face type"—like the threats of a "black list" in Saul Bellow's *The Victim*—suggest the low-keyed, but constant threats of the modern condition. For Levin, Cascadia College is virtually his last chance—a matter too serious to risk by disregard of an official memorandum. I suppose conventional satire might feature a bumpkin too ignorant of the complexities to entertain such thoughts, his wide-eyed appraisal of the situation exposing folly in the manner of a Huck Finn or Lemuel Gulliver. However, academic satire usually contains some interesting shifts in perspective. In our best writers, there is always a curious tension between a feeling that the System has been taken over by incompetents and an equal desire for promotions in that very System. It is the difference between a novel like *Lucky Jim* and *Up the Down Staircase*—the former concerned with making faces at the college while you work for tenure by publishing scholarly articles, and the latter in which you emerge as the System's only sensitive soul with hardly any struggle at all. Levin shares qualities with the protagonists of both these novels, combining a penchant for accident that easily makes him an American counterpart of unlucky Jim Dixson with the hard-core idealism of Bel Kaufman's heroine. The recurring trousers, Levin's idealism about the profession, his twinges of paranoia and, most of all, his slapstick schlemielism all combine to end his first class in high style. Surprised and somewhat heartened by the rapt attention of his new students, Levin—following the "bold-face type"—launched into the business of sentence diagram until only twelve minutes remained. At that point he "finally dropped grammar to say what was still on his mind"; I quote the scene *in toto*, letting Levin's comic victimhood speak for itself.

> . . . namely, welcome to Cascadia College. He was himself a stranger in the West but that didn't matter. By some miracle of movement and change, standing before them as their English instructor by virtue of appointment, Levin welcomed them from wherever they came: the Northwest states, California, and a few from beyond the Rockies, a thrilling representation to a man who had in all his life never been west of Jersey City. If they worked conscientiously in college, he said, they would come in time to a better understanding of who they were and what their lives might yield, education being revelation. At this they laughed, though he was not sure why. Still if they could be so good-humored early in the morning it was all right with him. . . . In his heart he thanked them, sensing he had created their welcome of

him. They represented the America he had so often heard of, the fabulous friendly West. . . . "This is the life for me," he admitted, and they broke into cheers, whistles, loud laughter. The bell rang and the class moved noisily into the hall, some nearly convulsed. As if inspired, Levin glanced down at his fly and it was, as it must be, all the way open. [Pp. 89–90]

There are, of course, other instances where Levin plays the slapstick schlemiel. In the mock seduction of Avis Fliss, Levin reenacts his abortive evening with Laverne as the scene shifts from pastoral barns to academic offices. Here, too, the comedy revolves around *coitus interruptus,* although this time Gilley adds a dash of paranoia to the proceedings. In the same spirit, Levin's accident-plagued ride to meet Nadalee at the motel suggests all the penchant for self-created failure that are traditional aspects of the schlemiel. And yet, the schlemiel of pratfall is far more at home on the vaudeville stage than in the confines of a novel. Levin's comic difficulties—the accidents seemingly earmarked for him and lurking around every corner—are established in the first hundred pages. Whereas a novel like Joseph Heller's *Catch-22* worked on a theory of reoccurring absurdity (Milo Minderbinder's mushrooming empire or the exploits of, say, Major Major Major Major), Malamud condenses for effect and then moves on to new thematic material. More than anything else, it is this failure to achieve a singleness of purpose which makes *A New Life* an artistic failure. The perennial bungler is more stereotype than character and when his role is split between that of naïve persona in an academic satire and moral Idealist in a corrupting world, the effect is a certain amount of distortion.

Levin's notebook gives perhaps the best clues as to the kinds of tensions which will ultimately become the focus of the novel—

> One section of the notebook was for "insights," and a few pages in the middle detailed "plans." . . . Among Levin's "insights" were "the new life hangs on an old soul," and "I am one who creates his own peril." Also, "the danger of the times is the betrayal of man." [P. 58]

We have come to expect that Levin's notion of a "new life" based upon geographical change is destined to fail a priori. As Mark Goldman has pointed out, Levin is the "tenderfoot Easterner . . . (always invoking nature like a tenement Rousseau). Now he took in miles of countryside, a marvelous invention." [7] But whatever the "new life" might be or how ironic such slogans ultimately turn out, it hangs very definitely on an "old soul." It is almost as if Levin's notebook be-

---

[7] Mark Goldman, "Bernard Malamud's Comic Vision and the Theme of Identity," *Critique,* 7 (Winter 1964–65), 105. Subsequent references to Mr. Goldman are to this article.

comes a private place of understanding, often at odds with his public behavior or the clichés on which much of the novel seems to operate.

In a similar fashion, the element of academic satire has, I think, been misunderstood by a number of critics who were quick to point out that they were equally indignant about schools like Cascadia (and teachers like Gilley). After all, "The danger of the times *is* the betrayal of man" and it is not hard to see how this statement was interpreted as having something to do with the preservation of the liberal arts, the humanities, and most of all, English literature. Ruth Mandel, for example, sees Cascadia College in the following terms:

> Here is a stereotyped, mediocre, service-oriented English department. The instructors are organization men of the worst kind, men who should know better, men educated in the humanities. The school is a Cascadian Madison Avenue, a school where the emphasis is on practical learning, prestige, school-board approval, and the well-rounded, shallow man who must be an athlete if he wishes to be accepted. The attack is devastating. Malamud's intentions are clear.[8]

But are they? If Levin is really to function as the traditional satiric persona, it seems odd that Malamud should fail to get his credentials straight. After all, S. Levin hardly comes "from a world of pastoral innocence," nor is he "the prophet come down from the hills to the cities of the plain; the gawky farmboy, shepherd or plowman come to the big city." [9] Rather, Levin ("formerly a drunkard") comes to this untainted (?) West from New York City, the very seat of Eastern corruption. He is, I suppose, a sort of reverse Nick Carraway who follows his dream of a liberal arts college westward—only to find, instead, freshman composition and departmental silliness. And yet, Levin often seems more like the Kurtz from Conrad's *Heart of Darkness* than the Carraway from Fitzgerald's *The Great Gatsby*. Far from being the innocent one who may see corruption and still refuse to understand it (Nick), Levin seems to be drawn into the evil System until he, too, becomes its victim. To be sure, Levin is virtually surrounded by academic absurdity: his chairman continually revises his *Elements of Composition*, 13th edition (which, naturally enough, is the required text of Levin's courses); another rewrites a dissertation on Laurence Sterne that no one will accept; still another cuts out pictures from old *Life* magazines for a proposed "picture" book of American literature. However, Levin is not paralyzed by what looks like the curious publish-or-perish character of Cascadia College; after all, he had some plans of his own.

8 Ruth Mandel, "Bernard Malamud's *The Assistant* and *A New Life:* Ironic Affirmation," *Critique,* 7 (Winter 1964–65), 117–18.
9 Alvin Kernan, *The Cankered Muse* (New Haven, 1959), p. 18.

(Levin) wondered if he could begin to collect material for a critical study of Melville's whale: "White Whale as Burden of Dark World," "Moby Dick as Closet Drama." . . . Levin began to read and make notes but gave up the whale when he discovered it in too many critical hats. He wrote down other possible titles for a short critical essay: "The Forest as Battleground of the Spirit in Some American Novels." "The Stranger as Fallen Angel in Western Fiction." "The American Ideal as Self-Created Tradition." Levin wrote, "The idea of America will always create freedom"; but it was impossible to prove faith. After considering "The Guilt-ridden Revolutionary of the Visionary American Ideal," he settled on "American Self-Criticism in Several Novels." Limiting himself, to start, to six books, Levin read and re-read them, making profuse notes. [P. 267]

The proposed articles—one has the awful feeling he has read them in some graduate seminar or other—serve a number of functions. First, they suggest the ironic dimensions of Levin's purity, a matter not nearly as important in the groves of academe as it will be in the regeneration of his moral fiber. After all, it is the "others" who have sold out, turning their talent from human concerns to more commercial ones—not Levin. His articles are filled to the brim with American guilt and Edenic innocence—all in the best traditions of Cotton Mather, Henry Adams, and the MLA. Levin may differ in degree, but not very much in kind. Of course, the titles are meant to be satiric, although I suspect that more than a few of Malamud's readers secretly thought that "The Stranger as Fallen Angel in Western Fiction" might not make a bad essay after all. My point is simply this: Levin's overriding concern is for moral preservation, both in the collective sense of America and in the individual sense of self. If his academic fantasies are those of a potential schlemiel, they must be seen in the larger context of Levin's moral structure. In a sense, the pettiness of Cascadia College is only a backdrop for Levin's more pressing concerns— his inability to love, his lack of commitment, his perennial death of the spirit.

However, it is in his last "insight"—"I am the one who creates his own peril"—that Levin unconsciously hints at the sort of self-knowledge traditionally associated with the figure of the schlemiel. It is the schlemiel, after all, who "creates his own peril" and Levin's "insight" is both an acceptable definition of the term and an accurate appraisal of his behavior thus far in the novel. Neither a "new life" in terms of geographical moves to a mythical West nor his romantic notions about the groves of academe can save Levin from himself. Whatever comic spirit derives from the incongruity of a Levin plunged into Nature, learning how to drive a car, or being initiated into the realities of Cascadia College fizzles out almost completely as he moves toward

Pauline and the larger complications of the novel. For a time, it looks
as if Levin will relive the legend of Leo Duffy. He arrived with a
Duffy-like beard, began his career in Duffy's abandoned office and
ended with Pauline. However, Malamud has more in mind for S.
Levin than one more academic martyrdom. Whereas a Duffy commits
suicide (the final "protest" and one that is sure to have "meaning"),
Levin gradually switches roles from academic complainer and/or critic
to moral bungler.

At one point in the novel, Levin tells Pauline about his first
"awakening," his initial encounter with the new life.

> For two years I lived in self-hatred, willing to part with life. I won't
> tell you what I had come to. But one morning in somebody's filthy
> cellar, I awoke under burlap bags and saw my rotting shoes on a
> broken chair. They were lit in dim sunlight from a shaft or window. I
> stared at the chair, it looked like a painting, a thing with a value of
> its own. I squeezed what was left of my brain to understand why this
> should move me so deeply, why I was crying. Then I thought, Levin,
> if you were dead there would be no light on your shoes in this cellar. I
> came to believe what I had often wanted to, that life is holy. I then
> became a man of principle. [P. 201]

And it is from Levin's mushrooming sense of "principle" that his link
to other characters in Malamud's canon is established. To be sure, his
concerns take in the vast range of contemporary problems (unlike the
more isolated concerns of, say, a Frankie Alpine), but the mechanism
is very much the same. For Malamud, the important thing may not be
that a Gilley or a Fabrikant are exposed, but rather that a Levin
finally acts. However, moral action is almost always a qualified com-
modity in Malamud's world, more an occasion for ironic failures than
spiritual successes. And if Levin's academic fantasies had a ring of
moral urgency about them, consider the following slice of Levin's
wishful thinking:

> He must *on principle* not be afraid. "The little you do may en-
> courage the next man to do more. It doesn't take a violent revolution
> to change a policy or institution. All it takes is a good idea and a man
> with guts. Someone who knows that America's historically successful
> ideas have been liberal and radical, continuing revolt in the cause of
> freedom. 'Disaster occurs if a country finally abandons its radical
> creative past'—R. Chase. Don't be afraid of the mean-spirited. Remem-
> ber that a man who scorns the idealist scorns the secret image of him-
> self." [Levin's notebook: "Insights"] Don't be afraid of names. Your
> purpose as self-improved man is to help the human lot, notwithstand-
> ing universal peril, anxiety, continued betrayal of freedom and op-
> pression of man. He would, as a teacher, do everything he could to
> help bring forth those gifted few who would do more than their teach-

ers had taught, in the name of democracy and humanity. (Whistles, cheers, prolonged applause.) The instructor took a bow at the urinal. [P. 230]

Meditations of this sort often occur in the john, as any disciple of either Norman O. Brown or Martin Luther would be quick to attest. However, Levin's fantasies have a rather elastic quality about them. They are able to expand until the savior of the Humanities in general and Cascadia College's English department in particular becomes the Christ-like savior of the entire world.

> He [Levin] healed the sick, crippled, blind, especially children. . . . He lived everywhere. Every country he came to was his own, a matter of understanding history. In Africa he grafted hands on the handless and gave bread and knowledge to the poor. In India he touched the untouchables. In America he opened the granaries and freed the slaves. [P. 273]

For Malamud, the giving of bread is a particularly important symbol. As I have suggested elsewhere, it encompasses such acts as Bober giving early morning rolls to the Poilisheh or a Yakov Bok (in *The Fixer*) giving matzoh to the wounded Hassid. During a symposium held at the University of Connecticut, Malamud kept stressing this connection, placing a strong emphasis on Levin's dream of giving bread and knowledge to the poor as evidence of both moral growth and the novel's "positive" ending. But the bread motif works in ways that are more subtle than mere fantasy. Much has already been written about the Protean character of S. Levin's name—from the ridiculously formal S. Levin to the more relaxed "Sam." Mark Goldman sees the line "Sam, they used to call me home" as particularly important because "their concluding words end the search for Levin, happily surrendering S. for Seymour, Sy for sigh, even Pauline's Lev for love, simply to identify with the real past." Evidently part of the contemporary critic's equipment is the ability to play name games with both ingenuity and endless patience. And while the shifting quality of "S. Levin" may not be nearly as challenging as, say, the possibilities of Moses Elkannah Herzog or almost any character from a Barth novel, I suspect the really crucial pun is centered on Levin's last name rather than the varieties of his first. As the "leven" of *A New Life* (a possibility Malamud would probably see as both silly and significant), he must come to terms with himself before there can be any bread. But the critics were inclined to disagree. They preferred to think of *A New Life* as a totally ironic (and not too terribly successful) piece of academic satire. They were annoyed that the novel ended wiht Levin forced to give up a college teaching career which had hardly even begun and his fantasies about doing even *more* "good" outside the profession did not help. The crux of the issue is freedom: in his imaginary articles, he muses that "the idea of America will always create freedom"; his fantasies at the john suggest that the betrayal of freedom is the very thing the self-improved man must combat; and finally, he rages to Gilley about Pauline's status as a "free agent." But, for Levin, "freedom" seems to be more entrapping than liberating. As Robert Alter puts it:

> Levin suffers the *schlemiel's* fate—ousted from the profession of his choice, burdened with a family he didn't bargain for and a woman he loves only as a matter of principle, rolling westward in his overheating jalopy toward a horizon full of pitfalls.

Perhaps this reluctance to see Levin leave the profession (as opposed to just Cascadia College) has something to do with the reasons Oregon State keeps asking Malamud back to lecture. For them, the reasons are purely pragmatic. To be sure, when the fictionized version of academic life in Corvallis was first published, it must have been painful reading indeed. However, in time, even *that* can be marketed, and I suspect that Oregon State has made much of the fact that Malamud once taught there. And, too, the mechanics of the situation also work on the most personal of levels. As the hard-boiled Jake Barnes might sneer, it is "pretty to think" that academic life can be better at some other school and Malamud's subsequent career at Bennington seems to suggest that it can. However, all of this says more about Levin's critics than Levin himself. He can accept Gilley's rather absurd condition that he never teach on the college level again because his ambitions are more oriented toward becoming a "savior" than a "professor."

As Levin abruptly exits from the profession, he rushes toward a salvation which, for all practical purposes, looks to be a surefire hell. At one point, Gilley gives Levin a dose of what Saul Bellow might call "reality instruction": "An older woman than yourself and not dependable, plus two adopted kids, no choice of yours, no job or promise of one and assorted headaches. Why take that load on yourself?" (p. 360). The lines might well have been Pinye Salzman's and the story, "The Magic Barrel." Like Salzman, Gilley has a talent for persuasion and his arguments are so sensible that Levin is reduced to the stature of schlemiel, his answer to Gilley's final question ("Because I can, you son of a bitch") suggesting his self-created victimhood. Like Finkle, it is Levin's zeal to affect a moral change, to create "a new life" that has unwittingly willed his destruction. And, like the final scene of "The Magic Barrel," the last lines of *A New Life* are packed with ambiguity.

> Two tin-hatted workmen with chain saws were in the maple tree in front of Humanities Hall, cutting it down limb by leafy limb, to make room for a heat tunnel. On the Student Union side of the street, Gilley was aiming a camera at the operation. When he saw Levin's Hudson approach he swung the camera around and snapped. As they drove by he tore a rectangle of paper from the back of the camera and waved it aloft. "Got your picture!" [Pp. 366–67]

On one hand, there is the terrifying "picture" of Levin's departure —the battered Hudson on the verge of breaking down and the human relationships inside very likely to follow suit—while, on the other hand, there is the "limb by leafy limb" destruction of both Nature and Humanity. Gilley may well have gotten one picture, but it is doubtful if he got the other. After all, "pictures" make up a large part of Gilley's sensibility: one thinks immediately of the "evidence" he collected against Leo Duffy and the stacks of *Life* magazines that make up his research. Perhaps all this concentration on visual media might please McCluhanites, but in the context of the novel Gilley's camera and his pictures suggest an unwillingness to demonstrate either human emotion (Duffy) or moral concern (Levin). His projected Picture Book of American Literature will be as much a failure as the sordid pictures of his personal life. Malamud once remarked that Gilley's last "picture" will leave a permanent impression on his mind but I suspect it is more consistent to imagine his plotting to replace the *Elements* with his "pictorial history"—a situation that should not be too difficult at Cascadia.

From *The Magic Barrel* stories to *A New Life,* Malamud creates one ironic triangle after another and suggests that moral bungling is at least as live a possibility as moral regeneration. However, with his latest novel, *The Fixer,* he changed gears in a number of important ways. Rather than drawing from personal experience (such as the fictionalized account of his unhappy days teaching freshman English at Oregon State) or spinning yet another yarn about a metaphorical lower East Side, Malamud turned to the mythic potentials of the Beiliss case. In a strange and probably inexplicable turn of literary events, Maurice Samuel's *Blood Accusation,* a highly documented account of the case, appeared at the same time. Malamud may or may not have counted this as good luck, but it does suggest that the moral overtones of this most famous of all "blood libel" trials is very much a part of the contemporary sensibility. And, too, the sales of both Malamud's "fiction" and Samuel's "fact" hint that these concerns are shared by those in the marketplace as well as by those who write for it.

Of course, *The Fixer* is only loosely based on the Beiliss case. As Robert Alter suggests:

One feels in *The Fixer* that for Malamud 1911 is 1943 in small
compass and sharp focus, and 1966 writ very large. The Beiliss case
gives him, to begin with, a way of approaching the European holocaust
on a scale that is imaginable, susceptible of fictional representation.

There are really two issues here: the first involves Malamud's
choice of subject material. Although moral growth of one sort or
another had nearly always been a part of the earlier canon, never before had response and occasion been so intimately joined in ways
which suggested the holocaust experience. The second issue is that of
employing the schlemiel as a fictional character who will be harmonious to both the theme and plot of his novel. Instead of the comic
asides which pulled *A New Life* in more directions than Malamud
could handle, the schlemiel of *The Fixer* unifies the novel structurally
and provides an easy index for his protagonist's growth.

Yakov Bok is a schlemiel in the most classical sense of the word.
Cuckolded and then deserted by his wife, he seems to have come from
a long line of those who were the innocent victims of absurd accident.

> His own father had been killed in an incident not more than a year
> after Yakov's birth—something less than a pogrom, and less than
> useless: two drunken soldiers shot the first three Jews in their path, his
> father had been the second. [P. 4]

And yet neither the death of his father nor the impoverished condition of his own life are sufficient to make a handwringer out of
Yakov. As the name "Bok" suggests, Yakov remains obstinate, the
Yiddish translation meaning either a goat or an unbendable piece of
iron, while the English "balk" characterizes his reluctance to move
forward. But it is only a short distance (linguistically at least) from
"Bok" to "Bog," the Russian word for the Christ. Yakov may begin the
novel as the would-be cynic who drank his tea unsweetened ("It tasted
bitter and he blamed existence"), but his speeches are filled with vague
hints of the knowing sighs which will come later on.

> In my dreams I ate and I ate my dreams. Torah I had little of,
> Talmud less, though I learned Hebrew because I've got an ear for
> language. Anyway, I knew the Psalms. They taught me a trade and
> apprenticed me five minutes after age ten—not that I regret it. So I
> work. . . . I fix what's broken—except in the heart. In this shtetl
> everything is falling apart—who bothers with leaks in his roof if he's
> peeking through the cracks to spy on God? And who can pay to have it
> fixed let's say he wants it, which he doesn't. If he does, half the time
> I work for nothing. If I'm lucky, a dish of noodles. Opportunity here is
> born dead. [Pp. 6–7]

But if, as Yakov puts it, "opportunity is born dead" in the shtetl,
perhaps things will be better in Kiev. However, Yakov finds himself

beleaguered by accidents along the way—none of which (ironically enough) he is able to fix. And, like other moral bunglers, it is Yakov's penchant for good deeds which seems to contribute to his misfortune. Spotting a peasant woman "wearing man's shoes and carrying a knapsack, a thick shawl wrapped around her head," he

> drew over to the side to pass her but as he did Yakov called out, "A ride, granny?"
> "May Jesus bless you." She had three gray teeth.
> Jesus he didn't need. . . . Then as the road turned, the right wheel struck a rock and broke with a crunch. . . . But with hatchet, saw, plane, tinsmith's shears, tri-square, putty, wire, pointed knife and two awls, the fixer couldn't fix what was broken. [P. 22]

The scene is merely a foreshadowing of more *tsoriss* to come. When he finally arrived at Kiev—ostensibly only a stopover on his way to Amsterdam—Yakov "went looking for luck," but finds a drunken member of the anti-Semitic Black Hundreds instead. What follows is an ironic parody of the Joseph story. In this case, Yakov or "Jacob" functions as a kind of biblical Joseph who finds himself in a foreign land and soon rises to the position of overseer. Of course, Yakov's position is not nearly so grand. He is merely the supervisor of a brick factory owned by the drunken man he once rescued from the snow. For a moment it looks as if the fixer has beaten the game. He moves into a non-Jewish neighborhood and, like Joseph, goes about the business of assimilation.

However, if the drunken Aaron Latke is the mock-Potiphar of this piece, his daughter, Zinaida Nikolaevna, plays the role of temptress, her frustration at Yakov's "morality" aiding his final imprisonment. At this point, Yakov makes much of the fact that he is "not a political person. . . . The world's full of it but it's not for me. Politics is not my nature." But in a scant twenty pages, Yakov finds himself arrested for the ritual murder of a Russian boy and on trial for his very life. And, again, it is his penchant for moral bungling which seems to have contributed to his defeat. In a scene which closely parallels the rescue of his anti-Semitic boss, Yakov saves a Hassid from the torments of an angry mob of boys and even offers him a piece of bread. However, it is Passover and the religious man will eat only matzo.

> Pouring a little [water] over his fingers over a bowl, he then withdrew a small packet from his caftan pocket, some matzo pieces wrapped in a handkerchief. He said the blessing for matzos, and sighing, munched a piece. It came as a surprise to the fixer that it was Passover. [P. 65]

The matzos, of course, are the basis of the ritual murder charge that has been brought against Yakov. The State claims that Yakov killed a Russian boy and drained his blood in order to make the ritual cakes.

At first Yakov, who is not observant and who was unaware "that it was Passover" until he saw the Hassid, refuses to take the questions of his Russian captors very seriously.

> "Are you certain you did not yourself bake this matzo? A half bag of flour was found in your habitat."
> "With respect, your honor, it's the wrong flour. Also I'm not a baker. I once tried to bake bread to save a kopek or two but it didn't rise and came out like a rock. The flour was wasted. Baking isn't one of my skills. I work as a carpenter or painter most of the time—I hope nothing has happened to my tools, they're all I've got in the world—but generally I'm a fixer, never a matzo baker." [P. 102]

However, it takes Yakov only a short time to realize that "I'm a fixer but all my life I've broken more than I fix." As the time he spends in prison begins to monopolize more and more of the book, Yakov becomes more conscious of his own role in his calamity: "If there's a mistake to make, I'll make it." The long and agonizing prison scenes (which have caused at least one reviewer to complain about needless repetition) make Yakov's sufferings realistic as opposed to merely metaphorical. Whatever else a Yakov may be, his chains and the inhuman treatment he receives are real. Unlike a Morris Bober who suffered "for the Law," or an S. Levin who had "suffering" built into his psyche, there are no a priori assumptions here for readers to suspend their disbelief about.

Furthermore, Yakov earns his rights as an Everyman. Caught in a web of bureaucratic absurdity, he suggests that "Somebody has made a serious mistake," only to find that the case against him is growing stronger every day. If a novel like Kafka's *The Trial* makes the point that his crime is merely "living"—and that message had a certain appeal for hand-wringing existentialists who saw most of life as an absurd waste of time anyhow—Malamud's protagonist takes a rather different tack.

> He feared the prison would go badly for him and it went badly at once. It's my luck, he thought bitterly. What do they say?—"If I dealt in candles the sun wouldn't set." Instead, I'm Yakov the Fixer and it sets each hour on the stroke. I'm the kind of man who finds it perilous to be alive. One thing I must learn is to say less—much less, or I'll ruin myself. As it is I'm ruined already. [P. 143]

Yakov's learning involves an understanding of his group identity, the Jewishness which he unsuccessfully tries to abandon and his own responsibility in the creation of his fate. There is much talk of "luck" in *The Fixer,* but as Yakov's speech suggests, there is a connection between Fate and individual posture. Yakov's stance is that of the classical schlemiel and he half remembers lines which are significant in this figure's history. The unacknowledged allusion ("What do they say?—'If I dealt in candles . . .'") is to the epigrams of Ibn Ezra which Theodor Reik's study, *Jewish Wit*, handles in the following way:

> The great Hebrew-Spanish poet Ibn Ezra (1092–1167) was exposed to the slings and arrows of a fortune as outrageous as that of any Schlemiel. Driven from place to place by poverty and restlessness, he wrote the self-destructive epigram: "If I should undertake to sell candles, the sun would never set; if I should deal in shrouds, no one would ever die." From these lines of a poet of the twelfth century, a direct line leads us to the humorous and pathetic figures that Charlie Chaplin created and who have their home in the Jewish East End of London.[10]

Of course the posture of self-destruction that Reik mentions has become the standard fare of contemporary comedians who make it clear that they are "losers"—and usually have been so since early childhood. However, this alone does not necessarily insure their schlemielhood. Equally important is the sigh of pathetic insight which sees the moment as both terribly important and, at the same time, rather inconsequential given the total scheme of things.

Yakov's learning comes slowly, interspersed by scenes in which momentary bits of self-humor are offset by the systematic torture of his captors. One by one his friends betray him—victims of bribery for the most part—until Yakov is left totally alone in his situation. Even his one Russian ally, Bibikov (a sort of Russianized Eugene Debbs who spouts lines like "If the law doesn't protect you, it will not, in the end, protect me.") is either murdered or, what seems more likely, is forced to commit suicide. Yakov, on the other hand, wears his prayer shawl under his suit ("to keep warm"), employing strategies of pragmatism in an attempt to stay alive.

The end result of Yakov's suffering is a kind of understanding which goes beyond the postures of the classical schlemiel. If the first stage in Yakov's development was a period in which he was the unlucky victim of external accidents (the material things that break and somehow cannot be "fixed"), the second stage involves a kind of internalized self-knowledge. Rather than the frenzied movement normally associated with pratfall, it is in an absolute lack of motion (represented both realistically and symbolically by Yakov's chains) that he begins to understand the gravity of the situation. The third stage, however, goes beyond the province of ironic self-knowledge usually reserved to schlemiels. For example, Yakov at one point understands that he

10 Theodor Reik, *Jewish Wit* (New York, 1962), pp. 39–40.

was the accidental choice for the sacrifice. He would be tried because
the accusation had been made, there didn't have to be any other
reason. Being born a Jew meant being vulnerable to history, including
its worst errors. [P. 143]

And, too, in the matter of his cuckoldry, Yakov both seals his fate as
classical schlemiel at the same moment that he rises above it. In their
endless attempts to extract a confession, the Russian authorities finally
allow his wife a short visit. At first Yakov is annoyed ("to betray me
again"), but he soon finds out that Raisl is more interested in the fate
of her illegitimate child than in complying with the Russians: she had
returned to their shtetl when the child was a year and a half old, only
to find that

> they blame me for your fate. I tried to take up my little dairy business
> but I might as well be selling pork. The rabbi calls me to my face,
> pariah. The child will think his name is bastard. [P. 289]

And so Yakov is forced to make a "confession" of a very different
sort than the one Raisl had originally proposed. Like the schlemiel of
the medieval story, Yakov acknowledges the illegitimate child as his
own.

> On the envelope, pausing between words to remember the letters for
> the next, he wrote in Yiddish, "I declare myself to be the father of
> Chaim, the infant son of my wife, Raisl Bok. He was conceived before
> she left me. Please help the mother and child, and for this, amid all
> my troubles, I'll be grateful." Yakov Bok. [P. 292]

In the medieval story, the schlemiel is first cuckolded and then
duped into believing that he is, in fact, the father of his child. His
lot was to live among neighbors who knew better and to be the butt of
their thinly-veiled jokes about the child's paternity. Yakov, on the
other hand, knows full well what he is doing; the child may not be
his, but he, alone, can give Chaim (the name, significantly enough,
meaning "life" in Hebrew) a life within the shtetl community. Normally the progress of a schlemiel ends with an ironic sigh, a realization
that his "great expectations" have been systematically unfulfilled. In
The Fixer, however, Malamud moves beyond the postures and sig-
nificances of a single life, suggesting that Yakov's learning can have an
effect upon future generations.

In the final scene of the novel, Yakov is driven through a teeming
crowd on the way to his "trial," and an almost certain death. There
are overtones of Camus' The Stranger, but with very important differences. Gone are the artful ambiguities which had characterized
Malamud's earlier work. Yakov Bok may be moving toward a literal
death, but one does not feel the ironies creeping in as they did with,

say, a Leo Finkle or an S. Levin. Bok began as accident-prone and morally neutral, the rather bitter and obstinate "Bok," but he exits with tragic dignity and a speech designed to warm the most political heart in Malamud's audience.

> One thing I've learned, he thought, there's no such thing as an unpolitical man, especially a Jew. You can't be one without the other, that's clear enough. You can't sit still and see yourself destroyed. [P. 335]

With *The Fixer*, Malamud proved that he could do his homework with regard to Jewish material. His portrait of the schlemiel, for example, draws more heavily from traditional Jewish literature than he ever had before. However, in the final analysis, the Beiliss case interested him for its allegorical implications rather than its historical possibilities. The concerns of *The Fixer* had been with Malamud from the beginning: his schlemiels tended to be moral bunglers moving haphazardly toward redemption. With Yakov Bok, they finally arrived.

The Syncretism of Bernard Malamud

by Sam Bluefarb

The College Edition of *The Random House Dictionary of the English Language* defines syncretism as "the attempted reconciliation or union of different or opposing principles . . . as in philosophy or religion." In this sense, Bernard Malamud may be said to be a literary syncretist, for he has not only made the attempt but has succeeded in reconciling and synthesizing a congeries of widely differing literary themes and styles. F. Scott Fitzgerald once said that "All good writing is *swimming under water* and holding your breath." [1]

Malamud has managed to bring off that difficult trick. For to create a unity out of a variety of disparate elements—which is what Malamud's syncretism is all about—amounts to a signal success in Fitzgerald's subaqueous literary analogue. Further, one also senses in Malamud that while the author is in control of his materials, it is a studied effort rather than an effortless study—again, a practice to which Fitzgerald's dictum is especially applicable. And of course one cannot speak of what Leslie Fiedler once referred to as the "breakthrough" in American-Jewish writing without taking Malamud and his work into serious account. [2] For of all American-Jewish writers writing today, he is perhaps the one who best brings together those sharply variant elements of style and theme in order to create a wider and deeper synthesis out of them.

Malamud has borrowed from a variety of sources; yet, excellent craftsman that he is, he has both assimilated and transformed them into something peculiarly his own. There are of course such obvious and diverse sources as Henry James, Dostoevski, the Bible, Nathaniel Hawthorne, and, incongruously, the surrealistic/hallucinatory humor of a James Joyce touched by the darker humor of the dramatists of the Theater of the Absurd. Even more obviously, there is the seminal

"The Syncretism of Bernard Malamud," by Sam Bluefarb. An original essay prepared for this collection.

[1] F. Scott Fitzgerald, *The Crack-Up*, ed. Edmund Wilson (New York: New Directions, 1945).

[2] Leslie Fiedler, "The Breakthrough: The American Jewish Novelist and the Fictional Image of the Jew," *Midstream* (Winter 1958), pp. 15-35.

influence of Sholom Aleichem and to a lesser degree that of other
Yiddish writers out of the *shtetl*. Apart from the tart humor of Leib
Peretz and Mendele Sforim, there is I. B. Singer's mysticism—two
strains which infuse much of Malamud's work, respectively marked in
such exemplary stories as "The Magic Barrel" and "The Jew Bird."
And there is the darker undercurrent of the black humor of the sixties
in Malamud's most recent novel, *The Tenants,* a humor that does not
only "spear" the establishment, but whose implications touch on a
kind of love-suicide pact between Jew and black man—in short, the
murderous consequences for both ethnic victims which come of
generations of (well-intentioned) stereotyping on both sides of the
ethnic divide. There is Job, certainly a character much diminished in
Malamud's work, more the *kleine menschele,* the little man of ghetto
or *shtetl,* than the towering figure of Old Testament tragedy, yet a
figure who must be reckoned with. In both the short stories and the
novels he comes to us in many guises: He is Manischevitz, the poor
tailor whose capacity for suffering—for reasons not even clear to Bok
initially—is tested to the *n*th degree; he is Morris Bober, the elderly
storekeeper in *The Assistant,* whose own human weaknesses and the
sufferings that derive from them are redeemed by a reborn "son"—a
rebirth that may be traced back to such a diversity of sources as Frazer,
Jessie Weston, and (not surprisingly) the death and the resurrection in
the *New* Testament. All three—Manischevitz, Bok, and Bober—have
their faith in God, humanity, and themselves sorely tested. But in the
process, as Jews, they become twentieth-century paradigms for all of
suffering mankind.

In bringing together the values of the past in their clash with the
impasses of the present, Malamud ranges over what Jonathan Baumbach has called the entire "landscape of nightmare," a terrain that
has come to be an inextricable part of the spiritual and social wasteland of twentieth-century life.

Although Malamud was (as an arrived writer) too young to have
become a part of the proletarian literary movement of the early
thirties, the influence of that movement is strong in his work. His
ambiances are those of poor Jews in and around ubiquitous lower
East Sides and Williamsburgs—where the time is perennially the
season of the Great Depression—not simply of relief agencies or of poor
shopkeepers on the verge of bankruptcy, but of the heart. However, in
Malamud, there is no obligatory conversion to socialism at the end of
the story, the *deus ex machina* which Michael Gold initiated in his
early *Jews Without Money* (1930), and which many writers of the
proletarian school—Jew and non-Jew alike—followed as almost blind
formula; the emphasis is placed more on the redemption of the individual than on the redemption of the social order. Redemptions do

take place in Malamud, but in a larger, more universal way, best exemplified in Frank Alpine of *The Assistant*; insights do happen, but these affect relations between individual and individual rather than those between the individual and his society, as, for instance, in the case of the Jewish landlord, Gruber, in "The Mourners"; and faith is regained after its near-loss, as in the instance of Manischevitz in "Angel Levine." So that while Malamud is not strictly a "proletarian writer," he has not only successfully synthesized a number of proletarian patterns and themes, but he has moved them onto a higher (less doctrinally rigid) plane of larger humanistic ends.

I have also mentioned Dostoevski as an influence on Malamud— or perhaps we should stay with the word "source"—for in such works as *Crime and Punishment* and *The Brothers Karamazov* the redemptive theme is crucial in the recognition of a way out of the maze of sin and guilt. As I have already suggested, the theme is one that touches on such diverse characters as Frank Alpine in *The Assistant,* Yakov Bok in *The Fixer,* as well as such widely disparate characters as the *shlimazel* Levin in *A New Life* and the man-of-little-faith, Manischevitz, in the short story "Angel Levine."

Further sources, as suggested, are Henry James and Nathaniel Hawthorne. Like them, Malamud fills his work with his own "quota" of expatriates, even though they are hardly the kind of expatriates, precious with an excess of sensitivity, who appear in Hawthorne and James, nor do they resemble the jaded characters of Hemingway's "other countries." A more obvious example of this garden variety in Malamud is Fidelman, the art student on an extended stay in Italy to study the works of the Renaissance painter Giotto; and another is that of Levin (or Freeman, as he crosses over to a symbolic alias) the floorwalker-tourist from Gimbel's vacationing in Florence. Interestingly enough, Malamud's expatriates—those Jewish "innocents abroad"— seem to carry out, almost mindlessly, the same functions as did their predecessors in James and Hawthorne—even to the extent of finding themselves in, and having to confront, that brilliant but hard, corrupt, and cynical Italian world of poor aristocrats and assorted *lumpens* ready to pounce.

Malamud, like Hawthorne, though perhaps not so extensively, has mined his own stake in the territory of the gothic: the darkness, the spectral gloom, the aching sense of the past—all these elements are represented. But in Malamud a certain macabre humor slightly diminishes the almost unrelieved "powers of blackness" that run through Hawthorne's work. Such chiaroscurist elements are eloquently evoked in the short story "Lady of the Lake" and in the collection *Pictures of Fidelman*. Both Freeman and Fidelman in those respective works, like their predecessor models in Hawthorne, must make their plunge into the past in order to come to know the loss of their present innocence.

Further, Malamud, like Hawthorne and James before him, may be said to write the travel tale. However, Malamud comes closer to Hawthorne, not just in his uses of the gothic past, nor even in his effort to tackle the guilt-innocence syndrome, as much Jamesian as Hawthornesque, as in limiting himself to the Etruscan landscape and its cities wherein a whole civilization is evoked. As he has shown in his novel *Stitch*, Richard Stern is perhaps another example of the Jewish-American writer who, in order to suggest the sense of Jewish, and more universally human exile, chooses Venice as the geographical locus of his characters' spiritual transformations and transfigurations. In this respect Malamud and Stern have something in common: in these tales of exile the preoccupation of these writers with the fate of their innocents abroad is perhaps more "American" than "Jewish"— and each of these strands seems to enhance the other. But there is a further twist: Hawthorne's sense of innocence and guilt was derived from that Calvinistic notion of "natural depravity" or sin, labeled by Melville the "power of blackness ten times black," which itself, though a far cry from Calvin, goes back to the Old Testament, a Jewish book, and incidentally (though significantly) a work that appealed far more to the Puritan/Calvinist vision than did the Christian New Testament. Thus the syncretism of Malamud lies in the recognition that he is both a very American and a very Jewish writer, each component of his literary personality giving a certain symbiotic as well as syncretic strength to its counterpart.

As in James—and Twain—many of Malamud's characters are (Jewish-American) innocents abroad. As Jews they are of course also re-enacting the traditional archetypal role as exiles and wanderers, a role assigned to them as much by Christian theology as by mythic literary patterns (The Wandering Jew). However, unlike Christopher Newman in James's *The American,* or the unsophisticated rubber-neck though verbally competent rube of Twain's *Innocents Abroad,* Malamud's characters are "educated," or they at least have some background which suggests the type, whether they are professors trying to "make it" in some Western desert of the beaux-arts (Levin in *A New Life*), or art students studying Renaissance painters, or even semi-educated floorwalkers. Whatever they are—Jewish, or anything else, though usually the former—all of them have one thing in common, their American, occasionally urbanized, innocence as opposed to the experience of the Old World, or their initiation into the New of some preposterous Cascadia out West (as, again, in *A New Life*).

If Malamud's work may be said to contain a major theme, it is perhaps that life is better than death—the title of a story in the collection

Idiots First; for no matter how deep the chasm of tragedy, or how intense the pain, a "live dog is still better than a dead lion." Of course, accompanying this commitment to life is also the frustration which is as much a part of life as its lack in the "state" called death. The story "Life Is Better than Death" is reminiscent of two of Henry James's stories, "The Beast in the Jungle" and "The Altar of the Dead." And like those stories, "Life Is Better than Death" attempts to come to grips with the problem of the relationships between men and women under the duress of peculiar spiritual and social circumstances. In Malamud's story, a widow and a widower see in their common loss a chance for a "new life." Further, the characters and the setting—two Italians in Italy—additionally indicate that Malamud is not a "Jewish" writer in the more parochial sense. Universals still hold, whether in the Italian Catholic milieu of Florence or in the Jewish Lower East Side of New York.

Another aspect of Malamud's syncretism may be seen in such a tour de force as *A New Life,* whose techniques he will further develop in the stories and the novels to come. In this work we again witness the attempted redemption of a sinner, a reformed alcoholic this time. But the redemption, or its attempt, takes the form of escape, the time-honored way in which countless protagonists have attempted to confront reality—or run away from it!—in the American novel. Even down to the direction of the escape, *A New Life* may be placed in the tradition of the literature of the Westward movement. However Levin, the main character, is an improbable, if not zany, latter-day escaper who instead of trying to adjust to the West, as previous westering escapers had done, tries to impose—in vain—his Eastern intellectual and humanistic values on this "New" West as part of his quest for a "New" Life. The results of course are predictable: Levin succeeds most hilariously and preposterously in changing himself much more than he succeeds in altering his environment. At the cost of an earlier, and innocent, crusading ardor, he attains a greater honesty—perhaps more toward himself than toward that symbolic, unchangeable constant, his environment.

As I have suggested, one of Malamud's major strengths is his ability to bring together in harmonious conjunction a large variety of disjunctive schools and styles. For example, his handling of the Yiddish-inflected English dialect of his characters seems to be unparalleled in Jewish-American writing. It is a dialect that possesses the Old World "heart" within the quick impatience of New World forms. But not until *A New Life* and *The Assistant* appeared was Malamud able to show that he was equally at home in the novel as in the short story. *The Natural,* his first novel, was more in the nature of a metaphysical *jeu d'esprit*—even to the counter-pun of the title itself—than a fully developed novel. To be sure, *A New Life* is a Jewish picaresque while *The Assistant,* because of its more melancholy undertones, is anti-picaresque. But Malamud's syncretism is a prime characteristic of these works, for in them he shows his ability to handle a variety of themes and techniques, and be at home in all of them.

The mythic pattern in *The Natural* is that of the Waste Land—a dry (baseball) season of no wins, the hopes (or prayers?) for rain (victory), and the "romantic agony" in their attempted attainment. Roy Hobbs, the baseball hero, is the "knight" in search of the holy grail of a game (or quest), which in this instance involves not the winning of a lady's favor but the World Series. And even the lady assumes the role of *la belle dame sans merci* when she "kills" Roy in the first of his incarnations, so that he may rise again "reborn." Roy's "knighthood" of course is derived from the ball club he is associated with; for Malamud, quite consciously, if somewhat heavy-handedly, has dubbed them the Knights. Admittedly, all of this fits too neatly into the mythic grail-quest pattern and the "victory" which is eventually Roy's. Yet as mechanical in its parallel of the medieval romance as it may be, or as derivative of T. S. Eliot's "Waste Land" as it obviously is, the end effect is to further illustrate Malamud's use of syncretism.

The Natural is replete with readily recognizable mythic elements. Any alert undergraduate in the humanities, or major in English or in anthropology, should be able to pick out such obvious symbolisms as the knight's search for the holy grail of his redemption through victory, a victory genuine in Hobbs's case because it is made all the more meaningful by his rejection of a false, as well as a cheap one. And an intelligent sophomore should be able to note both a father figure in the person of Pop Fisher, the club manager, and his symbolic function as a psychologically maimed Fisher King. Thus, though Malamud is no T. S. Eliot, he has woven Eliot's widely disparate Waste Land/grail motifs into this first novel—even though these occasionally seem to be more superimposed than fully integrated.

Further, Malamud's syncretism is roomy enough to include such diverse strands as the proletarian, the mythic, and the Dostoevskian. His ability to fuse such disparate elements within a single novel may best be seen in *The Assistant.* In this work there is the entirely successful synthesis of the proletarian strain—a fable of blindness and discovery—and of the mythic: the death of the father, Morris Bober, and his resurrection through his "son," Frank Alpine; and there is the Dostoevskian, in Alpine's sin against Bober—his participation in the robbery of the old man's store—a sin which will later lead to Alpine's repentence and redemption through his love for Morris's daughter, Helen, and his final conversion to Judaism, a conversion which would presumably include the acceptance of the prophetic and social values of that religion.

Malamud's syncretism has also drawn upon the best, or most useful, aspects of that split tradition—the Jewish-American and the Graeco-Hebraic—and brought them together in his novels and short stories as few other Jewish-American writers have done. Not even Saul Bellow, the most formidably intellectual of the lot, has succeeded in weaving these strands into his work quite as naturally as Malamud has done. Further, while Malamud (as already suggested) expresses the redemptive vision of a Dostoevski, the ambiguity of a Hawthorne, and the psychological probings of a James, he has also adopted the surrealistic mode of a James Joyce—a technique which the later Fidelman stories exemplify. Like Joyce, Malamud combines—though not always as successfully—the syncretism of Hebraism and Hellenism, and the fusions and the tensions that grow from both when they are polarized as symbolic antipodes. Thus he renders, like Joyce, the Hegelian unity of opposites. The result is the quintessential Irishman within the quintessential Jew: put another way, the Jew in Malamud, as in Joyce's Leopold Bloom (possibly the greatest portrayal of a Jew by *either* a Jew or non-Jew in twentieth-century fiction), has become the Jew-as-Everyman, just as Bloom, the Irish-Jew, becomes Bloom the Everyman-as-Father.

Pictures of Fidelman is the work that perhaps best exemplifies this Hebraic-Hellenic tension. The main character, Fidelman, *runs* both literally and figuratively through these stories. He is neither businessman nor Talmudist but, like Stephen Dedalus, an artist, or would-be artist and art critic. That Fidelman (or "faithful man") is an artist of sorts is especially interesting in view of the Judaic injunction against the creation of "graven images." But Fidelman's inner split—the Hellenistic side of his Jewish self—lies in the tradition of classical criticism. In a sense, Fidelman discovers or rediscovers his Jewish soul through Hellenic means, and is thus finally able to recognize the universal Everyman within himself and within the "two cultures."

A gift that incorporates, yet transcends, the purely syncretic in Malamud lies in his biting humor. Although much in his work is not pure satire, it drifts in that direction; yet what satire there is, is not very ambiguous. For in making his victims, who are almost always Jews, the object of our laughter, he also strongly implies ruthless censure of those who victimize those victims. By a classical Diasporic means—the use of inverted, self-directed humor, the shrug of resignation in a hostile world—Malamud manages to persuade us that laughter is at least one of a number of alternative means of vanquishing insanity.

Comedy, satire, humor, witticism all run through Malamud's best work. Even in *The Fixer*—hardly a humorous book!—these elements, though keyed low, may be seen in the posturings of Tsarist officials in their resplendent uniforms attempting to cower a poor, half-starved (but finally spiritually victorious) fixer. But pathos and comedy are present too, especially in the three collections of short stories, *The Magic Barrel, Idiots First,* and *Pictures of Fidelman,* all of which have also that admixture of comedy, pathos, and near or implied tragedy. However, unlike these elements in the work of such writers as Nathanael West and Edward Wallant, the comedy rarely manifests itself in the black humor of the alienated soul within a larger alienated society. Perhaps the one exception to this in Malamud may be seen in his novel *The Tenants.* For even behind the most alienated of Malamud's Jews stands an order, a sense of continuity—in spite of the non-Euclidean leap into the New World—that makes the Jew a part of a larger, long-lived tradition. In Malamud the victim-schlemiels, no matter how comical they may appear to be, are more the objects of our compassion than of our derision.

In sum, Bernard Malamud has synthesized a large number of Jewish literary strands and motifs within the larger tradition of Western literature generally, and American literature specifically. Yet by giving them that special Jewish pinch of salt, he has, if not transcended them, at least transformed those motifs into something no previous American-Jewish writer has done: he has created an influence which is considerably more than a mere ripple in the American-Jewish literary tradition.

Literary Blacks and Jews

by Cynthia Ozick

In 1958, in his celebrated collection *The Magic Barrel*, Malamud published a short story about a Negro and a Jew. It was called "Angel Levine," and it contrived for Manischevitz, a Job-like figure who has "suffered many reverses and indignities," the promise of redemption through a magical black man. Manischevitz has already lost his cleaning establishment through fire, his only son through war, his only daughter through a runaway marriage with a "lout." "Thereafter Manischevitz was victimized by excruciating backaches and found himself unable to work . . . His Fanny, a good wife and mother, who had taken in washing and sewing, began before his eyes to waste away . . . [T] here was little hope."

A black man appears. His idiom is elaborate in Father Divine style: "If I may, insofar as one is able to, identify myself, I bear the name of Alexander Levine." Manischevitz at first doubts that this derby-hatted figure is a Jew, but the Negro says the blessing for bread in "sonorous Hebrew" and declares himself to be a "bona fide angel of God," on probation. Of this Manischevitz is not persuaded. "So if God sends to me an angel, why a black?"

The angel departs, rebuffed by Manischevitz's distrust. Then "Fanny lay at death's door," and Manischevitz, desperate, goes "without belief" in search of the black angel. In a Harlem synagogue he witnesses a small knot of Negro worshippers in skullcaps bending over the scroll of the Law, conducting something very like a Baptist theology session: "On de face of de water moved de speerit . . . From de speerit ariz de man." Passing through a lowlife cabaret, Manischevitz is jeered at: "Exit, Yankel, Semitic trash." When at last he finds the black Levine, he is broken enough to burst out with belief: "I think you are an angel from God." Instantly Fanny recovers, and as a reward Levine is admitted to heaven. "In the flat Fanny wielded a dust mop under the bed . . . 'A wonderful thing, Fanny,' Manischevitz said. 'Believe me, there are Jews everywhere.' "

A distinction must be made. Is it the arrival of a divine messenger we are to marvel at, or is it the notion of a black Jew? If this is a story with a miracle in it, then the only miracle it proposes is that a Jew can be found among the redemptive angels. And if we are meant to be "morally" surprised, it is that—for once—belief in the supernatural is rewarded by a supernatural act of mercy. But the narrative is altogether offhand about the question of the angel's identity: Levine is perfectly matter-of-fact about it, there is nothing at all miraculous in the idea that a black man can also be a Jew. In a tale about the supernatural, this is what emerges as the "natural" element—as natural-feeling as Manischevitz's misfortunes and his poverty. Black misfortune and poverty have a different resonance—Manischevitz's wanderings through Harlem explain the differences—but, like the Jews' lot, the blacks' has an everyday closeness, for Manischevitz the smell of a familiar fate. To him—and to Malamud at the end of the fifties—that Black and Jew are one is no miracle.

A little more than a decade later, with the publication of *The Tenants,* the proposition seems hollow. Again Malamud offers a parable of black and Jew culminating in fantasy, but now the fantasy has Jew slashing with ax, black with saber, destroying one another in a passionate bloodletting. The novel's last paragraph is eerily liturgical—the word "mercy" repeated one hundred and fifty times, and once in Hebrew. Nevertheless *The Tenants* is a merciless book. Here are the two lines which are its last spoken exchange:

"Bloodsuckin Jew Niggerhater."
"Anti-Semitic Ape."

It took the narrowest blink of time for Malamud, who more than any other American writer seeks to make a noble literature founded on personal compassion, to come from "Believe me, there are Jews everywhere" to this. How was the transmutation from magical brotherhood to ax-murder wrought? Is it merely that society has changed so much since the late 1950's, or is it that the author of "Angel Levine" was, even then, obtuse? If the difference in Malamud's imaginative perception lies only in our own commonplace perception that the social atmosphere has since altered in the extreme—from Selma to Forest Hills—then "Angel Levine," far from being a mythically representative tale about suffering brothers, is now no more than a dated magazine story. One test of the durability of fiction is whether it still tells even a partial truth ten years after publication. The conclusion of *The Tenants* seems "true" now—i.e., it fits the current moment outside fiction. But a change in social atmosphere is not enough to account for the evanescence or lastingness of a piece of fiction. There are other kinds of truth than sociological truth. There is the truth that matches

real events in the world—in *The Tenants,* it is the black man and the
Jew turning on one another—and there is the truth which accurately
describes what can only be called aspiration. Even in the world of
aspiration, it is a question whether "Angel Levine" remains true. And
on the last page of *The Tenants,* when Jew and black cut sex and
brains from each other, Malamud writes: "Each, thought the writer,
feels the anguish of the other." This is the truth of invisible faith, and
it is a question whether this too can survive.

"The anguish of the other" is a Malamudic assumption, endemic in
his fiction. The interior of many of Malamud's fables resounds with
the injunction that for the sake of moral aspiration one must *undergo.*
Yakov Bok of *The Fixer* is an ordinary man with ordinary failings,
born a Jew but not yet an accountable Jew until he has undergone, in
his own flesh, the terror of Jewish fate. In *The Assistant* Morris Bober's
helper, the Italian Frank Alpine, formerly a hold-up man, becomes a
Jew through gradually taking on the obligations of a Jew, ultimately
even undergoing painful but "inspiring" circumcision. The idea of the
usefulness of submitting to a destiny of anguish is not a particularly
Jewish notion; suffering as purification is far closer to the Christian
ethos. Jewish martyrs are seen to be only martyrs, not messiahs or even
saints. Malamud's world often proposes a kind of hard-won, eked-out
saintliness: suffering and spiritual goodness are somehow linked. The
real world of humanity—which means also the real world of the Jews
—is not like this. "Bad" Jews went up in smoke at Auschwitz too—
surely embezzlers as well as babies, not only *tsadikim* but misers too,
poets as well as kleptomaniacs. Not one single Jew ever deserved his
martyrdom, but not every martyr is a holy man. For Malamud all good
men are Job.

Nevertheless there remains a thin strand of connection between Malamud's visionary "Angel Levine" and a commonplace of Jewish tem-
perament, between the messianic insistence on the anguish of the other
and the common sense of ordinary, "bad," Jews. The sociological—the
"real"—counterpart of Malamud's holy fables is almost always taken
for granted by Jews: it is, simply put, that Jews have always known
hard times, and are therefore naturally sympathetic to others who are
having, or once had, hard times. The "naturally" is what is important.
It is a feeling so normal as to be unrelated to spiritual striving, self-
purification, moral accountability, prophecy, Waskowian "witness,"
anything at all theoretical or lofty. This plain observation about par-
ticularized suffering requires no special sensitiveness; *naturally* there
are Jews everywhere, and some of them are black.

But what has surprised some Jews, perhaps many, is that this Jewish
assumption—this quiet tenet, to use a firmer word, that wounds recognize wounds—is not only *not* taken for granted by everyone else, espe-

cially by blacks, but is given no credibility whatever. Worse, to articulate the assumption is to earn the accusation of impudence. Nowadays the accusers would include numbers of Jews who point out how thoroughly racism has infiltrated the life of Jewish neighborhoods and institutions; Jews, they say, are as racist as anyone—maybe more so, in view of (the litany begins) those Jewish shopkeepers who have traditionally been the face-to-face exploiters of the black ghetto. For all these accusers, "Angel Levine" must seem not just dated, obsolete, a sentimental excrescence of that remote era when Jews were as concerned with CORE as they were with UJA—but *wrong*. And many young blacks writing today would regard its premise not only as not a moral hope, but as a hurtful lie. Or else would see Manischevitz's salvation as simply another instance of Jewish exploitation, this time of black benevolence.

Black distrust of this heritage of Jewish sympathy is obviously a social predicament, but it is, curiously, a literary one as well. If the distrust has caused a blight on the sympathy, it turns out also that the distrust antedates the withering of that sympathy. The historical weight of "Angel Levine" was this: Negroes are not *goyim,* not in the full oppressive meaning of that word. How could they be? Anti-Semitism is not properly a Negro appurtenance—it is not historically black, any more than plantation-slave guilt is properly a Jewish burden. Thirteen years later *The Tenants* appears to reply: but no, the black man is a *goy* after all; and perhaps always was. Between these contradictory and irreducible formulations Jewish astonishment came to fruition. It was as improbable for the Jew to imagine himself in the role of persecutor —or even indifferent bystander—as it was for him to imagine the black man in that same role. Yet by the late sixties Jews and blacks were recognizable, for and by each other, in no other guise. In a 1966 symposium in *Midstream* on the relations between blacks and Jews, the sociologist C. Eric Lincoln wrote: "One could argue the expectation that if the Jews are not especially moved by faith, then they ought to be moved by experience. Perhaps so. But the best way to forget an unpleasant experience is not by becoming implicated in someone else's troubles." If this sounded like a sensible generality, it was nevertheless shocking to Jews because it was so thoroughly contrary to the way Jews had been experiencing their own reality, their own normality.

But 1966 counts as almost recent; it is, anyway, midway in time between the redemptiveness of "Angel Levine" and the murderous conclusion of *The Tenants*—the corrosion of relations had already begun. It began perhaps not so much because of the emergence of black political violence and Jewish fear of that violence, and not even because anti-Semitism had again become the socialism of the militant masses, but more fundamentally out of the responsiveness of America itself:

the Jews have been lucky in America, the blacks not. Manischevitz's daughter—we can imagine it—moves out of the foul old neighborhood to Long Island; the black Levine, according to Malamud, has no place green to go but heaven.

Jews are nowadays reminded that this difference—America felt simultaneously as Jewish Eden and black inferno—has always been exactly the thing that called into question the authenticity of Jewish sympathy; that this disparity from the beginning made the Jews suspect to resentful blacks, that Jewish commitment to black advancement, much less black assertion, *had* to be undermined by the Jews' pleasure in an America open and sweet to them. The statement "The blacks have not been lucky in America" is used now as a reproof to these luckier Jews for the impudence of their empathy, and to show it up as a lie—an ineluctable time-bomb sort of lie: if Jewish identification with black causes was after all not intended to be traitorous, then it was destined by Jewish success to become so. That most American Jews are themselves less than eighty years distant from their own miseries in the Russian Pale is said to be wiped out by their American good luck, and all at once; Jews who lay claim to historical memory are ridiculed as pretentious or bullying—present security is taken for a mandatory form of amnesia.

But this very formulation—the hell of being black in America— which is today raised against Jews to chide them for the vanity and presumptuousness of assuming historical parallels, is nevertheless not tolerated when Jews themselves proffer it. Either it is taken as still another meaningless white *mea culpa,* or else as a sign of greenhorn uppityness: the Jew putting on airs in the pretense of a *mea culpa* he hasn't been around long enough to earn. Lack of sympathy is an obvious offense; sympathy turns out to be more offensive yet. The point is surprising but unsubtle. If the current wound-licking withdrawal of Jews is now seen as an outrage or an expected betrayal, what of that earlier, poignantly spontaneous Jewish concern? In the very hour of its freest, most impassioned expression, it was judged as a means to take the Negro's humanity away from him—even then. To illustrate this astounding statement one must turn from the social side to the literary.

Sociologists—I hope I am permitted this fractionally unfair jibe— arrive at their preconceptions cautiously and soberly, but it is the smoothness of their preconceptions they are all the while aiming for. Literary minds work rawly and unashamedly through their beliefs, and have the skeptical grace to arrive at no man's land. Both Jew and black in *The Tenants* are literary men. Their war is a war of manhood and of art. The book has no conclusion and stops in the middle of an incoherency. Eight years before the publication of *The Tenants,* five years after the appearance of "Angel Levine," at the absolute height of "Jewish concern" for the condition of being black in America, a Jew and a black, both literary men, acted out an adumbration of the tragic discord (this phrase is not too grandiose) of *The Tenants*. Their war was a war of manhood (what does it mean to be human) and of art (what are a writer's most urgent sources). Their clash led to no tangible conclusion and stopped in the middle of a double questioning: "how it seems to Ellison I cannot really say," Irving Howe wrote at the last, "though I should like very much to know." "You should not feel unhappy about this or think that I regard you either as dishonorable or an enemy. I hope," Ralph Ellison had already written, "you will come to view this exchange as an act of, shall we say, 'antagonistic cooperation'?"

("Each, thought the writer, feels the anguish of the other.")

The exchange is seminal and ought to be re-published all in one place for its superb documentary value—a collision rich in felt honesty and therefore somehow strange, hurtful and agonizing, eluding decent summarization. Ellison's side in particular is a remarkably useful notation in the history not so much of black as of Jewish self-understanding. That there is space here only to give the argument with the sort of crude speed one would ordinarily eschew is probably, for purposes of illuminating a single point, all to the good—that single point being the response of one profoundly gifted black writer to "Jewish concern."

It ought to be made instantly clear that nothing in Howe's "Black Boys and Native Sons"—the essay that triggered the debate with Ellison, first published in *Dissent* (Autumn 1963)—was overtly written from the viewpoint of a Jew. The essay was, first of all, a consideration of Baldwin and Wright, and finally of Ellison himself. Baldwin, Howe observed, had at the start of his career backed off from Wright's "nightmare of remembrance," hoping to "'prevent myself from becoming *merely* a Negro; or even, merely a Negro writer.'" And Ellison, Howe noted, was the "Negro writer who has come closest to satisfying Baldwin's program." Appraising Ellison's novel *Invisible Man,* Howe marveled at "the apparent freedom it displays from the ideological and emotional penalties suffered by Negroes in this country," but at the same time admitted he was troubled by "the sudden, unprepared, and implausible assertion of unconditioned freedom with which the novel ends." "To write simply about 'Negro experience' with the esthetic distance urged by the critics of the fifties, is a moral and psychological impossibility," Howe charged, "for plight and protest are inseparable from that experience." And while acknowledging that "the posture of militancy, no matter how great the need for it, exacts a heavy price from the writer," Howe's final sympathies came down on the side of Wright's "clenched militancy" and Baldwin's ultimately developed "rage."

As against Ellison's affirmation of America as a place of "rich diversity and . . . almost magical fluidity and freedom," Howe wrote:

> What, then, was the experience of a man with a black skin, what *could* it be in this country? How could a Negro put pen to paper, how could he so much as think or breathe, without some impulsion to protest, be it harsh or mild, political or private, released or buried? The "sociology" of his existence formed a constant pressure on his literary work, and not merely in the way this might be true for any writer, but with a pain and a ferocity that nothing could remove.

Afterward Ellison was to characterize these phrases as "Howe, appearing suddenly in blackface." The reply to Howe, an essay of great flexibility and authority, came in the pages of *The New Leader* the following winter, and what Ellison made plain was that he was first of all a writer and a man, and took his emotional priorities from that: "Evidently Howe feels that unrelieved suffering is the only 'real' Negro experience, and that the true Negro writer must be ferocious . . . One unfamiliar with what Howe stands for would get the impression that when he looks at a Negro he sees not a human being but an abstract embodiment of living hell."

In coming out for the autonomy of art, Ellison seemed to leave Howe stuck with all the disabilities, crudenesses, and ingenuousness of the militant Protest Novel. Yet in almost the next breath here is Ellison defending his own militancy as unassailable: "I assure you that no Negroes are beating down my door, putting pressure on me to join the Negro Freedom Movement, for the simple reason that they realize that I am enlisted for the duration . . . Their demands, like that of many whites, are that I publish more novels . . . But then, Irving, they recognize what you have not allowed yourself to see: namely that my reply to your essay is itself a small though necessary action in the Negro struggle for freedom." Here Ellison suddenly seems to be giving Howe a victory. Even in *not* writing the Protest Novel he is protesting; *by virtue of being black* his heart is instantly recognizable—by fellow blacks—as being in the right place, "enlisted."—And had not Howe argued, "But even Ellison cannot help being caught up with the *idea* of the Negro"?

This part of the argument—complex and blazing, essentially the classical quarrel between critic and imaginative artist, and between the artist's own two selves, the "esthetic" and the "engaged"—is also an uncanny fore-echo of one of Malamud's preoccupations in *The Tenants*. There, however, it is the Jew who assumes Ellison's overall position of the free artist committed first of all to the clean fall of his language, and the black man who expresses Howe's implacability.

What this reversal portends we shall see in a moment, but first it is necessary to look at Ellison's consideration of Howe as Jew. It comes very suddenly—and I think justly—in his reply, and points to the absence anywhere in Howe's remarks of the admission that he is a Jew. Whether or not Howe himself thought this relevant is not the issue: what is important is that Ellison thought it relevant, and scornfully rounded on Howe for having called himself a "white intellectual."

> . . . in situations such as this [Ellison wrote] many Negroes, like my-self, make a positive distinction between "whites" and "Jews." Not to do so could be either offensive, embarrassing, unjust or even dangerous. If I would know who I am and preserve who I am, then I must see others distinctly whether they see me so or no. Thus I feel uncomfortable whenever I discover Jewish intellectuals writing as though *they* were guilty of enslaving my grandparents, or as though the *Jews* were responsible for the system of segregation. Not only do they have enough troubles of their own, as the saying goes, but Negroes know this only too well.
>
> The real guilt of such Jewish intellectuals lies in their facile, per-haps unconscious, but certainly unrealistic, identification with what is called the "power structure." Negroes call that "passing for white." . . . I consider the United States freer politically and richer culturally be-cause there are Jewish Americans to bring it the benefit of their special forms of dissent, their humor and their gift for ideas which are based upon the uniqueness of their experience.

The statement reads admirably. But if Ellison wants to "see others distinctly," including Howe's distinctiveness as a Jewish rather than a "white" intellectual, he must not object to Howe's seeing *him* dis-tinctly, as a man participating in a certain social predicament—i.e., getting born black in America. Defining an individual's social predica-ment does not automatically lead to stripping him of his personal tastes and talents, as Ellison assumes earlier in his essay, when he speaks of "prefabricated Negroes . . . sketched on sheets of paper and superimposed upon the Negro community." Jews also have their pre-dicament, or call it their destiny, as Jews; but destiny is something profoundly different from a stereotype.

The second part of Ellison's remarks, ringing though they are, is where the real difficulty lies. If Ellison thought Howe obtuse because he visualized the black as a man in perpetual pain, if Ellison thought Howe was distorting his own more open perception of the effect on blacks of their civil inequities ("matters," Ellison wrote, "about which I could do nothing except walk, read, hunt, dance, sculpt, cultivate ideas . . .")—what could a Jew think of Ellison's projections? What could be "special" about forms of Jewish dissent which do not include dissent on behalf of others? * What else, in the eye of history, could "special forms of dissent" *mean* if not the propensity to be enlisted in social causes not intimately one's own? What could be the purpose of ideas based upon the uniqueness of Jewish experience if that uniqueness did not signify at least in part a perennial victimization, and if that experience did not expend itself beyond compassion into identification? How then does it happen that Ellison, in attributing so many useful and distinctive things to Jews, has it all add up to nothing less ugly than "passing for white"?

The trouble, I think, is a simple one. At bottom it is Ellison, not Howe, who fails to nail down the drift of distinctive experience, who imagines the Jew as naturally identifying with the white "power structure." Ellison has some of the psychology right, to be sure—it *was* a case of "perhaps unconscious" identification, but in a way Ellison was curiously unable to conceive of, except for the instant it took for him to ridicule the idea: "Howe, appearing suddenly in blackface." But Howe's call for the "impulsion to protest" was not a matter of burnt cork—he was not coming on as a make-believe Negro (and certainly not as a make-believe member of the "power structure"), but rather as a Jew responding implicitly and naturally, i.e. vicariously, to an urgent moment in history, applying to that moment the "benefit of [his] special form of dissent." That the "identification" was authentic, the vicariousness pragmatic, the dissent genuinely felt, untouched by manipulativeness or cynicism, the next several years in America rapidly made clear, the proof being the rise of black programs of "ferocity," both political and literary—which, interestingly enough, a Jewish critic was able to foretell through the exercise of his own familial sensibility.

In this interpretive re-telling, I have perhaps made Howe out to be too much the prototypical Jew. This may be unfair to him. I do not know his personal views or whether he would welcome this characterization. But the exchange with Ellison, at this distance and after so many reversals in the putative black-Jewish alliance (how long ago that now seems, how unreal the very phrase), has taken on the power, and some of the dread, of a tragic parable. Ellison's inability to credit the Jew with a plausible commitment was, as it turned out, representative not only of what was to come, but of what had long been. From the Ellisonian point of view, "Angel Levine" never *was* true: impossible for black man and Jew to share the same skin and the same

---

* Howe has written elsewhere that he became a socialist through realization of what poverty was. And it was the poverty of the rural South that brought it home to him, though at the very moment he was reading about it he was himself an impoverished youth living wretchedly in a Bronx tenement in the middle of the Depression. (That the connection was made through *reading* is perhaps also to the point.)

pair of eyes out of which to assess reality. Ellison's side of the argument, it seems to me, utterly undermines the "sociological" premises of "Angel Levine"—black and Jew are not, will never be seen to be, mutually salvational. But it is not only the non-fictive referents of the tale that are undermined. Little by little even the moral truthfulness begins to seep out of the vision itself—what was radiant, if illusioned, hope at the time "Angel Levine" was conceived has disintegrated into a kind of surrealism, an arbitrary act of art, set apart from any sources of life. Literature (even in the form of fantasy) cannot survive on illusion.

This is perhaps why Malamud went forward from the failed dream of "Angel Levine" to the warlike actualities of *The Tenants*. Ellison, meanwhile, is revealed by the passage of time to be not simply representative but prophetic. Society becomes for the black, if not yet magically fluid, then not nearly so much of a shut box as it is for Malamud's Jew in the claustrophobic world of *The Tenants*, or for the Jew in an America now seen to be inhabited by black as well as white *goyim*, with few temperamental allies. Black political fluidity has increased immeasurably since Ellison wrote, expressing itself in a kind of overall ascendancy of purpose, while Jewish political self-consciousness is static, confined to a handful of Congressional constituencies. But even then, while acknowledging the chasm between himself and the power structure, Ellison made it plain that he was at home in America in the most comfortable sense of country-culture. In the very same essay addressed to Howe there is an account of quail hunting in snowy Ohio fields, and a note of gratitude to Hemingway for having written so well on wing-shooting "that I could keep myself and my brother alive during the 1937 Recession by following his descriptions." Few Jews, even of the third or fourth generation, will recognize in themselves this sort of at-homeness with the land, whereas even urban Poles and Italians have land-memory to draw upon. What emerges from the encounter with Howe is that Ellison has a Gentile ease in America—an easier scorn, even, for its blemishes—that Howe and Malamud, with their bookish moral passion, have not. "I could do nothing except walk, read, hunt, dance, sculpt, cultivate ideas." It is almost as if the Jew can do nothing but cultivate ideas.

What happened between Ellison and Howe (behind the back, as it were, of literature) was bound to be seized on by the larger metaphor of the novel. In my own case I have not found it possible to think about *The Tenants* without first turning Howe-Ellison round and round; together they make a bemusing artifact in a reverse archaeology. Dig them up and discover, in genteel form, the savage future.

I came to rehearse their exchange because, in my first reading of *The Tenants*, I was, like many readers, rabidly discontent with Malamud's conception of his black character, Willie Spearmint, later called Spear. Willie Spear is a black writer who has the flavor of an Eldridge Cleaver rather than an Ellison; and this seemed to matter. Malamud, it appeared, had deliberately chosen—for novelistic bite and drama—an unruly spear-carrier, when he might have chosen a poised aristocrat of prose. And up against Spear he set the Jewish writer Harry Lesser, a man almost too fastidious in his craft. The balance was unequal, the protagonists unfairly matched, the Jew too hesitant and disciplined, the black too spontaneous and unschooled.

That the protagonists *have* to be a match for each other at first strikes one as important, because *The Tenants* is partly, despite its directness of language and gesture, a theater-piece designed as stately discourse. Though I admit the comparison is inflated, nevertheless one is put in mind of the eye-to-eye feud of Elizabeth and Mary Queen of Scots in Schiller's *Maria Stuart;* or of Shaw's Joan at her trial, another example of an elevated contest of societal interpretation. *The Tenants* is obviously barer and coarser than these—airless and arid, a flat plain pitting philosopher-king against philosopher-king. Except, for these two figures—the Jew and the black—the book is, by and large, unpeopled. The two writers meet in an almost empty tenement about to be torn down. Lesser still lives in his old apartment, refusing to move out until his novel is finished. Already ten years of his life have gone into trying to finish it. Willie is a squatter—hauls in a typewriter, rustles up an old table and chair, and begins—

The friendship that springs up between them is not really a writers' friendship. In a literary sense it is the relation of higher and lower. Lesser is always the pro, the publisher, authority, patron of opinion: he has published before, one book is moderately famous. Willie, out of the ghetto, is the rough-hewn disciple. Lesser is the cultivated representative of Society-at-Large, and when he speaks as writer he speaks not as a Jew but as a clear-cut descendant of the American literary tradition from Hawthorne to James—that very James, in fact, who, visiting the Lower East Side in 1904, worried about the effect of Yiddish-influenced impurities on his clean ancestral English. Lesser too feels himself superior: a natural inheritor, like James, of the language, while Willie is only a crude aspirant, likely to damage his material by clumsiness. Lesser observes:

> He has not yet mastered his craft . . . What can I say to a man who's suffered so much personal pain, so much injustice, who clearly finds in his writing his hope and salvation, who defines himself through it? He comes in the end, as in the old slave narratives, to freedom, through his sense of writing as power—it flies up and carries him with it—but mainly in the belief that he can, in writing, help his people overthrow racism and economic inequality. That his freedom will help earn theirs. The

Life he writes, whatever he calls it, moves, pains, inspires, even though it's been written before, and better, by Richard Wright, Claude Brown, Malcolm X, and in his way, Eldridge Cleaver. Their self discoveries have helped Willie's. Many black men live the same appalling adventure, but it takes a unique writer to tell it uniquely, as literature. To make black more than color or culture, and outrage larger than protest or ideology . . . Lesser sees irrelevancy, repetition, underdeveloped material; there are mistakes of arrangement and proportion, ultimately out of focus.

Reading this, it is easy to think: ah, but this is unjustly conceived. Willie is a straw man. Why not a black writer who is not only fully literate, but *accomplished?* Suppose Malamud had given us Ellison instead of Willie—then what? Lesser, like Ellison, believes first of all in the primacy, the loveliness, of the sentence; for him literature is the personal courage by which the language is seized. Beyond that lies propaganda. Granted that two-literary-intellectuals-talking-to-each-other does not make a novel (Mann and the Russians excepted), or, at least, would not make *this* novel, Malamud seems to be asking for the sort of resentment that would soon come to surround his formulation: Jewish Intellectual vs. Tough Black Militant. Unequal warfare in the Republic of Letters. Could it not—for fairness—somehow have been contrived as Jewish Intellectual vs. Black Intellectual?

There were, of course, good novelistic reasons why it could not. For instance, the conflict that eventually interposes itself between Lesser and Willie is not intellectual but rawly sexual. Willie has a Jewish girl friend, Irene, whom Lesser covets and ultimately wins. Irene is unfortunately a fiction-device and lives only intermittently. Her narrative task is to convert the two writers into enemies through sexual jealousy. Lesser's importuning landlord, Levenspiel, is also a fiction-device—he is there to give us the novel's pivotal "problem," to put time-pressure on a stubborn Lesser—but Levenspiel, by contrast, manages to live vividly: "Have a little mercy, Lesser, move out so I can break up this rotten house that weighs like a hunch on my back . . . Hab rachmones, Lesser, I have my own ambition to realize." All this is beside the point. Levenspiel and Irene and Willie's black friends who slide in and out from the wings are all interruptions in the dialogue between Lesser and Willie; they are pretexts for necessary "action," for novelistic progress. They are not what the book fundamentally intends.

If *The Tenants* progresses, it is not through plot but through revelation. The revelation is one-sided: it happens inside Lesser. We do not really know what happens inside Willie. And what happens inside Lesser is this: the clear realization that the black writer who shares his quarters and also his literary hopes is, more than he is writer, more than he is lover, more even than he is fleshly human being, a ferocious, a mythic, anti-Semite.

It is a revelation to Lesser because, at the start of their closeness, it did not "show." When Willie is angry at Lesser he says "white," he says "ofay," he does not yet see distinctly into his rage at the Jew. Lesser, himself a failing writer, views Willie as a possibly ascending one. All that is in Willie's way is technique. He tells Willie, "Not that you don't work hard but there has to be more emphasis on technique, form . . ." They discuss form:

> Lesser asks Willie to grant him good will. "I know how you feel, I put myself in your place."
>
> In cold and haughty anger the black replies. "No ofay motherfucker can put himself in *my* place. This is a *black* book we talkin about that you don't understand at all. White fiction ain't the same as *black*. It can't be."
>
> "You can't turn black experience into literature just by writing it down."
>
> "Black ain't white and never can be. It is once and for only black. It ain't universal if that's what you are hintin up to. What I feel you feel different. You can't write about black because you don't have the least idea what we are or how we feel. Our feelin chemistry is different from yours. Dig that. It *has* to be so. I'm writin the soul writin of black people cryin out we are still slaves in this fuckn country and we ain't gonna stay slaves any longer. How can you understand it, Lesser, if your brain is white?"
>
> "So is your brain white. But if the experience is about being human and moves me then you've made it my experience. You created it for me. You can deny universality, Willie, but you can't abolish it."
>
> "Bein human is shit. It don't give you any privileges, it never gave us any."
>
> "If we're talking about art, form demands its rights, or there's no order and maybe no meaning. What else there isn't I think you know."
>
> "Art can kiss my juicy ass. You want to know what's really art? *I* am art. Willie Spearmint, *black man*. My form is *myself*."

Up to the moment of Willie's conclusion—"*I* am art"—this exchange is only another chapter of Howe-Ellison, with Willie as Howe, speaking on behalf of "being caught up with the *idea* of the Negro," and Lesser as Ellison, speaking on behalf of the universal values of art and humanity. But the two positions, Ellison's and Willie's, intermingle somewhat. Willie, like Ellison, does not trust his antagonist to "know how you feel, . . . [to] put myself in your place." Addressing Howe, Ellison simultaneously denies and affirms universality: as a black man he considers himself first of all a man, one who despite external disabilities is pleased to walk, read, hunt, etc., like all men; but again as a black he denies that anyone not black can creditably take into himself the day-to-dayness of the black predicament. Willie accepts only the denial: only a black can know what it is to be black, no one else. As for "being human," not only does Willie reject the term "universal," but he sees himself as almost physiologically different ("Our feelin chemistry is different than yours"), and he goes further yet—he freezes himself into the image of a totem, a *"black man."* The statement "My form is *myself"* is beyond humanity, beyond even art. It stands for something more abstract than either: a political position taken at its most absolute. For a totem *is* an absolute politics: an object, an artifact, a *form* representing an entire people, together with its interests, its cult, its power, its history and fate. The totem has no fluidity, its being is its meaning. Willie has turned the politics of a group into an object—himself, *black man.* In Willie Art is Politics, Politics is Art.

This is why it would not have served Malamud's deepest intention if he had chosen not Willie, but a more "realistic," pragmatic, literate, humane, relatively political, less symbolic black for the novel. In *not* choosing an Ellison, of course, Malamud took on himself both a risk and a certainty. The certainty was the charge of "stereotype" and "blacklash," to which *The Tenants* has already been preëminently subject. The risk—a "stereotype" having indeed been chosen—was the failure of the novel as art. To a degree this *has* happened—to the very degree Willie's stereotyped expectations lead to banalities masking as passions. Something was necessary to stimulate Willie's active vengeance, so we are given a plot-fulcrum, Willie's girl Irene. In return for Lesser's stealing his girl, Willie destroys Lesser's work of ten years; the war is on. But Irene exists to accommodate neither Willie nor Lesser, but the exigencies of a made fiction. All this is too obviously and distractingly schematic—even the lineaments of "parable" cannot contain it—and if I seem to be bringing it up again now, it is only to contrast it with the novel's authentic passions. These are in the mimicry of Willie's writing. I will come to them in a moment.

Suppose, though, Malamud *had* chosen an Ellison-like character to confront his Lesser. The first advantage would have been safety in the world external to the novel: with equal contenders, fewer readers might have cried bigot. And internally, also, there would have been an advantage: the contenders might have met and if necessary separated on the *cultural* issues, as Howe and Ellison did, not on the extraneous ones of purloined women and violated manuscripts. ("But," Malamud might counter, "purloined women and violated literature are the stuff of Willie's culture.") It might even be argued that, if novelistic conflict was what was wanted, if dramatic misunderstanding and distrust were what was wanted, a fictionalized Howe-Ellison clash could have provided them as surely as Lesser-Willie, and with the black man's "humanity" intact, all stereotypes avoided and averted. Inside the air of Malamud's novel, Ellison—or, rather, "Ellison"—would still have found Jewish literary empathy suspect, as the actual Ellison did in the more open world of non-fictional debate; and there would not have occurred, between two civilized beings, the perilous contrast between the "civilized" Jew Lesser and the "savage" Willie. (As the book now stands, though, there is nothing to choose at the end between Willie's and Lesser's savagery.) And not only this: with "Ellison" instead of Willie to do battle with Lesser, the novel would have been intellectually richer, thicker, clearer, the parable more perfect, the fright more frightening because in seemingly safer hands.

With so much to lose from Willie, with so much to gain from "Ellison," why did Malamud opt for what is so plainly a grossness, a caricature, above all a stereotype?

Here is Willie at his grossest:

> ". . . You tryin to kill off my natural writin by pretendin you are interested in the fuckn form of it though the truth of it is you afraid of what I am goin to write in my book which is that the blacks have to murder you white MFs for cripplin our lives." He then cried out, "Oh, what a hypocrite shitass I am to ask a Jew ofay for advice how to express *my* soul work. Just in readin it you spoil what it says. I ought to be hung on a hook till some kind brother cuts off my white balls."

Ellison had complained to Howe (implying Howe was guilty of it too) that non-black writers tend to create "prefabricated Negroes . . . sketched on sheets of paper and superimposed upon the Negro community." Surely this quotation from Willie fits Ellison's imputations; Willie is unabashedly "prefabricated."

But the real question is: who cast this die, who prefabricated Willie? Not Malamud. The source of a stereotype is everything. When, in the late 1890's, William Dean Howells praised the black poet Paul Dunbar's dialect verse for having "the charming accents of the Negro's own version of our [sic] English," chiefly because it exploited "the limited range of the race," which was "the range between appetite and emotion," the stereotype imposed on Dunbar by a white critic killed the poet and the man; he died in bitterness at thirty-four, wretched over the neglect of what he regarded as his real work—"But, Ah, the world, it turned to praise / A jingle in a broken tongue." In the sixty or so years since Dunbar's death, the "jingle in a broken tongue" has entered the precincts of "soul," and the notion of "our English," when espoused by blacks, receives serious pedagogical and linguistic consideration as a legitimate alternative, a separate language with a distinctive grammar. The stereotype, emerging from Howells, was an in-

sult and a misappropriation; emerging from black pride, it begins to
gather the honors of honest coinage.

Malamud did not make Willie. He borrowed him—he mimicked
him—from the literature and the politics of the black movement.
Willie is the black dream that is current in our world. Blacks made
him. Few blacks disavow him. The black middle class, which is ambivalent about Willie, nevertheless does not disavow him—not simply
out of loyalty to the underclass (the loyalty is what is in doubt), but
out of covert gratitude.* Almost no black writer has disavowed Willie.
Ellison is the exception: ". . . what an easy con-game for ambitious,
publicity-hungry Negroes this stance of 'militancy' has become!" he
exclaimed to Howe, but that was eight years ago, and since then,
though Willie has grown louder and published amply (he is famous
as LeRoi Jones, for instance), Ellison has had nothing to say about
him. Surely Baldwin does not disavow Willie; he has become him.

In short, Willie is what he intends himself to be (which is also what
he is intended to be by those blacks who do not deny him): a totem,
emblem of a community unified in and through Willie's spirit, what
he calls his "form"—not man, as Ellison would have it, but *black man.*

What is the meaning of Willie in his self-declared "form"? Willie's
form takes up not freedom and fluidity, but unmovable hatred and
slavish vengeance. His vengeance is "literary" in two ways: the burning
of Lesser's book, and the creation of his own—but "his own" ends as
a travesty and spoliation of all humane literary values. Only through
the destruction of Jewish culture, says Willie's form, can black culture
arise. Lesser finds Willie's notes: "I have got to write better, Better and
Better. Black but better. Nothing but black. Now or never." And
whereas earlier—before the pivotal jealousy episode—writing "black"
for Willie had for the most part meant telling the poignant and honest
story of his ruined, scarred, and panicked childhood in the ghetto,†
now, writing black for vengeance, Willie dreams pogroms. For him
literature serves politics—not as propaganda consciously does, as an
"arm" or partner or extension or tool of politics—but intrinsically,

---

* Orde Coombs writes in a recent *Harper's* (January, 1972), "The thirty-to-forty-
year-old black who holds down a good job in the North must know that his present
success is a direct result of past tumult. All his talent, all his effort would not have
otherwise given him a toehold in television, in consulting firms, in brokerage firms,
in advertising, and in publishing . . . Many of these black men know they owe their
livelihoods to their poorer, more militant brethren . . . *In fact, only one group has
really benefited from the turbulence; and that is the middle class.*" (Coombs' emphasis.)

† Malamud has mastered the idiom typical of this fiction. For anyone doubtful
about Malamud's ear—or, rather, literary eye—a recent anthology called *What We
Must Be: Young Black Storytellers* (Dodd, Mead, 1971) is instructive.

below the level of rational motivation. Willie's only politics is co-
extensive with nearly the whole of his literary imagination; it is the
politics and the imagination of anti-Semitism.

Lesser finds another of Willie's notes:

> It isn't that I hate Jews. But if I do any, it's not because I invented
> it myself but I was born in the good old U.S.A. and there's a lot of
> that going on that gets under your skin. And it's also from knowing
> the Jews, which I do. The way to black freedom is against them.

Now that Willie has stopped seeing Lesser as a more experienced
writer and can think of him only as a Jew, Lesser too alters. He is rewriting his lost manuscript in fear and anguish, but the vision slips
from him, he is in terror of Willie. "I treated you like any other man,"
he tells Willie. Willie replies, "No Jew can treat me like a man," and
Lesser, afraid for his life, turns as savage as Willie, with this difference:
". . . it sickened him deeply," he remains self-conscious. Nevertheless
he gets an ax and chops up Willie's typewriter. On that typewriter
Willie had written pages of anti-Semitic (some of it "anti-Zionist")
poetry and prose, fantasying the murder of Jews. The work of the two
writers is contrasted. Lesser's destroyed book is about a writer's struggle to love. The writer is named Lazar Cohen; he is much like Malamud's Fidelman, an artist with a Jewish name who conceives of himself only as artist, almost never as Jew. Willie's stories are about blacks
torturing Jews. In one of them, "a Jew slumlord in a fur-collar coat,
come to collect his bloodmoney rents," is stabbed and killed by three
blacks, who strip his corpse naked and propose to eat it, but change
their minds. "He tastes Jewtaste, that don't tast like nothin good." The
story, as Lesser finds it in Willie's notes, ends:

> Then they [the murderers] go to a synagogue late at night, put on
> yarmulkas and make Yid noises, praying.
>
> In an alternate ending the synagogue is taken over and turned into
> a mosque. The blacks dance hasidically.

With the apparition once again of a black synagogue, with the word
"hasidically," Malamud suddenly and astonishingly blows in a whiff
of "Angel Levine"—are his blacks becoming Jews again? Lesser has a
fantasy: in a mythical Africa there is a double tribal wedding. A rabbi
presides. The chief's son, who turns out to be Willie, is marrying a Jewish girl, who is Irene. Lesser is marrying a black woman. The rabbi
exhorts the couples, "Someday God will bring together Ishmael and
Israel to live as one people. It won't be the first miracle." Inside his
dream Lesser says critically of it, "It's something I imagined, like an
act of love, the end of my book, if I dared."

But Malamud himself does not dare. "Angel Levine" is not merely out of date, it is illusion; at the close of *The Tenants* Malamud explicitly acknowledges that it is illusion. Lesser's ax—it is the final vision of the novel—sinks into Willie "as the groaning black's razor-sharp saber, in a single boiling stabbing slash, cut[s] the white's balls from the rest of him." It is curious, horrible, and terrifying to take in what Malamud in *The Tenants* openly posits: that the Jew in America, beginning as Howe did with a cry of identification with black suffering, is self-astonished to find himself responding now in the almost-forgotten mood of *zelbshuts*—the *shtetl*'s term for weaponry stored against the fear of pogroms. Lesser, a hesitant intellectual, is driven to hauling an ax. But *The Tenants* insists on more than this. Like much of Malamud's work, and specifically like *The Assistant* and *The Fixer*, it offers the metaphoric incarnation of a Malamudic text: whoever wants to kill the Jew has already killed the human being in himself.

It is not only no failing, it is the best achievement of the novel that Willie, its black militant, is a stereotype devoid of any easy humanity. The clichés appropriate for a political strategy are unsuitable for describing the soul of a living person. Given the extra-literary truth that black militancy, in and out of print, has now come to define itself if not largely then centrally through classical anti-Semitism, to bestow on a fictional Willie a life beyond his bloody fantasies would have been a savagery akin to Willie's own. To put it another way: to have ascribed to Willie the full and continuing aspects of a decent breathing human being *but for his hatred of Jews* would have been to subvert the meaning of human.

The Tenants is a claustrophobic fable: its theme is pogrom. It remarks the minutiae of a single-handed pogrom so closely that the outer world is shut out. There is almost no city beyond Lesser's tenement, and there are no white Gentiles in the novel, no faint indication of the identification with the Gentile power structure Ellison claimed Jewish intellectuals were seeking. In *The Tenants* the Jew has no allies. Jew and black fight alone in an indifferent world.

There is no means, at this juncture, of determining whether its current worldly truths will one day seep out of *The Tenants,* as the moral radiance of "Angel Levine" had ultimately, through subversion by history, to ebb into falsehood. But—for the moment—Malamud has abandoned the hopefulness of "Angel Levine" and drawn a parable of political anxiety. "Each, thought the writer, feels the anguish of the other" is the last flicker of that hopefulness but does not convince. Willie is Lesser's doom—Lesser, dreaming of love, rigorously apolitical, isolated in his esthetics, becomes the inescapable victim of an artist whose art is inseparable from butchery.

Yevtushenko, declaiming at the Felt Forum* that bombs and bala-laikas are in essence always separate, nevertheless speaks not for Lesser but for Willie. Yevtushenko's poem condemning the bombing of Hurok's office, and the death of a secretary there, moved everyone, who could disagree? But the poem is a cheat. To be horrified at the bombing is not automatically to assent to the purity of art. Mozart was played at Auschwitz, and it is a ruse to pretend that any natural "separation" of art keeps it unblemished by political use. Malamud, in plucking Willie out of the black writing that made him, has not invented the politicization of fiction. And in inventing *The Tenants,* Malamud ironically follows Willie—he has written a tragic fiction soaked in the still mainly unshed blood of the urban body politic.

* Yevgeny Yevtushenko, the Soviet poet, gave a reading in New York City the day after a New York group had bombed the offices of Sol Hurok, the agent responsible for booking cultural events in the United States. A young Jewish woman, a secretary in Hurok's office, was killed. Yevtushenko overnight wrote a poem in commemoration; it compared the girl's death to the gassing of Jews in Auschwitz, and declared that art and politics must be kept separate. The poem noticeably subverted its own thesis.

Malamud's Head (*Rembrandt's Hat*)

by Renee Winegarten

Here is another collection of short stories, the fourth by Bernard Malamud, with a beautifully resonant title. The very idea of Rembrandt's hat makes us think of artistic stature, of the highest accomplishment and most moving expression of humane understanding in art. At the same time there is something quirkily humorous about the hat considered in itself, distinct from the artist's head, and something grotesque in the thought that there might be any artist living to-day whom such a symbolically grand hat would fit.

In the title story, set in a New York art institute, a thoughtless voluble art historian wounds the susceptibilities of a reticent elder colleague, an unsuccessful sculptor in driftwood and welded iron with a taste for unusual headgear. He does so by comparing his colleague's cap to the hat he mistakenly remembers as having been worn by Rembrandt in a profound self-portrait. Thus he stands in for the critic who not only fails to hit the nail on the head but strikes the practitioner's thumb. Tension grows between the two men, until the theoretician, by thinking himself into the place of the frustrated and disappointed sculptor, suddenly realizes how lacking he has been in delicacy. For he has forced the sculptor to ask himself yet again "—but once too often—why am I going on this way if this is the kind of sculptor I am going to be for the rest of my life."

A reconciliation burgeons. At least it would appear that human failure can be overcome through insight even if limitations in the gift of artistic expression cannot. A hint of satire whose object is the restricted or misguided aspirations of modern anti-humanist art, together with a hint of touchingly modest self-criticism, of self-dissatisfaction on the part of the author himself, seem to be suggested here.

This tale and others like it make one wonder why so accomplished, so esteemed and ultimately successful a writer as Malamud—if success is to be judged by critical acclaim, academic assessment and consecration, winning the National Book Award for fiction, having a novel and

"Malamud's Head," by Renee Winegarten. Originally published in *Midstream,* 19:8 (October 1973), 76–79. Copyright © 1973 The Theodor Herzl Foundation, Inc. Reprinted by permission of the author and publisher.

a short story filmed (albeit unsatisfactorily) and stories published in
Playboy and *The New Yorker*—should concern himself to such a large
extent with struggling, frustrated novelists or failed artists. Typical of
the former was the novelist rather too obviously named Lesser, dreaming of "writing a small masterpiece though not too small" in *The
Tenants.* No doubt recognition came to Malamud comparatively late,
his first novel, *The Natural,* appearing when he was in his late thirties.
Moreover, in twenty years or so he has published five novels and four
collections of short stories (some of these stories, dealing with the tire-
some failed painter, Fidelman, featuring more than once), an output
which an ambitious writer might consider small. One guesses extreme
care, intense self-scrutiny and ready elimination.

Underlying Malamud's work is the dilemma of the conflicting claims
of art and life which preoccupied the writers of the nineteenth and
early twentieth centuries as much as the question of truth and illusion
bothered the artists of the High Renaissance and the Baroque. The
conflict was amusingly summarized in the epigraph to *Pictures of Fidelman*:

> The intellect of man is forced to choose Perfection of the life, or of the
> work. . . . W. B. Yeats.
> Both. A. Fidelman.

There seems little doubt that Fidelman here presents one of the bizarre
masks of the author himself who, if correctly reported, once told an
interviewer somewhat awkwardly, "I want my books to contain a feeling for humanity and to be a work of art."

Malamud, along with many other established writers, has suffered
from being ticketed. From small seedlings, preconceptions grow into
tall trees that obscure the view. So passionate and fearful a concern
with art—already adumbrated years ago in "The Girl of My Dreams,"
where long before *The Tenants* a manuscript is awesomely burned in
a (non-magic) "barrel," an Ibsenite image of the death of a spiritual
child or self that haunts Malamud's imagination—may surprise those
who tend to think of him largely in terms of what a critic once called
his "rather unconvincing fiddling-on-the-roof pastiche."

Paradoxically, however, it is when Malamud is most vigorously fid-
dling on the roof amid lit candles that he seems (to the present non-
American outsider at least) to be at his most American. His magic
barrels and silver crowns, whatever their scale, firmly belong in the
moral, allegorical realm of scarlet letters, white whales and golden
bowls. "The Silver Crown," with its wonder rabbi, tells us less perhaps
about any specifically Jewish predicament than about the universal opposition of spirituality and materialism. It also turns upon an unsatis-
factory father-and-son relationship, that theme beloved of American

writers which is to be found in "The Letter," in "My Son the Murderer" and, by extension, in "Notes from a Lady at a Dinner Party"
with its betrayal of the father-figure or father-substitute.

One can see why, when questioned by eager beavers regarding the
supposed oddity or mystery of stories with Jewish settings and para-
phernalia written by a self-confessed marginal Jew, Malamud tends to
read what sounds almost like a prepared statement or to turn the answer in a general American direction. Far more interesting than this
non-problem is his ambivalent attitude to the Jewish element in his
writing. On the one hand he conveys distaste for self-pitying Jewish
exploiters (the self-pity is a nice touch); on the other he exalts Jewish
spirituality while feeling doubts about certain manifestations of it.
The Dostoevskian symbolic doubles in his fiction can be seen as representing two contradictory inner voices. The relentless pursuit of one
figure by another would imply the secret urge to escape and remain
uninvolved as well as the call (through a sense of guilt) to the conscious
and willed acceptance of responsibility.

Ambivalence of this order is particularly clearly revealed in "The
Silver Crown," in a manner both wryly humorous and true, when the
distraught son cannot make up his mind whether the rabbi who proposes to "save" his dying father is a charlatan or not. Meanwhile, the
equivocal rabbi speaks the language of spiritual understanding which
is totally incomprehensible to the scientifically-trained son. Basically
"The Silver Crown" reverses the dénouement of an earlier story, "Angel Levine," where faith and trust in the dubious messenger of the
spirit restore a sick wife to her loving husband. There is a darkening
of tone in the more recent tale which suggests that lack of understanding for the life of the soul as well as insufficient love for a fellow creature can destroy the possibility of miracle, that is, of spiritual enlarge-
ment, a change of heart, reconciliation.

If "The Silver Crown" is the story most reminiscent of Malamud's
"magic barrel" manner, one of the best tales in the new collection
derives from that intensified awareness of the wider social and political
scene which has grown more marked since another story of tragically
misplaced distrust, "The German Refugee" in *Idiots First*. True, beneath much of Malamud's earlier fiction there lay his personal experience of the depression during the inter-war years and the intractable
fact of Nazi genocide. But now he tends to speak of social and racial
injustice in a broader sense.

Defining his political standpoint—at the time when he was being
honored for *The Fixer* in 1967—in opposition to the formalism of the
French "new novel," Malamud roundly declared that the atomic bombs
should never have been dropped on Hiroshima and Nagasaki, that the
fear fostered by Senator McCarthy had not yet disappeared, that the

Vietnam war was a cruel error. "After what one lives through, who runs from content? . . . What a fool I'd be not to say what I think of the world!" This unequivocally impassioned declaration, delivered by a writer distinguished for obliquity, a declaration which one read at the time with a certain surprise, pointed to the extension of his strong sense of moral responsibility in personal relationships, his enduring conviction that one is one's brother's keeper (no matter how unprepossessing or inimical that brother may be).

This conclusion could be drawn from the destructive enmity between a pair of struggling writers, one Jewish and one black, in *The Tenants*; and the same kind of concern permeates "Man in the Drawer," where the concentration of the short story enables Malamud to approach a terseness that sometimes eludes him in the broader expanse of his novels. "Man in the Drawer" probes the relationship between yet another symbolic literary pair, representing artistic withdrawal and commitment. On a visit to Russia a marginally Jewish American freelance writer named Harvitz (whose inadequacy can be guessed from the fact that he is writing on literary museums) finds himself dogged by Levitansky, a struggling half Jewish Russian writer who cannot get his work published in the Soviet Union. Not for nothing do Levitansky's heroes include the great Soviet Jewish literary martyrs Pasternak and Mandelstam.

Desperately Levitansky pursues the reluctant Harvitz because he sees in the suspicious, nervous American a veritable life-line. At last, he hopes, his suppressed voice may be heard if only Harvitz will arrange for publication of his stories in the United States. The four haunting Malamudesque stories attributed to Levitansky, significantly rather more spare and more bitter in tone than those of the master story-teller himself, reflect the integrity and courage of the Russian's social criticism. But Levitansky, unlike his own protagonist, does not have to burn his manuscript. A nightmare enables Harvitz to put himself in Levitansky's shoes—that process of imaginative substitution which serves as Malamud's shorthand for the flash of humane insight—and the American decides to fly out with the manuscript, realizing that the worst of the Russian's ordeal is still to come. This very fine and revealing long short story, a hymn to personal and literary courage and commitment, should surely be counted among Malamud's most memorable works.

Equally impressive in a different way is the last story in the book, "Talking Horse," a sadly humorous and allusive fable about the nature of the human being and the artist, the conditions of human fate and artistic destiny. It makes use of the ancient literary device of talking animals to satirize human beings, as well as the more modern Beckett-like machinery of the double vaudeville or circus act. "Q. Am I a man

in a horse or a horse that talks like a man?" asks Abramowitz, and he
goes on asking questions to which there are no answers. Goldberg, his
inarticulate owner-cum-partner, like fate itself, intersperses cruelty
with the odd kindness. Sometimes Abramowitz, like every artist, wishes
he were an ordinary farmhorse without the gift of expression; at other
moments he dreams of being endowed with the beauty and nobility of
the racehorse. He longs for freedom, considers the possibility of change,
and rises in revolt. Finally, after a struggle, he contrives to escape into
a fresh meadow as a "free centaur," like all aspiring beings ultimately
a mixed creature.

There is greater naturalness, ease and assurance here, less determined
striving for meaningfulness and universality than in some of Malamud's early writings. It seems almost as if the writer has succeeded in
coming to terms with the conditions of his gift (the way his imagination tends to engage through the presentation of a male characters for
instance, and to concentrate repeatedly upon the confrontation between two male figures, woman all too often proving to be a jinx).
Perhaps he himself has grown to accept that he is neither a farmhorse
nor a racehorse (named Rembrandt?) but a centaur—which, after all,
is a pretty rare and original thing to be.

The Promised End: Bernard Malamud's
The Tenants

by John Alexander Allen

I

Bernard Malamud's fifth and most recent novel, *The Tenants*, is vigorously alive. The dialogue and pace are brisk and racy; fact and fantasy combine with magical effect; the action mounts to a frantic climax. And the end is Armageddon. Before the final curtain, the two principal characters, once nearly friends, have, whether in fact or fantasy, brutally done each other in. Both are novelists. Harry Lesser is white; his subject, love; and Willie Spearmint (later Bill Spear) is black; his subjects, misery and hate. The two writers are the only inhabitants of a decaying New York apartment house, whose owner, Irving Levenspiel (a man with Job-like troubles), wants only to eject its final legal tenant—Lesser—so that he can tear it down. His dream is a row of shops with five floors of big-room flats over them—something, as he puts it, comfortable to his nature. Malamud's book is punctuated by Levenspiel's voice, like that of a mourning angel of creation, praying for mercy to a Lesser who will not leave his flat until his book (ten years in the writing) has been finished. As for Willie Spearmint, he is a squatter with no legal right to tenancy, only a pressing need. His first book is a fictionalized account of his tortured childhood, term in jail, progress toward becoming a writer; then this attempt gives way to a closer view of himself as child with a drunken whore for a mother; and his final efforts deteriorate into fantasies of blacks exterminating Jews. Neither writer can finish his book: Lesser's, entitled *The Promised End*, waits on his still inadequate understanding of love; Willie's, variously called *Missing Life, Black Writer?*, and *Book of a Black*, waits on his learning how to give form to fiction. As Lesser sums it up, Willie must "make black more than color or culture, and outrage larger than protest or ideology."

Lesser in a Jew. He has done Willie injury: shaken his confidence in his ability as a writer, stolen his white Jewish girl away while Willie, hunched over an ancient L. C. Smith, two-fingered his increasingly abortive messages of doom for whites—Jews in particular. Willie's conception of his manhood is inseparable from writing as a means to power and from his "normal sex life"—courtesy of his "sweet bitch." Hence his mounting rage against Lesser who has cut him off from both, castrated him as Willie sees it, and thus marked himself as Willie's victim. As Lesser's own identity is inseparable from his unfinished book about love, it is inevitable that Willie's revenge will take the form of burning Lesser's manuscript, his ten-years' labor, not to be duplicated from memory. The epigraph of the lost book is from *King Lear*—"Who is it who can tell me who I am?" And for the mourning Lesser the answer finally becomes "no one."

In the penultimate scene of *The Tenants,* Harry and Willie meet for their showdown in a dark forest glade somewhere in Levenspiel's deteriorating heap, now transmuted into aboriginal jungle. Accurately aiming blows at each other, they carry out what must be recognized as an exchange of roles: Lesser cleaves Willie's skull and brain with a jagged hatchet and Willie castrates Lesser with a razor-sharp saber. Lesser's thought at this critical moment points the significance of the promised end or image of that horror: "Each, thought the writer, feels the anguish of the other." Levenspiel occupies the stage alone as the lights go out in Malamud's book. He prays for mercy for himself, for Lesser and Willie, and for mankind: mercy, mercy . . . mercy (to the bottom of the page). End of the Novel.

II

The Tenants is about race hatred versus brotherhood, about art as the complement to life, and about what may be called symbiotic victimization—all developments of familiar concerns in Malamud's work.

The two sides of Malamud's treatment of black-white relationships can be studied in his short stories "Black Is My Favorite Color" and "Angel Levine." In the former story, one Nat Lime, the Jewish proprietor of a New York liquor store, wryly recalls his love affair with a widowed black woman, Ornita Harris, whom he wishes to marry. Not only does this good man love Ornita, but (as the title suggests) he has long felt a strong attraction to all blacks, to their very blackness and to the sorrows which derive from it. But his attempts to achieve brotherhood with persons of his favorite color have consistently been thwarted from the time when he attempted, as a child, to befriend a skinny black neighborhood boy called Buster Wilson and was rewarded for his kindness by a blow in the teeth from Buster:

> "What did you hit me for? What did I do to you?"
> "Because you a Jew bastard. Take your Jew movies and your Jew candy and shove them up your Jew ass."
> And he ran away.
> I thought to myself and how was I to know he didn't like the movies. When I was a man I thought you can't force it.

Nat Lime loses Ornita Harris after he is battered by three blacks when he is walking her home one night. After that, she decides marriage with him would be imposible, and she leaves town. And Nat, a lonely bachelor, is still stuck with unnegotiable love in the dour present. His black cleaning woman, Charity Sweetness, refuses to have lunch with him in the kitchen and eats her hard-boiled eggs in the solitude of the toilet. "If there's a ghetto," Nat says sorrowfully, "I'm the one that's in it."

So much for realism in story number one. In "Angel Levine" a visionary solution to the black-white stand-off is achieved. Levine, the title angel, is a black Jew who has returned to earth to earn his wings (at present mere nubs) by inspiring faith in a hard test case, a suffering white Jewish tailor, Manischevitz. It has never occurred to Manischevitz that a Jewish angel could be black, and when Levine comes in answer to his prayers, he cannot believe in him. As Manischevitz flunks his test, Levine is necessarily flunking his also, and he sinks into the iniquitous embrace of a red-hot black mama named Stella. But sheer suffering drives the tailor at last to acknowledge Levine as "an angel from God," whereupon Levine bursts into tears ("How you have humiliated me") and has soon soared off to heaven on "a pair of magnificent black wings." The Job-like troubles of the tailor ease, and the story concludes with his remarking to his wife, a hopeless invalid now restored and vigorously wielding a dust mop, "A wonderful thing, Fanny . . . Believe me, there are Jews everywhere." Humorous, yes. And of course most serious also. In fantasy, humanity triumphs over all that is divisive; the spirit triumphs, which is "the highest." All of which may suggest that the ending of *The Tenants*, while in one respect a promised end of horror only, also contains the seed of redemption. As each character, even in the moment of destroying his opposite number and being destroyed by him, feels in himself the anguish of the other, the mercy prayed for by Levenspiel becomes a redeeming possibility.

Actually, *The Tenants* is about equal parts realistic and fantastic, a combination which Malamud worked successfully in many of his best short stories and in his epic of baseball, *The Natural*. It is primarily the admixture of fantasy that keeps the book from bogging down in claustrophobic stereotype: the black writer trying to free himself of the incubus of a tormented past by writing about a black writer trying to do the same thing; the white novelist writing a book about a novelist writing a book about a novelist writing a book about the same problem that bothers Lesser himself: an incomplete humanity, an inability to love satisfactorily.

Among other things Levenspiel's apartment house is, from the beginning, also an island: Lesser is Crusoe finding his man Friday; Lesser and Willie, artists together, float between crowds whose cheers salute their achievement; shipwrecked Lesser, climbing from his raft, is greeted by a ravishing black girl, now his co-inhabitant. Or, the apartment is a jungle: Willie as cannibal devours the severed limb of a murdered white man; Willie and his cohorts, as missionaries, invade Lesser's hut and carry out a ritual destruction of its civilized accoutrements; the entire building becomes entangled in obscene and poisonous plant life, ripening to the dark glade of the final confrontation.

This fantastic confrontation, which is finally precipitated by Lesser's hacking up of Willie's L. C. Smith, is, in point of position, the book's ending. However, an equally fantastic passage which precedes the bloody duel by some twenty pages, can be considered an alternative ending. It is an elaborate scene of a double wedding in an African village: First, the village chief marries Lesser and Mary Kettlesmith, a black beauty in actual fact passed over by Lesser in favor of Willie's true love, Irene Bell (*née* Belinsky):

> His bride, holding in her hand a purple feather, says she will be kind. . . . Under a short maternity skirt her stomach is in flower.
> "You are married now," the interpreter says, "yet so by our customs the wedding is not done till when the first child be borned."
> "It's a long wedding," says Lesser.
> "You had your choice," says Mary.

A rabbi is present to perform the marriage of Willie to Irene: Says the rabbi:

> "If we stay convenanted to God it is easier to stay convenanted each to the other."
> "I will," says Irene.
> "Ain't no god been in my house or ever was," Willie says. "Like what color is he?"
> "The color of light," says the rabbi. "Without light who sees color?"
> "Except black."
> "Someday God will bring together Ishmael and Israel to live as one people. It won't be the first miracle."

Willie laughs, cries, then stands mute.

The scene concludes with Lesser and Irene having a last dance together:

"How do you account for this, Harry?"

"It's something I imagined, like an act of love, the end of my book, if I dared."

"You're not so smart," says Irene.

The miracle that will bring Ishmael and Israel together obviously hasn't happened in Malamud's book. He couldn't make it happen any more than Lesser could—except in fantasy. Lesser's personal problem is of course the same that keeps him from finishing his book and the same that keeps black and white at each other's throats until the miracle arrives: "I'm short of love in my nature, don't ask me why . . ."

III

Harry Lesser is not a particularly interesting character, is in fact defined, like many of Malamud's protagonists, largely by his run-of-the-mill decencies and equally common inadequacies. If he resembles an earlier product of Malamud's imagination, that character is Arthur Fidelman, subject of six stories assembled by Malamud to make up *Pictures of Fidelman*. Fidelman is an expatriate American in Italy, "a self-confessed failure as a painter" living at the expense of a sister, Bessie, to whom he never writes. When we first meet him, he is in Rome, planning to complete a scholarly book on the painter Giotto ("Last Mohican"). There he encounters his destined Dybbuk in the person of Shimon Susskind, a life-long refugee with no visible means of support. In the course of the story Susskind, goaded into retaliation by Fidelman's refusal to make him a present of his second-best of two suits (definition of charity: to give more than you can reasonably afford), makes off with Fidelman's uncompleted Giotto manuscript, which he burns, sheet by sheet, for a little warmth in the freezing closet where he lives. Caught up with at last by the enraged Fidelman, Susskind cries out, "Have mercy. I did you a favor. . . . The words were there but the spirit was missing." And Fidelman, inspired by a vision of St. Francis giving his gold cloak to a poor knight, shouts after the vanishing vagrant, "Susskind, come back . . . The suit is yours. All is forgiven."

Obviously, Fidelman and Lesser are kindred spirits, manifestations of Malamud's deep conviction that humanity must have priority over art. It takes us many pages in *The Tenants* to discover that Lesser has "an aged father he hasn't seen in years." Obsessed with trying to finish his unfinishable book, he ruminates, "About time I wrote him again."

Irene, his stolen sweetie, neglected by Lesser for the book, finally abandons New York for San Francisco, leaving no address with her farewell note: "No book is as important as me."

Like Lesser, Fidelman has trouble loving properly, though he is willing to exploit sex where he finds it. He keeps returning to the art which has rejected him, still hopeful that a minor masterpiece may be within his scope. One of Malamud's most poignant and telling parables of failed love is "A Pimp's Revenge." Here Fidelman has been working for years on a portrait of mother and child, using a snapshot of his mother and memories of himself at age ten. Love offers itself in the form of Esmeralda, surely Malamud's most enchanting heroine, a prostitute, aged eighteen, who moves into his studio. "Art isn't life," he tells her.

> "Then the hell with it. If I have my choice I'll take life. If there's not that there's no art."
> "Without art there's no life to speak of, at least for me. If I'm not an artist, then I'm nothing."
> "My God, aren't you a man?"
> "Not really, without art."
> "Personally, I think you have a lot to learn."

Briefly inspired by Esmeralda's love, Fidelman paints her into his mother-child portrait. Meanwhile, strapped for funds, he sets her back to work as prostitute, himself as pimp. The portrait shapes up. But it is no longer mother and child, it is pimp and prostitute. As such, it is in fact the minor masterpiece he has longed to paint. But of course, he can't keep his hands off it. A few strokes applied to the canvas one morning before Esmeralda wakes up is enough to spoil it utterly. Seeing the mess, Esmeralda comes at him with a bread knife, shouting "Murderer!" And that is the end of Fidelman's only success as artist. Later, he is done a favor by a homosexual glass-blower named Beppo. In judgment of Fidelman's works of art, Beppo tells him very simply, "Burn them all." He then slashes his canvases with a kitchen knife. "Have mercy," cries the agonized Fidelman. "Show who's master of your fate—bad art or you," Beppo replies. The two become lovers. "If you can't invent art, invent life." When last heard from, Fidelman is back in America, working as a craftsman in glass and loving men and women.

IV

Malamud has justly won a reputation as a superior writer by sticking tenaciously to a preoccupation which creates a kinship between all of his books but does not prevent them from being highly individual: He is always deeply concerned with a struggle between victim and exploiter or persecutor—a confrontation which gathers power naturally from his strong and enduring sympathy with the oppressed. If one asks of *The Tenants* whether Lesser or Willie Spearmint has the role of victim, the answer must be that each is the other's victim, finally. Willie, of course, has suffered from the burden of oppression which fell upon him at birth simply because he is black. His sense of injustice to himself does not, however, prevent him from waging war irrationally on Lesser as Jew and from declaring that the way to black freedom is against the Jews. Lesser, on the other hand, has no prejudice against blacks and does not really begin to feel victimized by Willie until he has stolen Willie's girl, Irene, and as a result begins to suffer feelings of guilt and fear. He makes an enemy of Willie by cuckolding him, a breach of faith which he rationalizes ironically in saying "I treated him like a man"; that is, he asserts that he has treated Willie no worse than he would have treated any other man. It turns out, inconveniently and indeed disastrously for Lesser, that Willie is not at all inclined to take his loss philosophically, that Irene is not merely Willie's play-thing but, as he says, "my bitch I love." Willie's deadly hatred of Lesser kills whatever chance Lesser may have had of pushing his own work through to a successful conclusion. Like the fictional writer in his book, "His life betrays his imagination." Willie has become his victim, and for that reason, he becomes Willie's.

The laws which govern the downfall of characters in Malamud's novels are difficult to formulate with confidence, but it is clear that sexual aggression on their part is consistently a prelude to disaster. The protagonist of Malamud's second novel, *The Assistant,* is a certain Frankie Alpine, a characteristically downtrodden hero who, as orphan, outcast and criminal, comes into the orbit of a poor immigrant grocer, Morris Bober, and his daughter Helen. When he enters the story it is as one of two hold-up men who rob Bober's store. Because of the guilt which Frankie thus incurs, he is bound to the family which rejects him as a goy, voluntarily becoming their victim until the conditions for his redemption are fulfilled. Just when it seems that Frankie has won the love of Helen, his evil alter-ego Ward Minogue (in the past the other hold-up man) reenters the story as Helen's would-be rapist. Losing con-trol of his own emotions while saving her from Ward's unclean em-brace, he takes advantage of her himself. This plunges him deeper than ever into outer darkness, and he must perform prodigies of patient service in order to win back the faith which he has lost. At last his suffering is sufficient and he is permitted his reward. But Malamud is never guilty of fudging in these matters. Despite repeated hints which associate him with Saint Francis, Frankie has no miracles to offer Helen. He is still poor, without prospects, uneducated. When, despite all this, Helen's love returns to its destined object, outcast and lady, each at one time the victim of the other, unsentimentally attain their hard-earned happiness.

The peculiar excellence of *The Assistant,* which is universally acknowledged, obviously springs from the same imagination which, in the most memorable short stories of *The Magic Barrel* and *Idiots First,* shapes the trials of immigrant city-dwellers into tight, parable-like form. Such materials, in Malamud's skillful hands, draw strength from the patient dignity and wry humor of simple people taking it on the chin and sometimes winning victories by the sheer persistence of their unpretentious virtues. Biblical overtones, like those generated by the shoemaker's Jacob-like courtship in "The First Seven Years," develop naturally when ageless human concerns are presented objectively in an idiom from which non-essentials have been pared away as though by centuries of understatement and forbearance.

Malamud's first and third novels—*The Natural* and *A New Life*—could hardly be more different from *The Assistant* and from each other. They deal respectively with the career of a baseball player and that of an instructor in English at a far-western college, their pace is leisurely, and their idiom for the most part is a standard American whose tendency to laxness and verbosity occasionally summons up the image of a writer grinding out his daily quota of pages whether he feels like it or not.

Despite their obvious differences in subject and style, however, one finds that *The Natural* and *A New Life* are linked by Malamud's recurrent pattern, faithfully at work. Roy Hobbs, the baseball player, and Seymour Levin, the instructor, are both victims and, as such, they go their tortuous way even as Frankie Alpine does, knocking off victims of their own en route to working out salvation. Both are ordinary men, so far as spirit and intellect are concerned, although they do possess the remarkable doggedness and resiliency without which no hero could complete the course in Malamud's obstacle race. Both are of obscure origin and, in young manhood, suffered poverty, indignity and despair. And the destiny of both is tied up with women: Roy Hobbs with a good angel and a bad, Seymour Levin with a lady whose blessing remains ambiguous to the end.

"A Malamud character," said the author in a *New York Times* interview, "is someone who fears his fate, is caught up in it, yet manages to outrun it. He's the subject and object of laughter and pity." This is an apt description of Roy Hobbs. As a sensational young pitching prospect about to try out for the Cubs, Roy makes his first mistake. Says the beautiful blonde who has lured hungry Roy to her hotel room, "Roy, will you be the best there ever was in the game?" "That's right," he replies. And she lodges a pistol bullet in his stomach. Thus the young player becomes a victim of Harriet Bird, a madwoman (or sane

Fate or Harpy) who specializes in curing attacks of pride in star athletes. But Roy Hobbs is hard to cure. The next time we see him he is thirty-four, has suffered for fifteen years in limbo, has converted himself into an outfielder and batting star equipped with a magical phallic bat called Wonder Boy, and is ready once again to set himself up for disaster: 1) by quite accidentally sleeping with a red-headed girl, Memo Paris, who properly belongs to teammate Bump Baily, 2) by indirectly and innocently causing the death of Bump, 3) by assiduously courting Memo Paris, who brings to bear on her unwanted suitor a Morgan le Fay-like evil magic, 4) by announcing once more on Roy Hobbs Day that he intends to be "The best there ever was in the game," 5) by refusing the love of one Iris Lemon (cast in the role of good fairy), and 6) by nearly killing Iris with a foul ball which he aims at Otto Zipp, a foul-mouthed pest who heckles him from the stands. For all of his ineptitude, however, Roy staggers home to moral victory. He is saved from actual responsibility for throwing the big game when he is legitimately struck out by a young pitching prodigy just up from the minors (himself at age nineteen), throws his $35,000 bribe in the teeth of the powers of evil, and learns that his brief amour with wholesome Iris is about to reward him with a son. In public disgrace, at the end of his career, impoverished, wrecked in health, he is cured at last of pride. "Hubris is poison ivy!" Exit Malamud's all-American victim, conqueror of himself.

Although in *The Natural* Malamud has enriched his story-telling with injections of Horatio Alger, Red Smith and Al Capp, a steady writer lies behind the gaudy extravaganza, keeping his eye on the ball. What happens when he tries his hand at an academic novel, drawing on his experience at a university a continent away from New York and from Bennington? If *The Natural* is slow in getting to where it's going, the progress of *A New Life* is positively glacial. It has been said that the book is our best academic novel, but this can certainly be challenged. The English Department at Cascadia is so quickly shown to be palpably and grotesquely dead on its feet, that Malamud is guilty, before he's done with it, of overkill. The pace begins to pick up half way through the book, precisely at the point where Seymour Levin seals his fate for better or for worse by making love in the Cascadian woods to Pauline Gilley, wife of the English Department's Director of Composition.

One reads almost to the close of *A New Life* before fully realizing that Levin has been summoned to Cascadia by Pauline Gilley (she talked Gerald Gilley into hiring him, drawn to his bearded face) precisely for the purpose of delivering her from death by boredom at the hands of Gilley. Gradually it also emerges that Levin is not Pauline's first lover: his predecessor, a wild Irishman named Leo Duffy, has been hounded from the College and is now dead. He was victim number one, and Levin's number is up:

> Let somebody else marry her, Levin thought. He had from the first resisted becoming her savior, or victim. She had in a moment of unhappiness after the death of a former flame picked him by chance from a pile of discards. She had marked him X in a distant port and summoned him across the continent. Did this casual selection make him responsible for her for life? Was he forever bound to the choice she had made?

The answer, of course, is yes. Like all of Malamud's heroes, Levin has a powerfully active moral nature. "He saw good in beauty. Good was as if a man's spirit had produced art in life." Levin is hooked by kismet and finds himself driving away from Cascadia with another man's wife. She is flat-chested and has big feet and physical and psychological problems. Her adopted children are anything but attractive. Malamud always succeeds in giving sentimentality the axe. But Pauline's flat chest has lately begun to bud. For the first time she is pregnant—by Levin. His academic career lies in ruins, he has no means of support. But his new life has been granted him: the victim's own reward; and the reward he offers the victim at his side.

V

It seems to have become popular to refer to Malamud's fourth novel, *The Fixer,* as a book which was overrated when it first appeared and which dwindles in the perspective of time. But this is a highly doubtful judgment. To be sure, the book probably suffers from a certain thinness in the author's knowledge of Russia and from the remoteness of the historical setting in Kiev in the years 1910–12. It is also true that the story has very little action. But it can hardly be maintained that Yakov Bok, the hero, is deprived of significance or interest by this circumstance.

The character Yakov Bok is based upon an historic Jew who was accused of murdering a Russian boy in order that his blood could be used for ritual purposes. Obviously, this incident and all that it entails are not so immediate to Malamud's own experience as what happens to Morris Bober, grocer, or to Seymour Levin, would-be college English teacher. But he knows Yakov Bok, and Yakov's history carries on all of the central preoccupations of Malamud's writing.

Yakov is Malamud's most memorable male character. He shares with many another of Malamud's creations an incorruptible honesty, a capacity for suffering and endurance, a reflective cast of mind, and a strong moral nature. All of these he needs in his long, painful, humiliating and infinitely tedious imprisonment. In addition to these qualities, however, Yakov possesses an unaffected humility, an intellect which never tires of questing within the narrow limits of his knowledge and experience, and a sweetness and gentleness of nature which are the more affecting in that he does not seem to recognize these qualities in himself. Although, like Job, he curses his fate, as well he might, he is devoid of self-pity. He has the charm of an intellectual who loves knowledge and reasoning for themselves but whose thought does nothing to weaken the responsiveness of his emotions. He is a seeker after truth without pretension. In reading Malamud's book one lives with Yakov for a long time in prison and he does not grow tedious. This is a tribute to Malamud's imagination and sensibility, and to his art.

The combination of qualities with which Malamud has endowed Yakov is essential to the effects achieved by *The Fixer*: revulsion against the persecutors of this good man, a sense of his superiority to them, and a belief that "he who endures to the end will be saved." Yakov is as slow to hate as he is to praise his own qualities, and it is only gradually that we come to appreciate in full how remarkable his forbearance is. Near the end of the book, Yakov declares that he has had "an extraordinary insight":

> "Something in myself has changed. I'm not the same man I was. I fear less and hate more."

The meaning of this insight can only be understood in the context of several incidents, real and fancied, which take place soon afterward. The first occurs when Yakov, although he knows that insubordination on his part will only give his captors an excuse to shoot him and prevent him from coming to trial, gives way to uncontrollable anger. Made to undergo one more humiliating search of his person, he flings his undershirt into the face of the Deputy Warden. The official draws his revolver and is about to shoot when he is interrupted by one of Yakov's guards:

> "Hold on a minute, your honor," said Kogin to the Deputy Warden. His deep voice broke. "I've listened to this man night after night, I know his sorrows. Enough is enough . . ."

At the cost of his own life, Kogin holds the Deputy Warden off until the Cossack guards arrive to take Yakov into custody. Yakov's anger is no greater than that of a jailor who knows what he has suffered.

The second incident takes place when Yakov is being driven along in a carriage to his trial. Looking out of the window he notices one of his guards riding a gray mare, and "he smiled a little at the Cossack for his youth and good looks." At this moment the carriage is rocked by an explosion. Someone has thrown a hand grenade, meaning to kill Yakov but instead killing the gray mare and tearing the foot off of the handsome Cossack. This is a kind of hatred Yakov could never feel.

Finally, Yakov finds himself imagining an interview with Tsar Nicholas himself. The Tsar is naked, and Yakov points a pistol at him. He is making up his mind whether or not to shoot. The Tsar asks whether suffering has taught Yakov mercy, and Yakov makes this reply:

> "Excuse me, Your Majesty, but what suffering has taught me is the uselessness of suffering. . . . Anyway, there's enough of that to live with naturally without piling a mountain of injustice on top. Rachmones, we say in Hebrew—mercy, one oughtn't to forget it. . . . In you . . . is missing . . . the sort of insight, you might call it, that creates in a man charity, respect for the most miserable. You say you are kind and prove it with pogroms."
>
> "As for those," said the Tsar, "don't blame me. Water can't be prevented from flowing. They are a genuine expression of the will of the people."
>
> "Then in that case there's no more to say."

And Yakov shoots the Tsar. "If the state acts in ways that are abhorrent to human nature it's the lesser evil to destroy it." Yakov's only personal hatred was against his wife, Raisl, who, in despair at being barren, had run off with another man. But she has visited Yakov in prison and told him that she has now given birth to a boy. He has acknowledged the child. Riding along on his way to be tried, "He felt an overwhelming hunger to be back home, to see Raisl and set things straight, to decide what to do." He thinks of the pogroms in which his own mother and father were killed. "Raisl, dress the boy and pack the few things we need, we'll have to hide."

VI

At one point in *The Fixer,* the liberal Investigating Magistrate, Bibikov, tells Yakov "There's something cursed, it seems to me, about a country where men have owned men as property. The stink of that corruption never escapes the soul, and it is the stink of future evil." It is, of course, quite natural that Malamud should have followed a novel about persecution of the Jews in Russia with one about the relationship of a Jew and a black in the U. S. The stink mentioned by Bibikov permeates every page of *The Tenants.* Levenspiel's all but abandoned apartment house reeks of human excrement, garbage, dead rats. Also, when Lesser first finds Willie Spearmint hard at work on his book, he notices that from the manuscript stacked beside him "an unpleasant odor rose." Could it be Willie's feet? the smell of fear? Later, reading Willie's soiled pages, Lesser notices the odor again. This time his theory is that the stink derives from "the festering lives the words created . . ." When he has read the book twice, he finds himself moved by "the affecting subject of the work," by Willie's belief that "he can, in writing, help his people overthrow racism and economic inequality. That his freedom will help theirs." Then it occurs to Lesser that Willie's tears may have "scorched the paper and stunk up the pages." And with that thought, he finds that the smell has completely disappeared. However, it is back again worse than ever (like a dead rat) later on, emerging from the garbage can where Willie has stuffed work sheets of stories now envisioning little more than wholesale slaughter of whites by blacks. Finally Lesser, utterly demoralized by his own life and futile efforts to write, notices that "A faint unpleasant odor rises from the paper." Two pages later, he hacks up Willie's typewriter with an axe, and the stage is set for the promised end.

The Tenants presents a vision of evil triumphant, the failure of charity and mercy. Willie and Lesser are equally to blame. Malamud is wonderfully impartial. There is humor in the book and hints of a not impossible brotherhood. At the height of his fury, Lesser peeks in at Willie at work: "Hey Bill, Lesser thought in the hallway, moved by the sight of a man writing, how's it going?" When Lesser leaves Willie a note wishing him good luck on his new book and accompanies it with six red carnations in a bottle, Willie doesn't thank him, but "once he remarked that there might be a diddle of black in Lesser's blood."

Malamud has no miracles to offer. But he doesn't knock miracles either.

Portrait of the Artist as *Schlemiel*
(*Pictures of Fidelman*)

by Leslie Field

I

For many, Bernard Malamud is a joy to classify. His published stories go back about three decades, but with his first novel, *The Natural,* written approximately twenty years ago, he enlisted in the Ring Lardner ranks of baseball-story writers (along with Mark Harris) —as they were to be joined years later by Robert Coover and then Philip Roth. For a short while Malamud became the interpreter of our then great American sport.

In *The Natural* Malamud saw baseball history as "the distillation of American life." He used real events to avoid contrivance and to reveal baseball as the ritual for expressing American life and its predicament. Other layers, Arthurian legend and Jungian mythic psychology, which are used to interpret the ritual, make baseball into a symbol of "man's psychological and moral situation." [1]

However, even in this early work one could see foreshadowings of what was to become a typical Malamud hero or antihero. Malamud's baseball hero became an "amalgam of the heroic myth and its democratic offspring, the Horatio Alger story." Roy Hobbs could be seen as a *failed hero* because he could not "act within" the prescribed mythology as any self-respecting hero should. [2]

After *The Natural,* Malamud continued to write short stories. In 1957 his second novel appeared—*The Assistant.* For this he received several national awards, and he became classified a second time, now as a Jewish-American writer—that class of hyphenated American

"Portrait of the Artist as *Schlemiel*," by Leslie Field. An original essay prepared for this collection.

[1] Earl R. Wasserman, "*The Natural*: World Ceres" (Fall 1965), in *Bernard Malamud and the Critics,* ed. Leslie A. Field and Joyce W. Field (New York: New York University Press, 1970), pp. 46–47.

[2] Frederick W. Turner, III, "Myth Inside and Out: *The Natural*" (January 1968), in *Bernard Malamud and the Critics,* pp. 113–118.

writers which includes Saul Bellow, Henry Roth, Philip Roth, and Edward Lewis Wallant—as distinguished from the Yiddish-American *Schmaltz* Industry housing the writers of ethnic sentimentality.

In *The Assistant,* a novel about a poor New York Jewish storekeeper and a young West Coast Italian-American boy who comes into his life, Malamud constructs two cultures—"the Jewish tradition and the American heritage." And he depicted a collision between Old World wisdom and New World practicality with its ethose of success. But it was also recognized that the characters in this novel existed "in an ironic relationship" to both worlds,[3] in many ways presenting a continuation of Malamud's twisted hero.

By 1958 Malamud had published his collection of short stories called *The Magic Barrel.* This book too received wide acclaim.

Then, just as one was getting used to Malamud the short-story writer, the baseball-story writer, and the Jewish-American novelist, he sneaked into another subgenre—that of writer of the academic novel—with the publication of *A New Life.* This was twelve years ago.

After *A New Life,* the short stories continued, and new ones were collected in *Idiots First* in 1963. Then in 1966 we had his novel *The Fixer.* This one was *not* about a baseball player, or an immigrant Jewish storekeeper in Brooklyn, or a young English instructor, but rather about a Russian Jew, a victim of early-twentieth-century anti-Semitism, of Czarist pogroms, of a grotesque ritual-murder plot.

Some dismissed *The Fixer* as merely another "historical novel" in the Dreyfus or Sacco-Vanzetti mold except that in this instance the victim was modeled on Mendel Beiliss, who had been accused of using the blood of a young Christian to bake Passover matzos. A little bit of enlightened Christian Russia, vintage 1913. Others, more perceptive, moved back and forth in the body of Malamud's work—from his early short stories, through *The Natural, The Fixer, The Tenants* (1971), and even to his latest stories collected in *Rembrandt's Hat* (1973)—to show significant patterns which, if they do not negate the periodic classifications of Malamud's work, at least put them into new perspectives, and certainly emphasize a more sophisticated and overall consistent schematization.

From Roy Hobbs of *The Natural* and Frank Alpine of *The Assistant,* through Seymour Levin of *A New Life,* Yakov Bok of *The Fixer,* Harry Lesser of *The Tenants,* and on through many of the short-story characters—especially Arthur Fidelman, who came to rest in *Pictures of Fidelman*—one sees the Malamud *schlemiel* used to realize a variety of themes and motifs.

One continues to see the *schlemiel* in the recent stories collected

<hr />

[3] Walter Shear, "Culture Conflict" (July 1966), in *Bernard Malamud and the Critics,* pp. 208–209.

in *Rembrandt's Hat.* In "The Silver Crown," for example, a young
biology teacher purchases a silver crown from a wonder rabbi for
$986, ostensibly to cure his father of cancer. The father dies. In "Man
in the Drawer" Howard Harvitz, a writer, leaves America to forget
his troubles, and with all the great expanse of Russia, he is the one
(selected?) to stumble on a Jewish taxi driver/author who pushes a for-
bidden manuscript on to him, one which can land the American in
trouble much more serious than that he had originally tried to escape
if he agrees to smuggle it out of the country. And in the story which
gives the collection its name we have a final scene showing Rubin, the
schlemiel, in the men's room "regarding himself in the mirror in his
white cap, the one that seemed to resemble Rembrandt's Hat. He wore
it like a crown of failure and hope." But of all the Malamud characters, early and late, one must return to Arthur Fidelman as the
Malamud *schlemiel par excellence.*

II

Through the pages of various standard dictionaries one looks in vain
for a workable definition of the *schlemiel,* that character who has become the beloved creature of Yiddish comic fiction. However, three
recent books—two of them scholarly, and one a rollicking dictionary
run-through of Yiddish terms—do supply us with what the dictionaries,
to their detriment, have failed to provide.

Ruth Wisse[4] has written a compact, scholarly little book which may
be subtitled "the birth and death of the *schlemiel.*" She traces the
schlemiel-type of character in literature back to its East European
origins, placing it in a socio-historical context, and then brings it up
to date in the post-Holocaust literature of the Jewish-American writers,
where, apparently, it had a brief flurry of popularity, reached a zenith
in Saul Bellow's *Herzog,* and then died quickly with Bernard Malamud's *Pictures of Fidelman,* Philip Roth's *Portnoy's Complaint,* and
the nonfictional *Making It* by Norman Podhoretz.

The *schlemiel,* she says, "is a character of folklore and fiction," but
he differs from the usual non-Yiddish comic or humorous or even
antihero character. Wisse analyzes the *schlemiel's* character in terms
of several different categories. The "political *schlemiel,*" for example,
is one who is always completely apart from or "out of step with the
actual march of events." As far back as the Middle Ages the Jew was
the actual or "potential victim" in a hostile society. In part, his
vulnerability was used as a humorous shield to soften the brutality of

---

[4] Ruth S. Wisse, *The Schlemiel as Modern Hero* (Chicago: University of Chicago
Press, 1971), pp. x, 3, *et passim.*

an alien world. Wisse probes "the historical irony," "the fools of folklore," "the social *schlemiel*," and the type known as the "Hassidic fool." For Wisse a folkloristic anti-intellectualism becomes the hallmark of the *schlemiel*. Humor emerges, for instance, when we have tales of fools in early Yiddish literature in which faith displaces reason. In hopeless situations for marginal peoples antirationalism becomes a sort of salvation. In effect, the *schlemiel* defines his own world, which bears no relationship to the world others know. Thus emerges a comic figure who seems to be a victim, but who, because he redefines his world, wins out in the end.

Both Wisse and Sanford Pinsker[5] see one strong double source for the Malamud *schlemiel*—the nineteenth-century Yiddish writers Mendel Mocher Seforim and Sholom Aleichem. Why was the humorous figure of the East-European Yiddish *schlemiel* brought over to America? Wisse asks. Moreover, how did he manage to survive in an American fiction and consciousness in which the down-to-earth American hero from Davy Crockett to Hemingway was deeply ingrained? One answer, Wisse believes, is that World War II was America's last large engagement in which it emerged as a clear-cut "winner." The years following were far less decisive. Increasingly, America appeared in a complex, confused, and shadowy light. More and more it took on the image of a "loser." Thus the rejection in American life and letters of the Hemingway heroes. The ground for a short while became fertile for the re-appearance of the Yiddish *schlemiel* à la Malamud and Bellow.

Wisse believes that the heyday for the *schlemiel* in Jewish-American fiction was the fifties and sixties and that the chief practitioners were Malamud, Bellow, Isaac Bashevis Singer, and Bruce Jay Friedman. But she further believes that we reach a pinnacle in Bellow's Moses Herzog, whom she considers the most excellent example of a *schlemiel* as a "liberal humanist"—and then we go downhill.

When we reach America of the Vietnam War, racial strife, and violence, losing becomes too stark, too concrete, and the two-decade flirtation with the *schlemiel*-figure is terminated. Moreover, in the last third of twentieth-century America, it is no longer impossible for the Jew to succeed within the framework of the larger society. Humorous, passive figures must disappear in an active society. Thus does Wisse see Malamud's Fidelman, Roth's Portnoy, and even the real-life Podhoretz of *Making It* as sounding a death knell for the *schlemiel* in modern American literature and life. There is, however, some evidence to suggest that Wisse may be premature in any funeral arrangements she may contemplate for the *schlemiel*. For example, even as Wisse formulated her concluding statements, Bellow and Malamud

[5] Sanford Pinsker, *The Schlemiel as Metaphor: Studies in the Yiddish and American Jewish Novel* (Carbondale, Illinois: Southern Illinois University Press, 1971), pp. 4, 22, *et passim*. (See especially pp. 45–71 of this collection.)

continued to hone their *schlemiels*—as Harry Lesser of *The Tenants* took on Willie Spearmint and Artur Sammler of *Mr. Sammler's Planet* confronted his black pickpocket and exhibitionist.

Pinsker, in *The Schlemiel as Metaphor,* covers some of the same ground as does Wisse, especially when he discusses "the *schlemiel* family tree." However, he often sees the *schlemiel* as an important part of Yiddish folk humor, which in itself is an offshoot of the Hassidic movement of Eastern Europe of the eighteenth century, a movement characterized by joyous, popularized didacticism.

Pinsker and Wisse seem to agree that the *schlemiel* is an Old World phenomenon, and an uneasy immigrant once he appears in America. After all, they point out, failure was a way of life for the oppressed Jew in the Old Country. In America he could succeed. Thus all logic would indicate that the *schlemiel* on Main Street would be an anachronism unless he adopted a new style, which, according to Pinsker, must be an "ironic posture."

For Pinsker, the Malamud *schlemiel* can be seen as "moral bungler" or "ironic hero." The typical Malamud *schlemiel,* in Pinsker's view, is "a moral bungler, a character whose estimate of the situation, coupled with an overriding desire for 'commitment,' invariably caused comic defeats of one sort or another." And from "The Magic Barrel" with Leo Finkle through Frank Alpine of *The Assistant,* Seymour Levin of *A New Life,* and finally Yakov Bok of *The Fixer,* Pinsker detects the many nuances of the Malamud *schlemiel.* Pinsker sees Malamud refining his various *schlemiels,* his "moral bunglers," who move "haphazardly toward redemption." Redemption, however, Pinsker believes, is elusive for Malamud's *schlemiels* until it is achieved by Yakov Bok.

It is perhaps left for Leo Rosten in *The Joys of Yiddish*[6] to balance the scholarly treatments given by Pinsker and Wisse. What or who is a *schlemiel?* he asks. One of his simple definitions is that the *schlemiel* is a foolish person, a simpleton. Or a consistently unlucky or unfortunate person; a fall guy, a hard-luck type, a born loser, a victim. Rosten recites a Yiddish proverb to illustrate: "The *schlemiel* falls on his back and breaks his nose." Or one sees a *schlemiel* as a clumsy, butterfingered, gauche type. He could be considered a social misfit, a naïve, trusting, gullible customer.

In Yiddish humor one often hears the words *schlemiel, schlimazl,* and *nebbish* used interchangeably. Rosten tries to set the record straight: "The classic attempt to discriminate between the [first] two types runs: 'a *schlemiel* is a man who is always spilling his soup— down the neck of a *schlimazl.* '" Or, to make a triple distinction: "The

6 Leo Rosten, *The Joys of Yiddish* (New York: McGraw-Hill Book Co., 1968). Rosten treats *schlemiel, shlemiel, shlemiehl, shlemihl, shlimazl,* and *schlimazel* on pages 343–349.

schlemiel trips, and knocks down the *schlimazl;* and the *nebbish* re-
pairs the *schlimazl's* glasses."

A fairly common view is that the most comprehensive definition of
the *schlemiel* has come from Golda Meir, the Prime Minister of Israel,
when, not too long ago, she whimsically traversed time and space to en-
compass a whole people as *schlemiel.* Half in jest, Mrs. Meir observed
that most of the world's oil was "in the wrong places." She said that
"Moses led the Israelites through the desert for 40 years and ended in
the one place in the Middle East with no oil."

When one listens to Golda Meir, Leo Rosten, Ruth Wisse, Sanford
Pinsker, and many others too numerous to mention, one cannot fail to
recognize one significant comic vein that Malamud mined through
his novels and short stories. And this comic vein is Arthur Fidelman's
heritage.

III

In addition to those of Pinsker and Wisse, one should consider
four other full-scale essays on Malamud's *schlemiels.* The first, by
Lois S. Lamdin, gives a general run-through of the *schlemiels* she finds
in Malamud's work. "They are fit protagonists in a fiction whose
central motif is the omnipresence of suffering, for they are born to
suffering, conditioned by it, and ultimately find the meaning of their
lives in learning to deal with it. As sufferers they serve as root symbols
for the condition of man." [7] Lamdin joins other critics in seeing the
Malamud *schlemiel* as a victim, who "if he can learn through his
suffering to accept the burden of his humanity, can achieve redemption." [8] She concludes by saying that the major Malamud *schlemiels*
"have used their membership in the brotherhood of *schlemiels* as
a passport to a higher order of humanity." [9]

The other three essays deal almost exclusively with *Pictures of Fidelman.* Barbara F. Lefcowitz says that "Malamud both depicts and parodies neurosis by juxtaposing two sets of values, the first composed of
the private world of Fidelman as victim and obsessional neurotic, and
the second of the socio-historical world of Fidelman as a victimizer." [10]

Robert Ducharme does more to place Malamud's book into perspective than any other critic. He sees "the themes of the book . . .
as fresh restatements of the author's consistent humanism." [11] But

---

[7] Lois S. Lamdin, "Malamud's *Schlemiels," A Modern Miscellany.* Carnegie Series
in English No. 11 (Pittsburgh: Carnegie Mellon University, 1970), p. 31.

[8] Lamdin, p. 42.

[9] Lamdin, p. 42.

[10] Barbara F. Lefcowitz, "The Hybris of Neurosis: Malamud's *Pictures of Fidelman," Literature and Psychology,* 20:3 (1970), p. 115.

[11] Robert Ducharme, "Structure and Content in Malamud's *Pictures of Fidelman,"
Connecticut Review,* 5:1 (October 1971), p. 27.

Ducharme devotes most of his essay to the form of *Pictures of Fidelman*. He describes the book as a "picaresque chronicle" or "a novel in the broad sense of Sherwood Anderson's *Winesburg, Ohio*." [12] Ducharme claims that the parts of Malamud's book "may stand as independent stories, but there is a definite sense in which they belong together . . . to form a self-contained narrative." [13] He further points out that "the book is like a series of pictorial tableaux, each story an image of Arthur Fidelman." Ducharme concludes that "throughout *Pictures of Fidelman* the ideas of suffering and responsibility have played a subtle and important thematic counterpoint to the central character's overriding quest for success in life and art. These themes and the character of Fidelman himself have drawn these six stories together into a loose novelistic unity they would not otherwise have." [14]

Christof Wegelin in his opening lines re-asks the question "What is an American?" posed early in our history by Crèvecoeur.[15] It was raised then in the context of Old World vs. New World standards, and as Wegelin points out, major American writers from Henry James through Scott Fitzgerald have used that same context. But there has been a change. A change from the innocent abroad to parity abroad. "Generally speaking, the White American in this fiction is no longer in conflict with the European but at one with him in cruelty, anxiety, need." [16] Wegelin goes on to use Fidelman as his "case in point."

IV

The collection of six stories called *Pictures of Fidelman* appeared in 1969, but the first of these, "The Last Mohican," dates back to 1958. Two others were included in Malamud's second collection. Two of the final three were printed later in magazines, and then all were brought together in a somewhat revised form as *Pictures of Fidelman: An Exhibition*.

We have in this collection or novel Malamud's antihero—Arthur Fidelman—conceived about fifteen years ago in "The Last Mohican" as a young Jewish-American art critic in Rome, who continued his adolescence as a would-be artist in Rome and Milan in "Still Life" and "Naked Nude," achieved *schlemieldom*'s young manhood—still as artist—in other Italian cities (in "A Pimp's Revenge" and "Pictures of the Artist") and, finally, emerged as an adult artist-*schlemiel* in

12 Ducharme, pp. 27–28.
13 Ducharme, p. 28.
14 Ducharme, p. 36.
15 Christof Wegelin, "The American *Schlemiel* Abroad: Malamud's Italian Stories and the End of American Innocence," *Twentieth-Century Literature,* 19:2 (April 1973), p. 77.
16 Wegelin, p. 78.

Venice. This was in the last story, "Glass Blower of Venice," where, ostensibly, our *schlemiel* discovers life and the true meaning of love, gives up art *per se,* and goes back to America to become a *mentsch* or human being.

So ends the saga of Arthur Fidelman—or is it only the beginning of an understanding not only of this book, but of much of the rest of Malamud?

Had Malamud simply given us the Yiddish figure of the *schlemiel,* we might have ended with farce or slapstick. However, in this story sequence, as in the novels, Malamud seems intent on unfolding his themes bit by bit as he reveals character. Fidelman's habitual pattern is that of apprenticeship or education. And the subgenre he is part of falls into that category which has been distinguished, by German criticism at least, as the *Bildungsroman.*[17]

We are in effect dealing with a sequence of stories or a novel focusing on development of character. When this development is confined to the professional sphere of the developing novelist or artist— the story tracing the growth of a hero as creative man—we have a *Kunstlerroman.*[18] The more common term is *Bildungsroman.* The term applies to *Pictures of Fidelman* as it does to James Joyce's *A Portrait of the Artist as a Young Man* and Thomas Wolfe's *Look Homeward, Angel,* even though Fidelman's destination is not that of Stephen Dedalus or Eugene Gant.

The form[19] of *Pictures of Fidelman* may be closer to that of Mark Twain's *Huck Finn* in that we have a combination of two subgenres: the *Picaresque* and *Bildungsroman*: i.e., the one portraying the episodic, seemingly indiscriminate movement of a character from place to place, and the other showing the growth of a central character amidst swirls of experience. In Malamud all is infused with the comic tone—the Jewish-American *schlemiel* in Italy working out and having his destiny worked out for him as he moves to ultimate discovery of self—and possibly salvation. Perhaps Arthur Fidelman is really not Huck Finn at all but rather Don Quixote. Or a Sholom Aleichem character. Or a younger Reb Yudel of S. Y. Agnon's *The Bridal Canopy.*

Pictures of Fidelman is introduced by three epigraphs, the first by Rilke: *"Not to Understand.* Yes, that was my whole occupation during those years—I can assure you, it was not an easy one." [20] The second is from Yeats: "The Intellect of man is forced to choose Perfection of

17 Harry Levin, *James Joyce: A Critical Introduction,* Revised Edition (Norfolk, Connecticut: New Directions, 1960), p. 41.

18 Levin, p. 41.

19 See also Ducharme, pp. 26–36.

20 Bernard Malamud, *Pictures of Fidelman: An Exhibition* (New York: Farrar, Straus & Giroux, 1969). All further citations from *Pictures of Fidelman* refer to this edition and are identified by page number parenthetically in the text.

the life, or of the work . . ." And the third is the terse utterance from
Fidelman himself: "Both."

If we trace our *schlemiel*-hero through the various stories we can
see him as through a prism: many different reflections. The six stories
are six episodes or pictures, which taken together form a portrait.

The first picture is taken in Rome. Young Fidelman, the would-be
art critic, has written the first chapter on his book on the painter
Giotto. His manuscript is stolen by a *luftmentsch*, a vagrant—a Jewish
nuisance named Shimon Susskind, a refugee from Israel. Susskind
chases Fidelman all over Rome, and then becomes the pursued. Fidelman catches up with him, retrieves the now empty briefcase which had
housed his papers, but is told by Susskind that the manuscript has
been burned. "I did you a favor," he says. "The words were there but
the spirit was missing" (p. 37). Or as Shlomo Carlebach, the great
Hassidic folk-singing rabbi would put it, the words are simply "the
black letters on a white background. Since both are from God, we
have Black Fire on White Fire. What is Black Fire? Words. Nothing
more. But the White Fire! That is the Spirit, the magic of the universe,
the Holy Flame which makes us see all and one another and pulls us
close together—as brothers." [21]

The title of Picture Number Two is "Still Life." Locale—Rome once
again. Instead of nuisance Susskind, Fidelman has Annamaria. He
rents part of the studio from her, moves in, and they both paint. But
Fidelman spends more time pursuing the woman than his art. What
follows is a series of eccentric misadventures. Ultimately he fumbles
his way into the young woman's heart by clothing himself as a priest.
In this guise he attempts a self-portrait "of the artist as priest." In a
flash Annamaria confesses *to* him ("Forgive me, Father, for I have
sinned . . ."), undresses *for* him, and is bedded *by* him.

In Picture Number Three the scene changes to Milan. Here Fidelman is a penniless artist, a petty thief, until he is seized by two
Mafia-like creatures (Angelo and Scarpio) and forced by them to slave
away in a Milanese brothel. The gangsters concoct a Damon Runyan-
like plan to steal a Titian nude and replace it with a Fidelman forgery.
Fidelman must do the forging and stealing—if he wants his freedom.
He does. But in the process he falls in love with his own work, the
forgery, steals it, and escapes. Before the denouement the antihero
suffers the usual humiliations reserved for all well-placed *schlemiels*.
Fidelman, slapped around by his captors and harried by the harpies in
the whorehouse, cannot concentrate on the painting he must duplicate.
He needs a live model. In a passage that reminds us of *Catch-22*, we
have the following:

[21] From a talking, singing, chanting, guitar-strumming evening by Rabbi Shlomo
Carlebach in West Lafayette, Indiana, February 21, 1971.

In desperation, on the verge of panic because time is going so fast, he thinks of Teresa, the chambermaid. She is a poor specimen of feminine beauty but the imagination can enhance anything. Fidelman asks her to pose for him, and Teresa, after a shy laugh, consents.

"I will if you promise not to tell anybody."

Fidelman promises.

She undresses, a meager, bony girl, breathing heavily, and he draws her with flat chest, distended belly, thin hips and hairy legs, unable to alter a single detail. Van Eyck would have loved her. When Teresa sees the drawing she weeps profusely.

"I thought you would make me beautiful."

"I had that in mind."

"Then why didn't you?"

"It's hard to say," says Fidelman.

"I'm not in the least bit sexy," Teresa weeps.

Considering her body with half-closed eyes, Fidelman tells her to go borrow a long slip.

"Get one from one of the girls and I'll draw you sexy."

She returns in a frilly white slip and looks so attractive that instead of painting her, Fidelman, with a lump in his throat, gets her to lie down with him on a dusty mattress in the room. Clasping her slip-encased form, the copyist shuts both eyes and concentrates on his elusive Venus. He feels about to recapture a rapturous experience and is looking forward to it but at the last minute it turns into a limerick he didn't know he knew:

> *"Whilst Titian was mixing rose madder,*
> *His model was crouched on a ladder;*
> *Her position to Titian suggested coition,*
> *So he stopped mixing madder and had'er."*

Angelo, entering the storeroom just then, lets out a bellow. He fires Teresa on her naked knees pleading with him not to, and Fidelman has to go back to latrine duty the rest of the day (pp. 83–84).

The setting for Picture Four is Florence. First Fidelman sculpts sorry-looking Madonnas, which he sells for a pittance to enable him to paint his masterpiece. One day he meets and takes as mistress Esmeralda, the prostitute. Meanwhile Fidelman struggles with his great painting. At first it is "Mother and Son." Then it becomes "Brother and Sister." And finally he calls it "Prostitute and Procurer"—the last after he gives up his hack-sculpting for the more lucrative and less tiring position of panderer to Esmeralda. At last he completes the painting. A masterpiece for certain. Both he and Esmeralda agree ecstatically. But Fidelman (or "F" as he is called in this story) can't let well enough alone. In the middle of the night he has the urge to rework the painting, and during the evening he succeeds in destroying that which was to have been the culmination of his five years' struggle.

Fidelman is a wanderer in Picture Five. He moves around Italy kaleidoscopically. It is all episodic, fragmented. A psychedelic mosaic. In one sequence he sculpts perfect holes in the ground which he then tries to exhibit—for a price. In true *schlemiel* fashion someone smacks him silly with his own shovel.

The final picture of Fidelman is taken in Venice. Here Fidelman finally stops painting and lives by doing menial work. Then one day he seduces Margheretta, the wife of Beppo, a glass blower. Naturally, the husband discovers his adulterous wife in bed with Fidelman. But all works out well because it turns out that the glass blower is a homosexual, who takes on Fidelman as lover and apprentice.

Beppo teaches Fidelman a craft, and instructs him in the arts of art, and love, and life. He destroys all of Fidelman's paintings because they are so bad. "Don't waste your life doing what you can't do. . . . After twenty years if the rooster hasn't crowed she should know she's a hen" (p. 198). And finally it is Beppo who directs Fidelman towards the future—"If you can't invent art, invent life" (p. 199). Fidelman gives Beppo back to his wife and in the last lines of the story we are told that "Fidelman sailed from Venice on a Portuguese freighter" and that "in America he worked as a craftsman and loved men and women" (p. 208).

V

So the artist as *schlemiel* ends his journey, gives up his artistic ambitions, and returns home. What has happened to him in the process? In one sense we can see Fidelman in terms of gain and loss. That is, in the six stories he loses "something valuable in order to gain a truth or further understanding." [22] What he loses almost always turns out to be something that he could well do without anyway—that which proves an obstacle to insight. Many perceive this "loss" as a controlling theme in Malamud's fiction. Some have seen it as a Henry Jamesian innocents-abroad theme. Others have called it Malamud's "addiction to failure." A *schlemiel* must fail, must fumble, must lose things, but in the end *may* somehow achieve a goal more meaningful than mere winning.

A few examples suffice: In "Last Mohican" Fidelman loses his manuscript, but as we saw, he finds out that Susskind really did him a favor after all: "The words were there but the spirit was missing" (p. 37). In "Still Life" Fidelman loses pride in himself but gains a mistress, whom he loves. In the succeeding stories he continues to lose—his sister's photo, his masterpiece, old values—as he moves closer

[22] Martin Tucker, *"Pictures of Fidelman," Commonweal* (June 27, 1969), p. 420.

to an understanding of himself. In the last story he loses everything in rapid succession—his mistress, her husband, all his paintings—but finally learns (so we are told) that he can regain his home and his somewhat ambiguous future.

Looked at another way, Fidelman may be understood in terms of the prison motif or metaphor.[23] In this respect he parallels the host of other Malamud *schlemiels* to whom everything happens. In *The Assistant* Frank Alpine is imprisoned in Moris Bober's dreary grocery store; *The Fixer's* Yakov Bok, the epitome of the uninvolved man, is "seized by history" and literally thrown into a Russian prison, where he is degraded and humiliated by his vicious anti-Jewish guards. Even as recently as *The Tenants* we have Harry Lesser and his self-imposed prison in a tenement scheduled for demolition as Harry tries day by day to complete the novel that refuses to be written. Fidelman is often his *own* prisoner also as a result of his bungling, his lust, his misdirection, and sheer chance. In "Naked Nude" he comes closer to Yakov Bok's situation in that he is actually held prisoner in a house of prostitution by the two gangsters. It may be that "the prison, like the *schlemiel* who is usually its chief inmate, is Malamud's way of suggesting that to be fully a man is to accept the most painful limitations." [24]

Often in the nick of time one's nemesis seems to change to guardian angel. Note again Susskind, who says after he steals the manuscript, "I did you a favor. . . ." Susskind's message to Fidelman over and over seems obvious: "You are not a critic! You are not an artist! Be yourself!" Thus did Susskind save Fidelman from himself in order to help him see within himself. And Fidelman, who all along spurned Susskind and begrudged him a suit of clothes, shouts, "Susskind come back . . . the suit is yours. All is forgiven" (p. 37). One small step toward salvation.

Self-centered and ambivalent Fidelman rejected his family and left America for his new life in Italy. Then, toward the end of his Italian journey, in a disjointed, partially eschatological section, he moves still closer to salvation by conjuring up his sister Bessie, who is on her deathbed in New York. He is able to offer her a final "hello" before she dies. The bond of blood holds fast. "It's as though you were trying to paint yourself into your mother's arms" (p. 122), said Esmeralda. Indeed, Fidelman, turn his back as he will, always seems to resurrect Bessie and their dear, dead mother. She may inhabit a Susskind or a Beppo—but as guiding shade she hovers and persists. A brief movement from fiction to life and one finds that the senior Mrs. Malamud's

23 Robert Alter, "Jewishness as Metaphor" (1969), in *Bernard Malamud and the Critics*, pp. 33–42. Throughout his essay (pp. 29–42), however, Alter interweaves the prison-*schlemiel* motif.
24 Alter, p. 35.

maiden name is in fact—Fidelman. Is Arthur Fidelman's darting about, then, a groping for his source? A movement toward reciprocation of maternal love? Elsewhere, we have seen, he offers love to Esmeralda, Teresa, Annamaria, Beppo's wife, and, finally, Beppo himself.

Put another way one can say that *Pictures of Fidelman,* a *Picaresque Bildungsroman,* "is an allegory of the artistic and moral life," [25] with the protagonist as bungler, scapegoat, sufferer, cad, pretender, loser, prisoner, innocent abroad—or *schlemiel.* He is a Leopold Bloom of many false starts, beset by many pitfalls, a man who is hit not only by the garbage but the garbage can as well—yet one who seems to win through and *may* gain salvation in the end by giving rather than taking, by rejecting lust for love, by abandoning the pretenses of art for the honesty of craftsmanship.[26]

Thus we return to the opening epigraphs: Rilke's *"Not to Understand"* is the starting place for the *schlemiel.* Then Yeats's "Perfection of the life, or of the work . . ." occupies a central position for the questing protagonist. But in the end for Fidelman the age-old talmudic principle is operative: *"Ein Brere*—I can do no other. There is no choice. I must reject *both* Rilke and Yeats so that I can understand, and then accept *both* life and art." What happens when life pits itself against art or art pits itself against life[27] is grotesquely demonstrated in the later book, *The Tenants.* In one sense Willie Spearmint represents life, raw force, black rage. And Harry Lesser, humane though he is, seems to be a manifestation of art, the esthetic principle. When their final, inevitable confrontation comes, they singlemindedly, monomaniacally dismember each other, oblivious to landlord Levenspiel's anguished refrain of *Rachmones, Hab Rachmones, Mercy, Have Mercy.* Fortunately, Arthur Fidelman is spared the horrible fate of Willie Spearmint and Harry Lesser. Fidelman has learned his painful lesson as they, apparently, have not. One must accept both life and art. *Ein Brere. No Choice.* It can't be either/or. It must be—*Both.*

25 Robert Scholes, "Portrait of the Artist as 'Escape Goat,'" *Saturday Review* (May 10, 1969), p. 33.

26 Scholes, p. 34.

27 Since this essay was written it has been revealed that Mr. Malamud rejects a life-versus-art approach to his work. "It isn't life versus art necessarily; it's life *and* art," he points out. Moreover, even the use of the concept of the *schlemiel* leaves him cold. He believes that "the *schlmiel* treatment of fictional characters . . . reduces to stereotypes people of complex motivations and fates—not to mention possibilities." For more on this matter see "Introduction" and "Interview" in this book.

Malamud's Trial: *The Fixer* and the Critics

by Gerald Hoag

Reynolds Price has remarked that there are no thick-skinned novelists; the domestic relationship with critics and reviewers is that of a
hateful and unbreakable marriage. If that is true, Bernard Malamud
must suffer more than most, because it appears that from the beginning he has tried his best to be a good spouse. The clearer marks and
developments in his first three novels, *The Natural* (1952), *The Assistant* (1957), and *A New Life* (1962), as well as in his most recent,
Pictures of Fidelman, suggest that in theme and method he has been
close to the center, neither conservative nor wildly experimental;
though not always lucky, he has tried his hand at the things reviewers
at a given time like to admire. Coincidence may be the key; all along
Malamud might have been following his natural bent. But the appearance is unpejoratively otherwise.

Malamud's fourth novel, *The Fixer* (1966), affirms the pattern. It is
a work of high literary intent that also, according to the author himself, bids for wide non-literary attention and approval. It appeared,
moreover, after some commentators, most notably Philip Roth, began
to grumble that Malamud seemed selfishly content with small private
issues rather than big public ones. The bulk of response has been cor-
respondingly greater than for any of his previous books, and it has
been so astonishingly varied and so often careless and superficial that
it may show, for our edification, how the normal critical process can
come almost totally to grief. I do not mean that all the "bad" notices
are necessarily wrong (some of the "good" ones are also wrong-headed),
but they again serve to demonstrate how far divided and ill-instructed
we are on what we expect a novel to do and to be.

At this writing, almost three years have passed since the appearance
of *The Fixer,* and in view of the original confusion, together with the
stir surrounding the recent film version, it is not too soon to begin a
reassessment. A sampling of the early reviews will illustrate the need
to ask again, very simply, what happens in this novel.

"Malamud's Trial: *The Fixer* and the Critics," by Gerald Hoag. Originally published in *Western Humanities Review,* 24:1 (Winter 1970), 1–12. Copyright © 1970
by University of Utah. Reprinted by permission of the author and publisher.

The situation, ironically enough, is less complex than that of any other Malamud novel. Yakov Bok, a Russian Jewish handyman, abandoning his religious tradition and his hope that his childless, delinquent wife will return to him, leaves his *shtetl,* his native village, for pre-revolutionary Kiev. Here he foolishly hides his identity in order to live and work illegally outside the ghetto. He is arrested and charged with the ritual murder of a Christian boy. Better than three quarters of the novel is concerned with Bok's stubborn endurance through two and a half years of brutal pre-trial imprisonment; the story ends as the trial is about to begin.

Whitney Balliett, of all the reviewers, brings the most fundamental and potentially the most devastating critical charge against *The Fixer* in his brief *New Yorker* evaluation. The constant outrages upon Bok's person become repellent: "The newest cuffing or kick in the groin is like the last." Virgilia Peterson, in *The Reporter,* also finds the bugs and pails of excrement at last monotonous. It would be easy enough to quibble about the varying intensity or psychological quality of suffering, but the implicit principle suggested by these reviewers, even if misapplied, is legitimate. The novelist's responsibility, even beyond accuracy or authenticity, is still, as Henry James says, to be interesting. Malamud's material in this case is inherently lurid, but he does not stand accused of cheap exploitation. And despite the conclusion of Virgilia Peterson that *The Fixer* lags behind historical accounts of the Mendel Beiliss case, on which the novel is based, because fact is superior to fiction, Malamud is clearly not interested in documentary realism. (Balliett's judgment, by the way, is grander and more absolvent: "Human misery does not catalogue well." If someone had long ago convinced Dostoevsky and some others of this principle, perhaps Malamud would not have found himself nose to nose with *The New Yorker* today.)

If Malamud is not trying merely to catch the drug store market or to emulate Zola's deadly, telling monotony, why does he expose himself to the Peterson-Balliett charge? The answer lies in the author's conception of Bok's character, and though the novel speaks well enough for itself, some of Malamud's statements about it may set us on the track.

Granville Hicks, in *The Saturday Review,* has quoted Malamud as saying that Bok has some of Dreyfus and Vanzetti in him as well as Beiliss, and that he wanted also to suggest the Jews under Hitler, a connection that would seem not to need uttering, except that it is not safe to assume anything. The *Time* reviewer finds Bok's troubles irrelevant: "It is an abdication for a novelist to reject the contemporary texture of the life about him and retreat into the horrors of someone else's history." There might be analogies between Czarist Russia and the present, "but an analogy is not a novel." Thus, into the garbage with Dostoevsky go *War and Peace, The Scarlet Letter,* and, by an analogical principle, most of Shakespeare.

The fact remains that Malamud intended to deal even more directly than in *A New Life* with public issues. He told Saul Maloff of *Newsweek* that, although he is not a political novelist (accounts are that he was relatively unaffected by the turmoil of the thirties), current issues have a growing impact on his work. Nevertheless, he said to Maloff, "My inclination has been to disinvent history." The historical Beiliss was too much a loser to be a hero; *The Fixer* is intended as a "gutsy, triumphant book, not a book about defeat and sorrow. I was writing about a folk hero. I was trying to move from history to mythology."

Somehow, Malamud's note of triumph does not ring clearly enough for some readers. Although Beiliss was in fact acquitted at his trial and the novel gives no sure hint of Bok's fortunes, *Time* has him flatly going to his death, and both V. S. Pritchett (in *The New York Review of Books*) and James M. Mellard (in *Critique*) claim the consistency of that probability. Admittedly, Mellard projects a Christ-like redemption of man to follow (*bok* means goat); but that role, while it contributes part of Bok's mythic substance, is oddly out of keeping with his final, belligerent self-awareness.

I think at least some of those who find *The Fixer's* movement stagnant, its scenes repetitious, or its material a rehash familiar from life or better done by Kafka, Orwell, and Koestler, are hoodwinked by a simplistic notion of the theme and situation. Balliett says that " 'Darkness at Noon' and '1984' are still the champions," and that recalls Hemingway's playful image of knocking off rival novelists in a kind of Golden Gloves tournament. But the practice of literature, as we are told by those who live it, is not simply a prize competition; Malamud's novel, like Orwell's and Koestler's, delivers something quite other than, as Balliett would have it, "just one message: Injustice is a terrible sin."

A one-dimensional reading of the theme and of Yakov Bok is not restricted to those who dislike the novel. Donald Fanger, writing in *The Nation,* also sees justice as the only issue in the novel, and right and wrong as absolutes. Bok has changed too little; he is "sinned against but not sinning, miserable but without cause for remorse, denying God without guilt or ill effect, whole, healthy, decent." In short, he is a melodramatic puppet, a parable figure. How do we square this with Granville Hick's notion—a fresh waft of over-praise, perhaps—that Bok is "one of the most fully rendered characters in modern literature"? We go at last to the novel itself.

II

As he leaves for Kiev, Bok is a narrow man, warped with bitterness and self-pity. "Charity you were always short of," Shmuel, his father-in-law, tells him, suggesting that Bok's wife Raisl has left him at least partly because he neglected his emotional and physical obligations. Bok responds, rather in the manner of the nineteenth-century novel, with a recital of his life's woes. (This expository artifice has bothered one or two commentators, but seems tonally in keeping with the calculated, almost stylized primitivism of setting and literary gesture that predominates throughout. Malamud has acknowledged a stylistic debt to such specialists in the Jewish folk idiom as Aleichem and Singer.) He ends by declaring: "I don't want people pitying me or wondering what I did to be so cursed. I did nothing. It was a gift. I'm innocent. . . . So please don't mention charity because I have no charity to give." Shmuel answers that he did not mean money but generosity of spirit, and Bok says, "Your daughter deserves nothing" (pp. 6–7).[1] Shortly afterward, in an equally mean-spirited way, Bok refuses a beggar alms and Shmuel a small loan (p. 14).

Bok is not so much losing his faith at this point as rejecting God as a meaningful contact. Instead of going to the synagogue, as Shmuel urges, he says he should go to the Socialist Bund meetings: "But the truth of it is I dislike politics, though don't ask me why. What good is it if you're not an activist? I guess it's my nature. I incline toward the philosophical although I don't know much about anything" (p. 17). In these comments Bok expresses his best and worst qualities: his clear sight of himself and, through much of the action, his isolating and debilitating pessimism. Malamud provides for Bok an intellectual touchstone, Spinoza, who seems appropriate enough as a Jewish free-thinker and a foe of tyranny, although Bok's real philosophical debt to him is never anything but vague. Any other strong-minded independent thinker would have served about as well, and one is reminded of the philosophical name-dropping, which seems mostly gratuitous, in Bellow's *Herzog.* Nevertheless, one key to Bok's growth is his adherence, as well as his changing response, to Spinoza.

As Bok's fortunes rapidly collapse and, through the long months in prison, as he gradually comes to see the hopelessness and astonishing magnitude of his role, he remains for a long time stubbornly passive. He is befuddled and narrowly resentful of what seems to him a wholly private disaster. The modern jargon word "activist," technically inappropriate in Malamud's text, negatively defines Bok's moral flaw. Only as the book ends can he formulate and accept his guilt and expiation: "One thing I've learned, . . . there's no such thing as an unpolitical man, especially a Jew." Then a couple of bromides that in another context might have come from the Birch Society: "Where there's no fight for it there's no freedom. What is it Spinoza says? If the state

---

1 Page references are to the cloth-bound edition of Farrar, Straus and Giroux.

acts in ways that are abhorrent to human nature it's the lesser evil to destroy it."

Is this all? Is Bok merely a composite of contemporary fashions—suffering Jew, sacrificial victim, the human lost in a mad society, existential saint turned militant? Even if so, such grand literary precedents for a popular alloy of this kind exist that it might be unfair to Malamud to cite them. What is Hamlet but a composite of well-worn Elizabethan themes and attitudes? Less invidiously, since *The Fixer* is at heart a conventional, intensive character study, the test is whether the incidents and devices serve effectively to give Bok the authoritative spark we expect in the novel of character. Do they make him a complex, convincing man?

In part, of course, the answer will be subjective. For example, Bok goes through a painful, unconsummated affair with Zina, the crippled daughter of his anti-Semitic employer. In what Robert Gorham Davis (writing for *The Hudson Review*) calls "a thoroughly novelistic scene unrelated to the real issues of the book," Bok fails to follow through when he sees menstrual blood. The word "novelistic," as Davis uses it, I take to be synonymous with "contrived," maybe even with some of the sense of "frivolous." The problem of justifying the scene is complicated by the concept of "real issues." Some very good novels do not have "issues," but I do not mean to revive that old argument here, because Malamud was, as he said, eager to have a few in *The Fixer*. Davis objects primarily to the novel's limited point of view. The issues are not put to a dialectic test because we see only the "visionary" imaginings of Bok, a "limited, crude, often unkind man" who seems unlikely to have such thoughts. "We have less the sense that they developed naturally or necessarily in Yakov than that they flowed from Malamud's mind into the emptiness of a prison cell." Bok is also unconvincing, Davis says, in the light of the experience of political prisoners since the time of Bok and Beiliss. A lot worse was to happen, and it did not make heroes of its victims. "Sheer luck decides who gets noticed. The suffering, . . . so terribly real to them, is unuseful to others and therefore goes unrealized imaginatively." But if I understand Malamud's stated aims and the impact of the novel itself, this is precisely the condition *The Fixer* is out to correct. Davis' strategy of the avuncular "we" should not obscure the fact that he is forcing his own issues on the novel. The crisis with Zina seems irrelevant to him and Bok's developing thought seems unnatural because, I suspect, he is far less interested in character development than he is in polemic.

Bok's response to Zina is complex and revealing. First, it glosses vividly his wrecked marriage to Raisl, whom we see only briefly late in the novel. From the beginning he is reluctant and passive. His kindness to Zina does not come from compassion or even real interest: "Al-

though he tried to think of her as possibly a friend she remained
strange to him. He was strange to himself." His sexual response is tem-
pered by deep fears that are both ethnic and psychic. "Excitement and
foreboding flowed into one feeling. No, he thought, it's a Russian
woman. . . . For himself he was willing to experience what there was
to experience. But let her lead." When he discovers her condition, he
exclaims that she is "unclean," and he remembers Raisl's modesty and
cleanliness during the menstrual time. Although he had "felt for an
instant an anguished pity" for Zina and had warned her not to lie with
him if she is a virgin, his first concern all along is his own security. Sex
itself holds no rewards for him: "At my age it's nothing new. It means
nothing." He worries about being discovered with her, and finally, even
before he sees her blood and leaves her pleading, he has decided:
"Things are bad enough, so why make them worse?" (Pp. 49–53.) Bok's
sexual boredom and self-protectiveness here help explain his failure
with Raisl. He is bitter because his marriage is childless, but as is later
demonstrated, the biological flaw, which is symbolic of and parallel to
the psychic flaw, lies with Yakov.

Bok's encounter with Zina works relevantly on at least two other
levels. In an elementary way, it makes plausible the malicious and
damaging testimony Zina gives after Bok's arrest. Finally, in Bok's
minimal ability to see Zina at least in some sense as a person, we have
the seeds of his later strength, the unbreakable humanity that enables
him to cling bloody-fingered to his sanity during the prison ordeal and
finally to grow because of it.

The growth is slow partly because of that same virtuous stubborn-
ness. Bok's sexual repulsion to Zina's being "unclean" is instinctively
Jewish, and so are various instincts and mannerisms that plague him
in his blundering attempt to "pass" and thus find new identity and a
spurious peace. His attempt at ethnic escape is an obvious but effective
irony in the novel. As a freethinker, he is charged with a fictitious
crime from a Russian folklore that posits only the most fanatic Jewish
Orthodoxy. In bitter cold weather, he huddles in desperation in a
prayer shawl brought into his cell to entrap him. His beard grows
long and in boredom he recites fragments of the Psalms, although he
knows the guard may use this at the trial as evidence of his devoutness.
While he recites, he laughs inwardly, knowing that God is pitiless. His
political diffidence is also a source of irony when he is accused not only
of Zionism, but of revolutionary Communism. Yet the irony is only for
the reader; Bok, waiting for his indictment, seems for a long time
angrily, miserably unaware of it. "I am not a revolutionist. I am an
inexperienced man. Who knows about such things? I am a fixer" (p.
226). As for his Jewishness, he is simply resentful: "He was sick of *their*
history, destiny, blood guilt" (p. 227, italics mine).

Later, however, when a guard smuggles the New Testament to Bok, he reads it for the first time and weeps for Christ, the "strange Jew, humorless and fanatic," who died while "God was on the other side of his mountain" (p. 232). Now with bitter humor and a new perception of irony, he recites telling passages to the Christian guards. So a change occurs, barely perceptible here but finally significant.

Interspersed with these incidents is the endless catalogue of physical miseries that seem monotonously repellent to some readers—the beatings, the fever and dysentery, the chains, the heat and cold, the humiliating sadistic bodily searches several times daily. Malamud surely wants the reader to share with Bok, subjectively, his physical suffering. And while one kick is like the last ("Who makes comparisons?" Bok would say), the context in which they are delivered changes, as does the man who receives them. At some appropriately obscure point, the blows and insults cease to be matters of his private, gratuitous misfortune and somehow become positive moral episodes for Bok. Inductively he comes to the doctrine of passive resistance; he senses that each successful endurance increases the frustration and brutality of the guards and prison officials, and this increases his hope that if his indictment and trial come to pass, he can win. This is his general sense, and yet his suffering is no easier. He is wrung between hope and despair in a rhythm that parallels, as Mellard has suggested, the round of seasons and that reinforces the heavy sense of passing time and loss of youth that weighs more than anything on Bok.

To catch the quality of time, a task most peculiar to the novel, especially in the last hundred years, is to share a large challenge with Tolstoy, James, and Proust, among others. Simple length or undifferentiated repetition will not catch it; giving the sense of it, however tricky or impressive the task, is frivolous or sterile in literary terms without, for want of better words, a certain weight of human importance. If we think of Malamud's project in these terms, considering his past achievement and the fact that he is willingly working in the enduring bright shadows of Kafka, Orwell, and Koestler, we will in fairness read him at least with close attention.

III

Perhaps the change in Bok first begins to tell when, after his reading of the New Testament, a pitiful, coughing priest comes to his cell to beg him to forgive and be forgiven. "I forgive no one," Bok says (p. 236), earning himself a new round of tortures, and his refusal comes not so much from hostility as from a need to affirm his innocence and to stand independent of the whole alien system that accuses him. It is a positive act.

He begins to see, however, that he cannot be independent of history, and roughly from this point he will no longer be entirely strange to himself, as he was with Zina. His very suffering thus begins to define him to himself. After the Deputy Warden seizes his New Testament and throws loose pages of the Old into his cell, Bok reads and pieces together his biblical knowledge, on request obligingly rocking back and forth "like they do in the synagogue" for his captors (p. 241). He puzzles over the human image of God in the Old Testament, the indifferent talking God, endlessly sponsoring new covenants that will be broken. He compares this God to that of Spinoza, a God silent, immanent in nature and the mind, but Bok cannot accept either concept. "Nobody suffers for him and he suffers for no one except himself. The rod of God's anger against the fixer is Nicholas II, the Russian Tsar. He punishes the suffering servant for being godless" (pp. 240–241). Thus he now accepts personally the Jewish context of his experience.

Earlier he had been aware of his ethnic burden, but in a different way. "Being born a Jew meant being vulnerable to history, including its worst errors. Accident and history had involved Yakov Bok as he had never dreamed he could be involved. The involvement was, in a way of speaking, impersonal, but the effect, his misery and suffering, were not" (p. 155). After the incidents involving the Testaments, however, Bok falls for a time into a feverish delirium, in which he sees a bloody pogrom, and a Christian child fearfully runs from him in spite of the fixer's cry: "Stop, I love you" (p. 250). Tsar Nicholas II lectures him on the damage the Jews have done to Russia.

Even beyond this point, however, Bok's isolation, as well as his intellectual honesty, prevents his full identification with the peril of the Jews. In an emotional scene, Shmuel, who has bribed a guard to see him, warns Bok to turn back to God: "Without the covenant we would have disappeared out of history." In response, Bok lashes out bitterly: "Nature invented itself and also man. Whatever was there was there to begin with. Spinoza said so. . . . When it comes down to basic facts, either God is our invention and can't do anything about it, or he's a force in Nature but not in history. A force is not a father." But his resentment now is of the Jewish concept of God, and not of the Jews themselves. When Shmuel urges him to be patient with God's justice, which is "for the end of time," Bok answers, "I'm not so young any more, I can't wait that long. Neither can the Jews running from pogroms" (pp. 256–258).

Before long, chained to the wall after Shmuel's visit is discovered, Bok despairs and resolves to force the Russians to kill him. In a dream, however, he envisions Shmuel's corpse with a bullet hole in its forehead, and he realizes that his own death may signal the beginning of a pogrom. "What have I earned if a single Jew dies because I did?

Suffering I can gladly live without, I hate the taste of it, but if I must suffer let it be for something. Let it be for Shmuel" (p. 273).

Bok's ethic of suffering is hardly new, either to the mind of man or in Malamud's novels, each of which turns on a similar discovery. Roy Hobbs in *The Natural* fails to profit, to break out of himself, and so he fails in every crisis. When Iris tries to school him in the virtue of suffering, he retorts: "All it taught me is to stay away from it. I am sick of all I suffered." Bok has found a use for pain, but he is not so flat or unbelievable a character that he cannot share Roy's sentiment. Julius Ostrovsky, his lawyer, brings Bok news of Shmuel's natural death and tries to comfort him by citing his role as scapegoat: "I would be honored to be in your place." But Bok rejects his consolation: "It's without honor. . . . It's a dirty suffering" (p. 305).

Nevertheless, without his developing response to his misfortunes, he could not meet Raisl on the terms he does when she appears at the prison. At first, to be sure, all his old resentments well up. Yakov and Raisl, again in an older convention of fiction, rehearse their lives together, and the scene vindicates Malamud's method. The language is spare, stark, unobtrusively rhetorical. Raisl's explanation of her desertion will serve as an example:

> ". . . What bothered me most were the curses and dirty names. Because I slept with you before we were married you were convinced I was sleeping with the world. I slept with no one but you until you stopped sleeping with me. At twenty-eight I was too young for the grave. So, as you advised, I stopped being superstitious and at last took a chance. Otherwise I would soon have been dead. I was barren. I ran in every direction. I flung myself against trees. I tore at my dry breasts and cursed my empty womb. Whether stayed or left I was useless to you, so I decided to leave. You wouldn't so I had to. I left in desperation to change my life. I got out the only way I could. It was either that or death, one sin or worse. I chose the lesser sin. If you want to know the truth, Yakov, one reason I left was to make you move. Whoever thought it would come to this?" (P. 286.)

Bok's anger drives Raisl to tears, and he softens, admitting his share of guilt, explaining: ". . . it takes me a long time to learn. . . . Still I've suffered in this prison and I'm not the same man I once was. What more can I say, Raisl? If I had my life to live over, you'd have less to cry about, so stop crying" (p. 288). The talk is full of clichés, as spoken language in times of stress is especially apt to be. It is also thick with Yiddish cadences and idioms, much indeed, Whitney Balliett notes, as one might hear sometimes at Miami Beach. The fact is that it works.

The worst of the ordeal for Bok is the news that Raisl has borne a bastard child by a wandering Jewish musician. Briefly Bok goes out of control, but responds at last in a way radical for him. Raisl issues the challenge in commenting on the musician: "He fathered the child but he's not his father. Whoever acts the father is the father" (p. 290). In his most symbolically redemptive act, Bok writes out a declaration of his own paternity. Raisl confirms his new and hard-earned place as a man when she leaves. " 'Yakov,' she wept, 'come home' " (p. 292). If God is not a father, Bok, as far as he can, will try to be one.

Yakov Bok's moral and psychological journey to this point seems clear enough, indeed, hardly to call for recharting here, except that so many professional readers have overlooked it while stressing other real or imaginary matters in the novel. But *The Fixer* has a chilling twist of its own, which marks it off from most other novels of moral redemption. In the scene with Raisl, Bok is the once proud agnostic who has come, in a familiar if no less convincing way, to what is at heart the Judao-Christian moral ideal. His horrid life now has meaning and purpose, and in a sense what happens to him does not matter.

But Bok is neither a conventional saint nor a conventional anti-hero. His object is to beat the Russians by surviving until his trial happens. If one unconscious effect of the rack on which they hold him is to make Bok a better man, what will yet another turn of that screw accomplish? If great suffering and heroic endurance can produce Faulkner's Dilsey, can yet a little more pain produce Rap Brown?

As Bok rides in the black carriage, much like one which recurs in his dreams, to the trial, he falls again into a hallucination about Nicholas II, who sits ill and naked before him. After a long and improbably coherent debate about the novel's political "issues," Bok shoots the Tsar in the breast, despite the frantic protests of Bibikov, the just Investigating Magistrate who had been hounded to his death for supporting Bok early in the case. Nicholas has been pleading with Bok, asking if suffering has not taught him "the meaning of mercy." Bok replies, "what suffering has taught me is the uselessness of suffering" (p. 333). As he previously tells Bibikov in a dream, "I'm not the same man I was. I fear less and hate more" (p. 319). The wobbling carriage, damaged by a bomb, draws on, and, jolted back to consciousness, the fixer muses: "As for history . . . there are ways to reverse it. What the Tsar deserves is a bullet in the gut." Then his thoughts on the cost of freedom, previously cited, follow, and his final inner cry: "Death to the Anti-Semites! Long live revolution! Long live liberty!" (Pp. 334–335.)

"Mythology" need not try to avoid the familiar, or even the trite and obvious. I am not sure what Malamud means when he uses that tired and troublesome word, but I would guess that he intends to have Yakov Bok embody for us hidden impulses or patterns in our own experience, or perhaps to engage us afresh with axioms of the most primary sort that we know well enough but have ceased to feel. The

business of suffering and what it can bring us to is one such axiomatic
pattern, but I believe the dominant one is represented in Bok's changing attitude toward life itself. His final thought follows his surprise
that the bomb thrown at the carriage has not killed him: "If you
were a certain type death stayed its distance. Your afflictions were from
life—a poor living, mistakes with people, the blows of fate. You lived,
you suffered, but you lived" (p. 330). Here again, Bok at last projects
his own pattern outward.

IV

I have heard it offered that Bok may be an image of the biblical
Hosea. Such a connection would be consistent with Malamud's earlier
archetypal method, as Mellard and others have noted, and Bok himself
at one point, thinking of Raisl, sympathizes with Hosea's anguish over
his harlot wife. He reads the biblical lament personally, in spite of the
allegorical gloss that takes Hosea's wife to be Israel (p. 242). The passage Bok reads (Hosea 2:2–7, Revised Standard Version) is prophetic
for him. Raisl, after many hardships and the loss of her lovers, comes
back like Hosea's harlot to her husband. Spiritually, as in the biblical
promise, a new fruitfulness ensues, although Bok merely assumes fatherhood of Raisl's bastard and although she has conceived in contrast
to God's warning to the Israelites: ". . . they shall play the harlot,
but not multiply" (4:19). The correspondences cannot be carried much
further. The Jews of Russia are not engaged as are Hosea's Israelites in
venereal idolatries. Unlike Hosea, Bok, who comes to assume something
like the role of prophet and leader, remains bitterly unfaithful to
Jehovah. If, as some scholars argue, the heresy of Hosea's Samaria is
adherence to the Adonis cult, and Bok can be taken as an anti-Hosea,
there may be some profit, as Mellard suggests, in connecting Bok's
dream murder of Nicholas with the ritual death of the Old King and
the trial itself with the Chapel Perilous. But so much for that kind of
play; the key to myth in *The Fixer* is not allusion. It lies rather in
the skill that raises a neutral anecdote to cosmic exemplum in the
natural course of tale-telling.

In other ways that I may only suggest here, the novel is texturally
rich. The recurring imagery of dark birds, picked up from the black
eagle that is the emblem of a Russian anti-Semitic society, is evidence
of Malamud's demonstrable skill, here and elsewhere, at what E. M.
Forster calls rhythm in fiction. Concrete detail in *The Fixer* is rarely
a mere matter of scene-setting. One paragraph describing the *shtetl*
will illustrate:

> They rattled along a rutted dusty street with thatched cottages on one
> side, open weedy fields on the other. A big-wigged Jewess, sitting on her

doorstep, plucked a bloody-necked hen between her knees, as she cursed out a peasant's sow rooting in the remnants of her potato garden. A pool of blood in the ditch marked the passage of the ritual slaughterer. Farther on, a bearded black goat with a twisted horn, tethered to a post, baaed at the horse and charged, but the rope around his neck held and though the post toppled, the goat was thrown on its back. The doors of some of the cottages hung loose, and where there were steps they sagged. Fences buckled and were about to collapse without apparent notice or response, irritating the fixer, who liked things in place and functioning. (P. 15.)

The old woman, an image of Russian Jewry, is also an omen of the sort one finds in myth. The goat is a comic symbol suggesting Bok himself and also an omen. The disorder makes possible some important, if conventional, character exposition. Malamud's attention to small matters, his effort to make almost every detail count in some multiple way, never flags. Two of the three guards, who might have been mere instruments of brutality, gradually become ambivalent victims of their own system and of Bok's heroism. For the most part, Malamud's full powers and experience seem to be at work.

The chief flaw, to my mind, is in the use of dream and hallucination. The Tsar is more like a historical reference book than a figure in a vision. The other dreams are too often creaking expository artifices rather than convincing bits of experience. Nevertheless, if one is sensitive to the central action of the novel, which involves the inner growth of the protagonist and not the often monotonous circumstance, even the repetitions take on increasing interest, and a tension inexorably builds. *The Fixer* can claim almost the economy and control of *The Assistant,* and, if that is what a reader looks for, a much clearer perspective upon current events.

In summary, Yakov Bok is neither too good a man to be interesting, nor too dehumanized to change. The intracranial point of view does not restrict us entirely to Bok's thoughts and feelings, as Robert Gorham Davis claims; the fixer is veritably besieged with the talk of others with varying claims upon him. After the imprisonment begins, the other characters are presented as a series of dramatic foils to illuminate Bok and challenge his perspective. They come to him alternately with periods of dream or introspection, in a rhythmic arrangement common enough both in fiction and drama, and since external events are limited, a heavy burden of interest and attention rests upon these characters. Hence, even the minor ones are often vividly drawn. The heavy focus on Bok's private anguish that Davis justly notes will make him seem irrelevant, moreover, only if Malamud fails to convince us of the fixer's representative qualities. I believe Bok's psychic troubles could hardly be more familiar to the twentieth-century reader, and therein lies the daring of the author's plan. The occupational hazard of the mythologist of contemporary experience is that the reader, like Huck Finn, may just say "I been there before." The outcome for such a novel depends heavily on subjective response, the mood of the moment. More than others, the mythic novel may need time to be judged.

We have come around again to a season of crisis when writers, along with professors and other artists, are being exhorted to man the barricades, to subordinate art and scholarship to propaganda. *Time*'s clumsy misreading of *The Fixer* is suggestive of attitudes in journals of far greater intellectual pretensions. While *Time* says Malamud should be relevant, however, Charles Thomas Samuels in *The New Republic* says that *The Fixer* is an attempt at political and social relevance that should not have happened. Malamud, Samuels argues, is especially skilled as a novelist but also politically naive, and the Beiliss material is unsuited to his gifts. ". . . writers like Malamud constitute a precious national resource: an image of discipline and craft without which, ironically, even the problems they are said to neglect can never be solved." Caught in such a crossfire, who can win?

Samuels' proper feelings about the value of craft, however, are hard to reconcile with his failure to see that, while Bok's (*ergo* Malamud's?) politics may be simple, his make-up as a man is not. An honest reassessment will show, I think, that Malamud has been sufficiently engaged with his times all along. It seems to me one of the more tedious realities of the day that, so soon after the thirties and forties, we feel we must tell novelists what to write about and (so prescriptively) how.

In the Heart of the Valley: Bernard Malamud's
A New Life

by Richard Astro

Bernard Malamud, formerly a New Yorker, arrived in the Pacific Northwest in late summer of 1949 to take a position as Instructor of English at Oregon State College. He was met at the train station in Albany, Oregon by the Director of English Composition at the small, technically-oriented land-grant institution, who drove the new instructor through the farm-filled Willamette Valley, ideally situated between the Cascade and Coastal mountain ranges, to Corvallis (the name is derived from the Latin and means "in the heart of the valley"), a quiet but not unattractive community of about 10,000.

In New York, Malamud had attended C.C.N.Y. (B.A., 1936) and Columbia University (M.A., 1942) as well as Brooklyn College, Hunter College, and New York University. He had taught English at Erasmus Hall and Chelsea High Schools. Additionally, he had written "Bulldog Drummond" radio scripts and had published reviews in *Atlantic Monthly* and *The New York Times Book Review* and short stories in *American Prefaces, Threshold,* and the Washington *Post.* At Oregon State, he was assigned four sections of English Composition in a rigid and closely supervised program which emphasized "the writing of short expository themes, and the study of those elements of grammar, punctuation, spelling, and diction which are prerequisites to the writing of effective expository prose in any professional field." [1]

Malamud taught composition at Oregon State for more than a decade, and he endured the drudgeries of the department "theme room" (where all student papers were filed), grading "technical reports," and monitoring group final examinations in composition with at least a passive tolerance. It was, of course, during his stay in Oregon that he wrote his first two novels (*The Natural* and *The Assistant*) and his

"In the Heart of the Valley: Bernard Malamud's *A New Life*," by Richard Astro. An original essay prepared for this collection.

[1] This statement appears in a document entitled "A Statement of Current Standards for English Composition" which was circulated to the English department staff during the early 1950's.

celebrated volume of short stories, *The Magic Barrel,* for which he was awarded the National Book Award in 1959. But there was a department policy stating that only those members of the faculty with Ph.D.'s might teach literature classes. And despite the fact that he was promoted to Assistant Professor (in 1954) and to Associate Professor (in 1959),[2] Malamud was annually given large doses of composition with only an occasional section of an introductory literature course and a short-story writing class to break the monotony.

It would seem only natural for Malamud to resent having to teach almost exclusively the kind of course which, in even the most enlightened university, tends to depress the spirit and stifle the creative imagination. And Malamud was angered by the policy of "literature for Ph.D.'s only," particularly during his later years at Oregon State when it seemed possible that his own work might one day become the subject of doctoral dissertations. Nevertheless, Malamud generally was regarded as an effective composition teacher by his students and as a concerned member of the composition staff by most of his colleagues. He served on the Composition Textbook Committee and on the department's Uniform Grading Committee.[3] And Walter Foreman, who served as Director of Composition from 1952 until 1965, recalls that Malamud was a competent teacher who graded his themes promptly and meticulously and was rarely, if ever, the subject of student complaints.[4]

Malamud left Oregon State in the spring of 1961. He had come to Corvallis an unknown writer, though with a genuine talent that can be seen in even his earliest stories and reviews. He left as a national figure, a novelist of significant accomplishment and even greater promise in a time when few serious writers were having success trying to understand, describe, and make plausible the bizarre facts of contemporary life.

Malamud's years at Oregon State had a formidable impact on his personal sensibility as well as on his art. Many of his experiences at the college were, of course, highly negative, particularly when he felt that his literary achievements had been ignored by people who should have known better. Nevertheless, he remained on the faculty (in on-leave status) until 1964, and though he has gone on to Bennington and to international fame, he maintains close friendships with former colleagues (*The Malamud Reader* is dedicated to an Oregon State pro-

2 It should be mentioned that Malamud's promotion to Associate Professor did not come easily. It was opposed by some members of the staff because the novelist did not have the Ph.D.

3 Malamud also helped innovate the Liberal Arts Lecture Series and the Foreign Film Program at Oregon State.

4 Walter C. Foreman in conversation with Richard Astro, June 5, 1973.

fessor and his wife), and he has even returned to Corvallis for summer visits.

Most importantly, though, Malamud's experiences in Corvallis and at Oregon State College serve as the backdrop for his third novel, *A New Life,* which was published late in 1961. The book chronicles the search for love and meaning by Sy Levin, a thirty-year-old former drunkard from New York, who takes a job teaching English Composition at Cascadia College, a small school in the Pacific Northwest where education consists of teaching students "how to work" and where "there are no geniuses around to make you uncomfortable." [5] Levin finds his "new life," all right, but it is not what he had hoped for. He is thrust into the world of campus politics and into some strange experiences in sex and love. He fumbles through most of the novel, and when he finally does "the right thing," it costs him his job.

At first glance, *A New Life* seems just another academic *roman à clef,* one more example of that sub-genre of literature we call the college novel which records the inevitable encounter between an intellectual's dream and academic reality by a bitter man who never should have entered the academy. Certainly, this is the way it was viewed by many Corvallis townspeople (one of whom launched a blatantly anti-semitic attack on the novelist) and by many of Malamud's more insensitive colleagues at Oregon State who accused the instructor of being "ungrateful." Even some of Malamud's friends viewed the book principally as gossip. And English Professor James Groshong was severely criticized by many of his colleagues when he suggested in a review for the Corvallis *Gazette-Times* that *A New Life* is a complex and difficult book which should not be read quickly and discarded.[6]

A New Life is in large measure a *roman à clef.* Almost all of the major characters have real-life equivalents, though Malamud worked hard to avoid direct correspondences by making many of his characters and situations carefully constructed composites of two or more people and events. Orville Fairchild, the reactionary Head of Cascadia's English department and author of the hated *Elements of Grammar* (used in all composition classes) is patterned on a former Oregon State professor, as is Composition Director Gerald Gilley, Levin's antagonist, who prefers teaching composition to literature and who prefers golf and photography to either (Gilley particularly dislikes Thomas Hardy whose reputation in America was, curiously enough, the subject of Malamud's Master's thesis at Columbia). The sympathetically drawn

---

[5] Bernard Malamud, *A New Life* (New York: Dell, 1961), p. 38. All further citations from *A New Life* refer to the Dell edition and are identified by page number parenthetically in the text.

[6] See James W. Groshong, "Trouble in the West: Malamud's New Book," Corvallis *Gazette-Times,* October 5, 1961.

Joe Bucket who wears army surplus shoes and who for years has been working on a dissertation on "Disorder and Sorrow in Sterne" has an equivalent in Oregon State's English department, as did George Bullock, who prepares lists of teachers hard on athletes for Cascadia's athletic department, and C. D. Fabricant, the department scholar whose liberalism initially attracts but finally repels Levin. Even the character of Leo Duffy, the radical instructor who was dismissed shortly before Levin's arrival and in whose footsteps Levin eventually treads, is based upon a man who pursued drastic reforms in Oregon State's composition program prior to 1949, though happily, unlike Duffy, he has not committed suicide.

The city of Easchester, "a small town" where there "isn't much doing unless you get outdoors or are interested in football and such," (12) resembles Corvallis, though Malamud does manipulate geography in the interests of his plot. But it is clearly Corvallis that the novelist is describing when he writes that

> The town, though attractive, was much of sameness. It had grown in a semicircle around a bend in the Sacajawea and now extended thinly to the western and northern hills; surrounding the long rectangle of green campus and red-brick college buildings. Downtown was a treeless grid of boxlike store and small office buildings, unimaginative and verging on abstraction. The goods in store windows supplied its only color. Around the business district were many old-fashioned double-pediform houses, mainly carpenter-built on small plots of ground, squeezed together; some were redeemed by gardens, shrubbery and trees, whose apples, plums and walnuts often rotted on sidewalks as Levin walked, evoking in him guilt for the waste. Farther out, past the campus, appeared the modern ranch houses with picture windows; tilted roof types; and split-levels climbing the hills. The fraternity and sorority houses were the most magnificent of the community. (72)

Though there are colleges like Cascadia throughout America, a fact Malamud must have realized when he received letters from faculty in a number of schools congratulating him on describing "their" English departments so well, Cascadia is undeniably Oregon State; where there have been fly-casting classes for college credit and where, though great improvements in the service of the humanities have been made by thoughtful faculty and administrators, there are still no graduate programs in the liberal arts.

But while *A New Life* is what Leslie Fiedler calls "Malamud's valedictory to one college he was about to leave for another," [7] an indictment of an educational system which in many ways did not agree with him, it is also much more. For one thing, it is a novel about the Amer-

[7] Leslie Fiedler, *Waiting for the End* (New York: Dell, 1965), p. 146.

ican West and about a wanderer for whom, at least initially, the West
is another word for magic. Levin's quest for what he calls "my manifest
destiny" is founded on that American dream of a golden age patterned
on the land of the heart's desire.

"My God, the West!" Levin exclaims on his first day in Easchester
as he imagines "the pioneers in covered wagons entering this valley for
the first time." (8) But as the story unfolds, Levin learns (actually he
is told by C. D. Fabricant) that the pioneers who settled the West are
gone, replaced by the pygmies whose "great fear is that tomorrow will
be different from today." (103) Moreover, it is ironic that it is Fabricant
who laments the passing of the frontier spirit in Easchester, since he is
himself a fraud whose individualistic sentiments in the end give way
to expedient political considerations. Early in the novel, Gilley tells
the impressionable Levin that "one of the things you'll notice about
the West is its democracy." (9) But it soon becomes apparent to the
new instructor that the "democratic spirit" of Easchester is no more
than equalitarianism—the achievement of the identical average.

As John Barsness has noted, Levin must also learn what all Western
dreamers have been forced to recognize: that a clear break with history
is impossible, and that a belief in freedom cradled in nature—in the
Garden as a source of redemption—disregards the obvious continuity
of culture and experience as it is carried over the mountains to the
West.[8] Like A. B. Guthrie's settlers in *The Way West* who travelled
to the same Willamette Valley a century earlier, Levin brings his "bag-
gage" with him. And while he hopes that "a new place will inspire
change—in one's life," (20) he finds that in terms of his personal
geography, Easchester is still very much in the East.

Initially, Levin is inspired by the "distant mountain ranges laden
with forests, the vast sky piled high with towering masses of golden
clouds," (8) and so is convinced he did the right thing when he left
New York. But his wonder is gradually replaced by his sober reflections
that the present is drenched with the past; Levin's musings about his
former unhappiness stand in the way of his aspirations. He anticipates
"participating" in the "Western experience," but he really does nothing more than rake his landlady's lawn, collect the ubiquitous Easchester walnuts, and admire (from a distance) the fertile fields, the cloud-
decked skies, and the "fluttering, honking" formations of birds.

At one point in the novel, Levin approaches a liaison with a more
than willing coed named Nadalee Hammerstad like a Western knight-
errant, "his lance at his side." Driving the fifty miles from Easchester
to Nadalee's cabin on the coast, he even sees himself as "stout Cortez

---

[8] John A. Barsness, "*A New Life:* The Frontier Myth in Perspective," *Western American Literature*, III (Winter, 1969), 298.

—Balboa that is." (143) Levin and Nadalee consummate their passion, and he continues to think "of Nadalee endlessly," but his chivalric spirit is depressed by tortured reflections that he had really "got her without deserving to—fruit for teacher—a mean way to win a lay." (154–155)

> His escape to the West had thus far come to nothing, space corrupted by time, the past-contaminated self. Mold memories, bad habit, worse luck. He recalled in dirty detail each disgusting defeat from boyhood, his weaknesses, impoverishment, undiscipline—the limp self entangled in the fabric of a will-less life. A white-eyed hound bayed at him from the window—his classic fear, failure after grimy years to master himself. He lay in silence, solitude, and darkness. (155)

And as Levin thinks about his sordid past which has discolored his affair with Nadalee, he falls "into sadness, an old kind; this lonely man remembering this lonely man in the dark of a dirty room." (155) In the end, Levin's experience leaves him frightened "because he thought he had outdistanced it [the past] by three thousand miles. The future as new life was no longer predictable." (155)

Later in the novel, Levin begins his affair with Pauline Gilley (wife of the Composition Director) in the lush greenery of a nearby forest under the open Western sky, the spaciousness of which suggests total freedom and possibility. In the end, though, Levin's passion gives way to feelings of seediness for having committed adultery with Gilley's wife, and Pauline is no longer Levin's mythic heroine, but a flat-chested neurotic who gives him a literal pain in the butt.

Levin ultimately accepts responsibility for Pauline (who has become pregnant by him) and her two children, and the novel ends as Levin and his charges leave Easchester in search of a still newer life. But Levin has accepted the painful fact that despite the genuine beauty of its surroundings, Easchester has not been the never-never land of his romantic dreams. For the instructor whose present cannot blot out a tortured past, it has not been a garden of renewal. Moreover, Levin finds that Easchester is simply a town with a campus like towns with campuses everywhere—plagued with commercial morality and educational philistinism with its fear of creative people and creative criticism. As Levin drives out of town in his old Hudson, he stops "for a last look at the view to the mountains."

> "Beautiful country."
> "If beauty isn't all that happens." (335)

Malamud affirms that beauty, the emblem of the Western dreamland, is simply not enough. And this is the lesson which Levin has had to learn through his agonizing odyssey to Cascadia.

But although Levin fails as the adventuring Western hero ("I failed this place," he tells Pauline [335]), in the larger picture he triumphs. Malamud shows, of course, that redemption cannot be achieved simply by moving from New York to a rural Western valley, but he does suggest that salvation is possible when there is a change in the heart of the man. S. Levin, "a man of thirty still running after last year's train," (190) does discover through his experiences in Easchester that man's spirit is the only source of human freedom. And, like Frankie Alpine in *The Assistant* and Yakov Bok in *The Fixer*, he is another "metaphorical Jew" who gradually adopts that unique code of morality by which, as Ihab Hassan puts is, a man becomes a *mensch*.[9]

More than an academic novel, more than a treatment of the flawed dream of the mythic West, *A New Life* is Levin's story—a personal allegory in which the hero, though beaten and chastized by life, emerges with the kind of liberating insights about humanity which make life bearable. And if we can accept Theodore Solotaroff's thesis that for Malamud "Jewishness is a type of metaphor" for "the tragic dimension of anyone's life and for a code of personal morality and salvation that is more psychological than religious,"[10] and I think we can, then *A New Life* can be read as what James Groshong calls a "sociology of the Jew in America."[11]

In the course of his ordeal, Levin learns that life is holy and that the living of it is important. And it is this realization by a man who is willing to involve himself in life even though that involvement eventually damns him that makes one what Levin calls "a man of principle." A *schlemiel* who has done almost nothing right in his life, who has always managed to say and do the wrong thing at the wrong time, Levin is "chosen" (literally—by Pauline Gilley, who selected his application because "your picture reminded me of a Jewish boy I knew in college who was very kind to me during a trying time in my life" [331]) to emerge through repeated failures with an understanding of the beauty of morality. Morality, Levin learns, is "a way of giving value to other lives through assuring human rights." And the instructor holds fast to this principle, though it means that by sticking it out "chained to her [Pauline's] ribs," he willingly sacrifices the "freedom to feel free."

Even his determined attempt to confront and engage the philistine academy of Cascadia bears redeeming fruit. For Levin learns as he leaves town that through his efforts, *The Elements* has been removed from the composition curriculum, that the Dean has approved his idea

9 Ihab Hassan, *Radical Innocence: Studies in the Contemporary American Novel* (Princeton: Princeton University Press, 1961).

10 Theodore Solotaroff, "Bernard Malamud's Fiction: The Old Life and the New," *Commentary*, XXXIII (March, 1962), p. 198.

11 Groshong, "Trouble in the West."

for a Great Books program, and that Gilley (who late in the novel replaces Fairchild as department head) has decided to give literature
classes to some members of the faculty without Ph.D.'s.

Still, Levin's success is sharply qualified. A teacher committed to the
humanistic tradition, he is forced to agree to Gilley's unreasonable demand that he never again teach on the college level. And there is something distinctly pathetic about the way he leaves the novel—driving out
of town with a pregnant woman he no longer loves and with her two
children who do not love him. In short, the affirmation of life in *A
New Life* is distinctly ironic, and the book's main theme seems to be,
as Sidney Richman notes, "success in failure—failure in success." [12]
Levin, the unfrocked idealist, drives off into an unheroic and unre-
ceding future, with all the hope, Malamud seems to imply, that the
modern man of principle can cherish in the troubled times in which
he lives.

Thematically, *A New Life* is Malamud's "largest novel." In it the
novelist expands his horizons (beyond those of *The Natural*, *The Assistant*, and *The Magic Barrel*) by creating and populating a world
large enough not only to carry his main theme of human connection,
indebtedness and responsibility, but also able to sustain a love story,
a Western adventure, a comedy, and a study of American academic
life. But because the vehicle which Malamud chooses (the college novel)
cannot support his tale of human suffering and regeneration, the novel
ultimately fails. In short, Malamud's problems in handling the materials of the academic *roman à clef*, in addition to the implicit short-
comings of the genre itself result in a book in which the author attempts to show that there is a narrow zone of freedom where man can
escape the grim determinings of history, but which is actually an ironic
tribute to precisely those determinings he sets out to criticize.

A New Life is a novel divided against itself, and it comes apart less
because of Malamud's deficient sense of the West (as Fiedler suggests),[13]
than because Malamud knows too much about the workings of a college. In those sections of the novel which deal with Cascadia's English
department, Malamud treats his subject exhaustively. He ignores no
minutiae, however uninteresting and unimportant, that will help him
indict Cascadia's intellectual aridity. Consider, for example, Gerald
Gilley's explanation of how the college lost its liberal arts curriculum:

> "They were taken from us, Sy. I won't go into the whole long story but
> there's a history of some nasty pitched battles for funds between us

---

12 Sidney Richman, *Bernard Malamud* (New York: Twayne, 1966), p. 93.
13 Leslie Fiedler, "Crimes and Punishments," *American Judaism* (Spring, 1967),
reprinted in *The Collected Essays of Leslie Fiedler* (New York: Stein and Day, 1971),
p. 153.

and our sister institution, Cascadia University at Gettysburg.—That, if you have checked the map, is our capital city, a hundred miles north of here, where they still rib us as 'southerners,' to say nothing of 'aggies' and 'hay palace.' Politics get steaming hot every biennium when the state budget is in the works, and I guess some of our alumni took it into their heads that it might make things easier all around to bring CU right down here to Easchester—they're the younger institution, 1878, and we have a lot more land than they do—and incorporate us both into one big super-university with one physical plant, which would, of course, have saved the taxpayers lots of money in the long run. Well, for too many reasons to mention, the plan didn't come off. Their alumni in the legislature raised a stink—they're always had the law and journalism schools and as a result can influence public opinion almost any way they want—and they got their own bill through, separating CC and CU more than we were in the first place. There was talk—as I've many times heard the story—of removing *us* to the Gettysburg campus, but then they decided to settle for certain punitive measures, which in this case were nothing less than cutting out our upper-level courses in the liberal arts, which people here thought weren't so important anyway, so we'd be two absolutely different institutions and theoretically uncompetitive." (28)

Now all this is a fairly accurate transcription of the historical conflict between Oregon's two major state institutions, but it does little to amplify the conflict between east and west or the sorrows of Levin.

Or, take Orville Fairchild's monologue about his tenure as head of Cascadia's English department:

"I've fought the good fight. *The Elements* was born here. The department, in my time, grew from three to twenty-one. Yet the path was not always without thorns: We've had hard times, when the administration gave us almost nothing to live on. I scrimped to save. I had to pare down salaries, occasionally causing friction, I confess; still, what had to be done had to be done. The first duty of a good leader is to carry out orders. I did as I was ordered. At one time I ran the cheapest department on the Coast, and frankly I was proud to keep the college solvent and functioning during times of crisis. Dean Feeney felt as I did. He's also a careful man with a dollar. We have to be—we're not a rich state. The dean and I saw eye to eye. I have in my papers at home a letter from him commending me for my efforts in the college's behalf. I'm proud of it." (53-54)

Again, this is an effective rendering of the depression world-view of several members of the department in which Malamud taught, where administrators took pleasure in keeping salaries low so that they could return money to the state, but the detail in which it is presented draws attention away from the novel's major themes. The same is true of the lengthy reports on the activities of various members of the English faculty who play inconsequential roles in the novel and the excessive parodies of *The Elements* and its satellite workbooks. These were subjects of obvious interest to Malamud which, I must confess, cannot help but amuse (or infuriate, as the case may be) anyone who has ever taught in Oregon State's English department. But the novelist presents them in such cumbersome detail that they are plodding and listless and detract from what is otherwise a serious novel in affirmation of the human spirit. Even Gilley's cryptic final remark to Levin: "Got your picture," which has perplexed at least one critic,[14] and which Malamud has unsatisfactorily explained as suggesting a coming change for the better in Gilley's attitudes,[15] is best understood not in connection to anything in the novel itself, but rather in relation to the character of the original on whom Malamud's portrait of Gilley is based. It is a house joke—and in serious fiction house jokes do not make for good comedy.

As a matter of fact, Levin is himself diminished as a character in those scenes set in Cascadia's English department. At the college he merely agrees, laughs, gasps, sighs, exclaims "tst-tst," groans and nods. It is only when he is off-campus that his expressions grow to sentences, his sentences to paragraphs and he becomes the kind of character who can carry Malamud's moral theme.

Malamud's experiences at Oregon State affected him deeply, and despite his attempt to use those experiences as a backdrop for his tale of Levin's search for meaning and purpose, there are just too many scenes and portraits in the novel which are mere personal justifications. Indeed, perhaps the most effectively drawn member of Cascadia's English department is the spectral Leo Duffy to whom Levin finds himself drawn in "self-love" and whose role as an advocate of liberal educational programs and as the former lover of Pauline Gilley prefigures similar activities by Malamud's protagonist. And perhaps the reason why Duffy functions so well in terms of Malamud's moral theme in *A New Life* is that he is the one member of Cascadia's English department whose original the novelist never met.

Beyond the question of Malamud's circumstantial involvement in English department affairs at Oregon State-Cascadia, lies the larger issue of the value of the academic novel itself. For viewed realistically, it must be conceded that the college novel is a vulgar literary form. As Leslie Fiedler notes, such books are "hopelessly middlebrow, muted where they pretend to be moderate, melodramatic where they pretend to be tragic, commonplace where they pretend to be wise."

[14] Ruth B. Mandel, "Ironic Affirmation," *Bernard Malamud and the Critics,* ed. Leslie A. Field and Joyce W. Field (New York: N.Y.U. Press, 1970), p. 270.
[15] See Mandel, p. 270.

And this is, surely, their essential flaw, the clue to why they inevitably end by falling into the very attitudes they begin by satirizing. Certainly most of them seem not so much transcendent explorations of the failures of institutions of higher learning as depressing symptoms of the way in which such institutions subserve the flight from excellence and the parody of high art represented by the triumph of midculture in our lives.[16]

The two major themes of the college novel, Fiedler notes, "the teacher as liberal and innocent victim of social repression, and the teacher as lecher and guilty seducer of the young" demand "cliché rather than truth, since their end is titillation rather than insight." [17]

It is certainly true that Malamud intends to reflect Levin's quest for love and life in the account of Levin's difficult pilgrimage over coastal mountains to Nadalee, who in Levin's office "nuzzled her hard little breast against Levin's lonely elbow" and whom the instructor undresses in his thoughts despite his realization that "she was his student and he her instructor, in loco parentis, practically a sacred trust." (130) But the whole incident never really progresses beyond the stock student-professor sexual encounter with its overtones of what Fiedler calls "garden-variety pornography." [18] Similarly, no matter how thoroughly we may sympathize with Levin's plight in the illiberal atmosphere of Cascadia where, as Gilley happily notes, "life is peaceful" and where "what we don't want is trouble," the instructor's lament about being engaged in "a great irrelevancy" teaching composition in an unknown corner of a cold-war America which, "in the best sense of a bad term" is distinctly "un-American," smacks of popular-front politics. "I worry I'm not teaching how to keep civilization from destroying itself," (109) Levin groans and then laughs "embarrassedly." And we laugh embarrassedly too, at a character whose insights are reduced to the stock truths of the ritualistic liberal.

Fiedler suggests that more ambitious and subtle practitioners have tried to liberate the college novel from "the limitations of exotic reverie and ritualistic liberalism" by a form of thematic inversion whereby the instructor is more seduced than seducing and where the liberal clichés of the academy are satirized rather than eulogized." [19] True to form, Malamud has Nadalee attempt to use her encounter with Levin to get a higher grade (to which, ironically, she is actually entitled), and he launches a devastating assault on C. D. Fabricant who abandons his liberal views when those views threaten his career. Addition-

[16] Fiedler, *Waiting for the End*, p. 141.
[17] *Ibid.*, pp. 141, 142.
[18] *Ibid.*, p. 142.
[19] *Ibid.*, p. 143.

ally, there is more than one occasion in the novel when Malamud seems to make Levin's militant assault on the barricades of illiberalism seem ridiculous, as for example when the instructor pompously affirms that "The liberal arts—as you know—since ancient times—have affirmed our rights and liberties. Socrates—." (29) And perhaps it is because of statements like these that while we "feel" for Levin the man, we really do not like Levin the professor. Moreover, while these aspects of Levin's and Fabricant's behavior are principally valuable in that they add slightly to Malamud's presentation of the novel's dual themes (the corruption of the West and the quest through suffering for salvation), their real appeal is parasitic in that their overriding interest is restricted to the genre to which they belong and requires an intimate knowledge by the reader of the kind of characters they are meant to mock. In short, Malamud's rendering of life at Cascadia—as it was before and as it is during Levin's year at the institution—simply does not transcend its occasion which it must do if it is to serve as a meaningful background for a work of serious fiction.

In an article written shortly before the publication of *A New Life,* Philip Roth noted that the modern writer has his hands full trying to make credible an American reality which stupefies, sickens and infuriates. And Roth points to Malamud as one of several talented writers whose early works (*The Natural, The Assistant,* and *The Magic Barrel*) indicate that the author has not found "the contemporary scene a proper and sufficient backdrop for his tales of heartlessness and heartache, of suffering and regeneration." [20] Even when Malamud writes a baseball story, says Roth, referring to *The Natural,*

> it is not baseball as it is played in Yankee Stadium, but a wild, wacky baseball, where a player who is instructed to knock the cover off the ball promptly steps to the plate and knocks it off; the batter swings and the inner hard string core of the ball goes looping out to centerfield, where the confused fielder commences to tangle himself in the unwinding sphere, then the shortstop runs out, and with his teeth, bites the center fielder and the ball free from one another.[21]

Perhaps it was for the purpose of making Levin's story—which is certainly a tale of "heartlessness and heartache, of suffering and regeneration"—more credible that Malamud turned to situations and characters he knew well. Unfortunately, neither the genre of the college novel itself nor Malamud's handling of materials of that genre was sufficient to support his important cultural and moral themes.

It is certainly true that the position of the writer without the cus-

[20] Philip Roth, "Writing American Fiction," *Commentary,* XXX (March, 1961), p. 229.
[21] *Ibid.,* p. 228.

tomary academic degrees is bound to be a difficult one in a tradition-bound university. And as Fiedler notes, the difficulty of his position is compounded when he is also "A Jew among Gentiles, an Easterner among Westerners . . . or simply an urban type among provincials." [22] Bernard Malamud was all of these things, and it would be simple to predict that his tenure at a school like Oregon State would have a decidedly negative effect on his art; that having to develop those special qualities of character one must possess to endure the endless succession of academic quarters in such an institution might steal time otherwise spent more profitably. But Malamud has been a writer who has worked well alone—away from places where literary "fads" and "trends" are born and die—and so Oregon State, where he wrote three significant volumes of fiction, may have provided a perfect setting where his talents could ripen. When, however, he attempted to use his experiences at that college as the source and background for a story about man's sad, uneasy but heroic adjustment to the way things are, his setting failed him. From his characterization of Frankie Alpine in *The Assistant* to that of Abramowitz in *Rembrandt's Hat*, Malamud has always operated best in that parish of immediacy where the reader can respond to his characters' meager humanity. But in *A New Life*, we see less of the heart of the man than we see of the heart of the valley, and the result is a backhanded slap at the academy which is curiously interesting, but which does not contain the sort of stuff from which great fiction can be made.

[22] Fiedler, *Waiting for the End*, pp. 145–46.

From Bernard Malamud, with Discipline and with Love (*The Assistant* and *The Natural*)

by William Freedman

Ah yes, the Fifties. Who can forget them? That was the Eisenhower decade, the decade before Civil Rights, before Viet Nam, before Berkeley, before The Living and naked theaters, the decade when presidents knew their places, Blacks and dissenters knew theirs, students, actors, and audiences theirs. In the Fifties if you didn't like what was going on —if indeed you were sufficiently awake to know what was going on and to know you didn't like it—you muttered something about next year and reported for work the following morning—ten minutes early. It was the decade of discipline; and art, doing its duty, reacted to life, whether through confrontation or self-conscious rejection and recoil. Discipline was one of the principal items on the literary menu, the specialty of the house if the restaurant happened to be kosher.

Discipline is no recent visitor to the house of fiction. It comes with the artist's territory; it is the architect as tenant. When Voltaire advises the cultivation of our gardens, Conrad the salvatory attention to busy work, Hemingway the stoic code, they speak of what they know. Each is translating out of his own creative experience and the recommendations are translatable back to their probable source: the disciplined business of authorship.

But during the Fifties we had something to keep the subject dangling before us like a grotesque puppet. We had the lingering memory of the War to end all thought of the end of war; and we had the bomb. The thought of recent past and likely future sent us scurrying in several directions. To some it suggested the need for a tighter leash on the not-so-latent beast. Human beings, even the most cultivated and sophisticated, were capable of savagery to which cannibalism was cycling in the park. Beneath it all we were fiends and we had better do what we can —all we can—to keep the fiend beneath it all. To others—we call them

Beats—it suggested an Epicurean indulgence of the moment, each of which threatened to be the last. And it sent others—the overwhelming majority—back to the mindless absorption in the task of simply getting on, to the business of sweeping past and future under the rug of real and invented need. One way or another the questions of discipline, restraint, and self-control were on our minds, even if only, like the white bear we challenge ourselves not to think about, in the futile attempt to force them off.

Some read the Holocaust more closely and read more. They saw in the examples of Nazi and Jew a mad paradox of discipline. On the one hand discipline, a vital acquisition in our drift from caves to cities, was put at the service of our most atavistic instincts. If the Nazis used discipline, presumably the mark and tool of civilization, as an instrument of savage massacre, the Jews, contrary to its preservative function, seemed to use it in the passive acceptance of their own annihilation. Discipline to destroy others. Discipline to facilitate ones own destruction. Neither could be allowed again and the thoughtful, many of them writers, many of them Jewish writers, began to look harder for alternatives.

The artist who is also a Jew has a historical step on the field. His preoccupation with discipline is as much a part of his racial as of his professional heritage. According to the legend, before God gave his Law to the Israelites he went among all the other nations and asked of each, "Will you accept my Torah, my Law?" All refused it. At this, God came to Israel and asked, "Will ye accept the Torah?" They inquired, "What is written therein?" He answered, "Six hundred and thirteen commandments." And they replied, "All that the Lord has spoken we will do and we will hear." As Morris Bober would say, others had more sense; the Jews accepted. They were "The Chosen People," a very mixed blessing indeed, for it meant that in exchange for the most precious gift in God's possession, "the future world," the Jews had bound themselves to the 613 commandments—ethical rules, social duties, religious beliefs, dietary regulations, etc. And as Mark Zborowski points out in *Life Is with People,* his classic study of the East European shtetl (the smalltown Jewish community), "All life was oriented toward rigorous fulfillment of the commandments." Freud offers in *Moses and Monotheism* another explanation for the renunciatory character of Judaism —penitential submission to the hated father, "the consciousness of guilt because of that hostility, the bad conscience because one had sinned against God and continued so to sin." But the result is the same, and the consequences, though less prominent, are still very much in evidence. Judaism is a religion of what Freud calls "instinctual renunciation," and Jews pride themselves on their restraint, their self-control, their future-orientation that enables them to abstain from immediate gratification in the interest of long-range goals. In exchange for the blessings of "the future life" they will accept the Yoke of the Law or any other yoke that promises a brighter future, particularly *fur der kinder*. Those who seek to understand, like Jesus Ortiz, the assistant to Edward Wallant's Pawnbroker, the secret of Jewish worldly success, must begin here. The Jew will prepare, principally with education; he will endure, and he will wait. He will complain interminably about the yoke of his endurance, but he revels in the yoke as he revels in his complaints, for he interprets his renunciation as a mark of higher spirituality; and in terms of success as we habitually measure it, it pays off.

This is the heritage of the Jew and the Jewish author, and Jewish fiction is a window to it. Andre Schwarz-Bart's *The Last of the Just* (an unhappily forgotten book) logs the shamanic initiation of a latter day Just Man in search of his soul and his mission. Wallant's *The Pawnbroker*, tale of a concentration camp survivor, studies a defensive renunciation of feeling tantamount to death. Bellow's "heroes," particularly Joseph (*Dangling Man*) and Henderson, grope their way out of chaos toward order, accommodation, and discipline. "Hurray for regular hours!" shouts the no longer dangling man in the book's last lines. "And for the supervision of the spirit! Long live regimentation!" And Philip Roth, the hopelessly exceptional rule-maker, brings the tradition —along with a variety of others—to a delightfully agonizing (what could be more Jewish?) counter-climax in *Portnoy's Complaint*. Having lived through the 50s, not to mention the 40s and part of the 30s, with his eternal Jewish earth mother, goddess of fear, inhibition, repression, and constipation, Portnoy has had it up to there (yes there!) with restrictions, and with the orgiastic fury of the rebel he lights out for the territory of the female crotch: he ain't been there before.

But among Jewish writers none is more provocatively or more habitually concerned with the subject of discipline than Bernard Malamud. And the two novels he wrote between 1950 and 1959, *The Natural* (1952) and *The Assistant* (1957), bear the still tender scars of World War II. Both probe the animal nature of man, reveal a fearful mistrust of instinctual behavior, and struggle toward an answer in discipline and love. Discipline not at the expense of others, not at the price of self; but discipline in the service of others and toward a fuller realization of self.

The Natural is a baseball story, but beneath the uniform it is a mythic tale of pride, impulse, guilt, self-destruction, and the failure of self-control. Roy Hobbs is a congenital bad-ball hitter, a Knight who chases the wrong women and the wrong ideals even more persistently than he chases the wrong pitches; and though he gets away with both pursuits for a while, in the end, as inevitably he must, he pays. Roy's sin is hubris. He wants too much and he wants it for himself. His ambition, as he audaciously announces on his "Day," is "to become the greatest there ever was in the game." His fans feared the brash procla- mation "might tempt the wrath of some mighty powerful ghosts," as ultimately it does, but his dream is more than audacious. More dam- agingly it is aggressive, a goal reached over the fallen bodies of com- petitors, each of whom looms not as a man but as an obstacle, and each of whom is clearly associated with the figure of the father, whom Roy did sometimes "want to skull." The inevitable litter of the parricide dream are guilt, self-hatred, and the impulse to self-destruction, and the habitual accidents and blunders that trip the questing Knight at the door of every chapel are not the inexplicable mysteries he imagines. Nor are they the fortuitous agents of a hypostatic fate. Ultimately we make our own fate, and Roy makes his of the symptomatic "accidents" that cloak his deepest needs. The premature celebration of the pennant is an act of hubris that tempts fate, but fate is inert. It will not respond to mere temptation; it must be met. The compulsive gluttony with which he "celebrates" and which cuts him down just before the crucial last series with the second place Pirates is pathological. It at once feeds his craving for self-annihilation and serves as a misguided attempt to satisfy still another buried hunger, a longing for expiation and purifi- cation. What Roy has not yet learned is that love and dedication to the needs of the larger group—the family, the team, mankind—are the true grail, not the triple devils of fame, wealth, and beauty he self-destruc- tively pursues.

In the end he does locate the true grail in the person of the un- beautiful Iris and his child inside her, but it is too late. Although at last he has glimpsed the proper dream—"suffering," Iris had told him, "teaches us to want the right things"—he lacks the discipline, the habit of renunciation that builds a future and separates the successful grail Knights from those who strew the way. And that same failure obscures the dream itself. Roy is, at the end as at the start, a bad-ball hitter, a man who in his crying need for redemption cannot escape the impulse to overreach. Midway through the final game of the season, the playoff on which all depends, he moves to renounce the sellout he had agreed to in exchange for the temptress Memo Paris and the financial security she demands. We pay for our sins, however, often and ironically in the very act of inadequate atonement, and Roy, who should have been content with the fourth ball that would have kept the team alive, lunges for it instead—and strikes out. Hubris has to an extent yielded to redemption as his principal motivation, but bad habits, like corrupt goals, do not die with an expiatory gesture of the will; they must be gradually and painfully burned away. Even at the last he was thinking of himself—"only a homer with himself scoring the winning run would truly redeem him"; still he lacked the discipline to moderate his goals and to subordinate personal gain to larger dreams. The result is as familiar as it is inevitable: symbolic murder of another father figure, Pop Fisher, the team's manager to whom the pennant is almost literally a matter of life and death, and for Roy failure on triumph's edge.

What we need are the right goals, "the right things" which suffering teaches us to want, possible, non-destructive things like love and service and self-sacrifice. The price is discipline, self-control, the capacity for renunciation, for we live in a world where homemade fate smacks its lips around the corner and where our own aggressive impulses, plaguing guilt and self-hatred chase us up the street, our heads turned back, stumbling into its arms. Roy Hobbs learns the lesson too late, and when his sellout is exposed and the newsboy begs him to "Say it ain't true, Roy . . . he wanted to say it wasn't but couldn't, and he lifted his hands to his face and wept many bitter tears."

Only the most obstinately literal-minded will deny that *The Natural* is deliberately patterned along the lines of the mythic grail quest. It is Sir Percival at the bat. Roy plays, appropriately, for the Knights, and wields a phallic bat affectionately dubbed "Wonderboy," with which, in his first professional game he knocks the cover off the ball and brings the rain to the drought-parched stadium. This is good clean academic fun, but at times the mythic trappings become somewhat cumbersome, weighing the characters down, obscuring their humanity, and occasionally pulling the story in embarrassingly unplotted directions. Malamud's next and probably finest novel, *The Assistant,* likewise shows the author's unashamed familiarity with the stuff of myth and ritual: it is a fusion of initiation rite and initiatory quest. But Malamud is more at home in a Jewish grocery store than he is on the ballfield, and the dressing is mixed to suit the salad, not the other way around. What Malamud wants to say determines how, when, and whether he will employ the materials of rite and myth; there is little if any pull in the opposite direction.

"Initiation lies at the core of any genuine human life," writes Mircea Eliade in *Rites and Symbols of Initiation.* And this is true for two reasons.

> The first is that any genuine human life implies profound 'death and resurrection.' The second is that, whatever degree of fulfillment it may have brought him, at a certain moment every man sees his life as a failure. This vision does not arise from a moral judgment made on his past, but from an obscure feeling that he has missed his vocation; that he has betrayed the best that was in him. In such moments of total crisis, only one hope seems to offer any issue—the hope of beginning life over again. This means, in short, that the man undergoing such a crisis dreams of new, regenerated life, fully realized and significant. . . . Such a renewal is the result of every genuine religious conversion.

Eliade's description of the initiate's crisis reads like the constitution of a club to which we all belong, but Frank Alpine, the Assistant, could make just claims to chairmanship. The account fits him with uncanny precision but for one point: his vision of failure does arise, at least in part, from a moral judgment on his past. Frank is trapped in an endless circle of uncertain origin but proved result. Like Roy Hobbs he wants too much too soon. Lacking a clear sense of where he is going, he is afflicted with a compulsive over-eagerness to arrive. He is the drowning man who, by lunging at what at least may be driftwood, only succeeds in pushing it further away:

> I work like a mule for what I want [he tells the Jewish grocer, Morris Bober], and just when it looks like I am going to get it I make some kind of a stupid move, and everything that is just about nailed down tight blows up in my face. . . .
> With me one wrong thing leads to another and it ends in a trap. I want the moon so all I get is cheese.

Alpine's trap is a fatal circle of guilt, recrimination, and failure. An impatient, often criminal act leads to guilt. Self-hatred born of guilt demands punishment in the form of another self-destructive gesture which adds to the weight of guilt, renews the demand for punishment, engenders another crime, and so on.

The only way out of the trap is through the definition of clearer and nobler goals and the acquisition of the eminently Jewish talent for renunciatory staying power, for the self-discipline that makes such goals attainable. The book plots the assistant's initiation under the tutelage and guidance of Morris Bober, the aging, and chronically suffering Jewish grocer, and of Bober's daughter Helen, the guilt-ridden dreamer with whom he falls in love (The story of Jacob and Rachel floats just beneath the surface). Frank begins to work in Bober's dismal store as an act of expiation. In a mad vision he had imagined himself destined for greatness in a life of crime, and the paupered Morris Bober, as both their lucks would have it, had been his first victim. Service in the store, then, begins as atonement—twelve hours a day, seven days a week virtually without pay—but it gradually develops into something more. The store is in effect the cabin, or cave (it is variously described as a "cave" and a "tomb"), where the tribal initiate dies out of the old life in order to begin a new one as a full-blown member of the tribe. The "tribe" in this case is of course the Jews, the Rabbi or priest is Morris Bober (a bobo Moses or Martin Buber), the store's ledgers the Holy Books, and the inevitable apron the prayer shawl. There is no need to insist on these parallels. The point is unmistakable. Frank Alpine, the restless Italian drifter, undergoes through the imposed discipline of the store, through conversations with and the example of the infinitely enduring grocer, and for the love of his employer's daughter, a process of initiatory *rediscovery*. "The perilous journey [of the hero]," observes Joseph Campbell in *The Hero with a Thousand Faces*, "was a labor not of attainment but of reattainment, not discovery but rediscovery. The godly powers sought and dangerously won are revealed to have been within the heart of the hero all the time." Frank Alpine undergoes the painful process of rediscovery, of locating that better self he knows lies buried inside him beneath the dirt of his compulsive behavior. He does not become a Jew so much as he discovers what Malamud elsewhere affirms: that in an important sense "all men are Jews."

The store confines him, restricts his movements, and inhibits his impulses. The grocer teaches him the habit of endurance with hope, interprets for him the Law his people received on Mt. Sinai (Morris is the English equivalent for Moses, and the name Alpine may be intended to suggest that Frank too must climb a mountain to make his Covenant). He teaches him the duties and ethical strictures that separate man from beast (Bober from Alpine at this point) and for which we must suffer; to suffer for the Law is to suffer for others. "What I like to know," demands Alpine almost defiantly, "is what is a Jew anyway?" "The important thing," replies Bober, "is the Torah. This is the Law —a Jew must believe in the Law. . . . This means to do what is right, to be honest, to be good. . . .

> 'I think other religions have those ideas too,' Frank said. 'But tell me why is it that the Jews suffer so damn much, Morris? It seems to me that they like to suffer, don't they?'
>
> 'Do you like to suffer? They suffer because they are Jews.'
>
> 'That's what I mean, they suffer more than they have to.'
>
> 'If you live, you suffer. Some people suffer more, but not because they want. But I think if a Jew don't suffer for the Law, he will suffer for nothing.'
>
> 'What do you suffer for, Morris?' Frank said.
>
> 'I suffer for you,' Morris said calmly.
>
> Frank laid his knife down on the table. His mouth ached. 'What do you mean?'
>
> 'I mean you suffer for me.'
>
> The clerk let it go at that.

Alpine is at this point still in darkness, but he is brought nearer the light by the grocer's daughter. Helen provides the assistant with a more specific goal, with something to suffer for—herself and her love. And she offers more specific instruction, bred of her own torment, on the question of means. Helen had yielded her body without love to another man. The price, paid and repaid daily, was guilt and self-hatred, but unlike Frank she knows the way out of the encircling trap of transgression and self-hatred.

She tells him he must develop discipline. The idea fascinates him; it touches the root of his need:

> Often since the time Helen had been in his room he had recalled her remark that he must discipline himself and wondered why he had been so moved by the word, why it should now bang around in his head like a stick against a drum. With the idea of self-control came the feeling of the beauty of it—the beauty of a person being able to do things the way he wanted to, to do good if he wanted . . .

But instruction alone is not adequate to the needs of conversion. Frank Alpine is, as he repeatedly insists, not the man he once was. He has changed; but not completely. He is not yet in control of his urges, his hungers, his aggressive and self-destructive impulses. The lessons of *The Natural* are the lessons of *The Assistant*. Habits nourished a lifetime do not readily loosen their bite. Nor can past sins be brushed away with a flick of the will; as Roy Hobbs learns to his grief, they may begin to draw blood in the very act of imperfect atonement. Ironically, the grocer catches Alpine with his hand in the till not when he is stealing but when he is borrowing back a fraction of the money he has finally begun to repay in a futile attempt at absolution.

To die out of the old life and be reborn is not the work of days; "to do what he had to do he needed years." But Frank is at once a wiser and a more fortunate man than Roy Hobbs. He learns what he must do and he is given the chance to do it. In Malamud's world, however, full recognition and reversal come only after all external supports have been removed; they come when the assistant has lost all outward assistance and is thrown back entirely on his own resources. Instruction is a necessary first step, but ultimately the initiate must face the dark alone. Not until his theft is discovered and he is evicted from the store like Adam from a dubious Eden, and not until his importunate love drives Helen all but irredeemably beyond his reach does he arrive at a full understanding of the tragic pattern of his life and the basic goodness —and Jewishness—of his buried self. This is the hero's moment of reattainment, of rediscovery.

When Bober's death removes another prop, Alpine has his chance. He has worked his way back into the store during the grocer's illness; Morris had never mentioned the thefts to either his wife or daughter, and the store is the family's only sustenance. It is also Frank's only hope, and his use of it indicates that like the initiate he is, he has found his personal identity in the identity of the tribe. Alpine, like Yakov Bok, the hero of Malamud's *The Fixer*, discovers himself through the private recapitulation of the sufferings, trials, and history of the larger group. And like Bok he discovers that his personal identity is indistinguishable from his group identity: one is discovered—or rediscovered—in the process of discovering the other and is in fact the other. But he can touch his tribal and thereby his personal soul only when forced back entirely upon and into himself, for the group soul sleeps in the private spirit and is discovered only in the ordeal of isolated responsibility. When everything else is gone, we discover ourselves and our intimate connection with, and responsibility to, everything else.

Morris Bober has died, his dream of a college education for his daughter apparently buried in his plain wooden coffin. To give his life meaning, Helen knows she must in some way, though it will take years, earn her degree. By quietly and self-effacingly dedicating himself to the realization of that dream, by working day and night, without encouragement but with discipline and with love, to send Helen through school, Frank breaks out of the circle of his personal hell and enters the divine circle of service. Morris gave to Frank his virtually barren store and the invaluable tradition of suffering for others with discipline, endurance, and with hope. With these gifts Frank will see to Helen's education, one purpose of which is to give posthumous meaning to the grocer's pathetic life. Thus each life gains meaning by what it gives to the next, and the divine circle of the Law, of doing for others, curves back on the point of its origin: the meaning of Morris Bober's life.

When at the end Frank is circumcised and becomes a Jew he ritually confirms the completed act of psychic conversion. But the event is more than mere ritual confirmation. The fact that it takes place in April, and that he becomes a Jew "after Passover" is particularly meaningful in the context of the season symbolism of the novel. The psychic and seasonal setting of the action is winter, the Sacred Time of the initiation of novices, and the eager anticipation of spring, the season of life, of renewal, weighs heavily on everyone's mind. To Helen it represents the season of fulfillment through love, release from the winter of her sexual guilt; and it is on a "warmish" "spring-like" late February night that Frank precipitously takes her on the grass. It is also a premature celebration of spring that kills Morris Bober who insists on shovelling snow without a coat on the last day of March and contracts pneumonia for his lone impulsive gesture. "Tomorrow is April," he reminds his wife. "What kind of winter can be in April?" The last of March is not April, but when Frank converts it is April, the season of renewal, and it is after Passover, the season of deliverance. The act is as appropriate as its timing. The circumcision is the mark of the Jew's covenant with God—his acceptance of the Yoke of the Law and his submission to a disciplined life dedicated to the fulfillment of God's commandments. And it is also a painful "ceremonial mutilation," a symbolic substitute for castration that, in Freud's view, signalled the initiate's submission to the father's will. Frank Alpine has submitted to the father's will, to the will of Morris Bober and to the will of his own conscience—the father as superego. What Roy Hobbs childishly destroys, Frank Alpine maturely accepts. But perhaps most importantly, he signals his acceptance in an act symbolic of sexual renunciation. He has been painfully transformed from "uncircumcised Dog!", from undisciplined beast, to circumcised Jew, the "man of stern morality."

Chronology of Important Dates

(See "Works of Bernard Malamud" for publication dates)

Personal

1914   Born Brooklyn, New York, on April 26, to Max and Bertha Fidel-
            man Malamud

1928–32   Student at Erasmus High School, Brooklyn

1936   B.A., City College of New York

1942   M.A., Columbia University; thesis on Hardy's *The Dynasts*

1945   Married to Ann de Chiara on November 6

1947   Son, Paul, born

1952   Daughter, Janna, born

1956   Lived in Rome and traveled in Europe

1963   Traveled in England and Italy

1965   Traveled in U.S.S.R., France, and Spain

1968   Trip to Israel in March

Professional

1940–49   Taught English in New York City evening high schools

1949–61   Oregon State University, Corvallis, Department of English, in-
            structor to associate professor

1961–   Bennington (Vt.) College, Division of Language and Literature

1966–68   Harvard University, visiting lecturer

Awards and Recognition

1956–57   *Partisan Review* fellowship in fiction

1958   Rosenthal Foundation Award of the National Institute of Arts and
            Letters for *The Assistant*

Daroff Memorial Fiction Award of the Jewish Book Council of America for *The Assistant*

Rockefeller grant

1959 National Book Award for fiction for *The Magic Barrel*

Ford Foundation Fellowship in humanities and arts

1964 Member of National Institute of Arts and Letters

1967 Member of American Academy of Arts and Sciences

National Book Award for fiction for *The Fixer*

Pulitzer Prize in literature for *The Fixer*

Notes on the Editors and Contributors

JOYCE FIELD, co-editor of this volume, teaches at Purdue University. She has published in *Modern Fiction Studies, The Journal of Popular Culture,* and the *Journal of Reading.* She was co-editor of *Bernard Malamud and the Critics.*

LESLIE FIELD, co-editor of this volume, teaches at Purdue University. He has published in various journals, was co-editor of *Thomas Wolfe's Purdue Speech: Writing and Living* and *All the King's Men: A Critical Handbook,* and editor of *Thomas Wolfe: Three Decades of Criticism.* He was also co-editor of *Bernard Malamud and the Critics.*

JOHN ALEXANDER ALLEN teaches at Hollins College, Virginia. His poems have appeared in many periodicals and are collected in *The Lean Divider.* He has published a thematic anthology, *Hero's Way: Contemporary Poems in the Mythic Tradition,* and his criticism has appeared in a variety of journals, including *Shakespeare Quarterly.*

RICHARD ASTRO teaches and is an administrator at Oregon State University. He has edited *Steinbeck: The Man and His Work* and *Hemingway in Our Time,* and has written *Steinbeck and Ricketts: The Shaping of a Novelist.* He has also contributed essays to various journals, including *Modern Fiction Studies* and the *Windsor Review.*

SAM BLUEFARB teaches at the Los Angeles Harbor College in Wilmington, California. He has published *The Escape Motif in the American Novel: Mark Twain to Richard Wright* and he has also published widely in a variety of journals. He is presently at work on a novel.

WILLIAM FREEDMAN teaches at the University of Haifa, Israel. He has written on English literature and Jewish fiction in journals such as *Modern Language Quarterly* and *Modern Fiction Studies.* His poems have appeared in many periodicals and he has just completed a book on Laurence Sterne.

NORMAN SHELDON GREBSTEIN teaches at the State University of New York at Binghamton, where he has been director of the Graduate Program in English. Among his other writings, he has published *Sinclair Lewis, Perspectives in Contemporary Criticism,* and *Hemingway's Craft.*

GERALD HOAG teaches at Wichita State University. In addition to his work on Malamud, he has written on Coleridge, James, and Virginia Woolf.

CYNTHIA OZICK is a novelist, short story writer, and critic. She has published *Trust,* a novel, and *The Pagan Rabbi and Other Stories.* She was the recipient in 1973 of the Award of Literature of the American Academy of Arts and Letters of the National Institute of Arts and Letters.

SANFORD PINSKER teaches at Franklin and Marshall College, Lancaster, Pennsylvania. In addition to his book, *The Schlemiel as Metaphor: Studies in the Yiddish and American Jewish Novel,* he has published essays in a variety of journals, including *Critique,* the *Saturday Review,* and *Modern Language Quarterly.*

RENEE WINEGARTEN, literary critic and essayist, who lives in England, is a frequent contributor to journals on both sides of the Atlantic. Her book, *Writers and Revolution,* is to be published by Franklin Watts in 1974.

Works of Bernard Malamud

Stories

"Benefit Performance," *Threshold*, 3 (February 1943), 20–22.

"The Place Is Different Now," *American Preface*, 8 (Spring 1943), 230–242.

"Cost of Living," *Harper's Bazaar*, 84 (March 1950), 142ff.

"The First Seven Years," *Partisan Review*, 17 (September–October 1950), 661–671.

"The Prison," *Commentary*, 10 (September 1950), 252–255.

"The Death of Me," *World Review*, 26 (April 1951), 48–51.

"The Bill," *Commentary*, 11 (April 1951), 355–358.

"An Apology," *Commentary*, 12 (November 1951), 460–464.

"The Loan," *Commentary*, 14 (July 1952), 56–59.

"Girl of My Dreams," *American Mercury*, 76 (January 1953), 62–71.

"The Magic Barrel," *Partisan Review*, 21 (November 1954), 587–603.

"The Mourners," *Discovery*, 5 (January 1955), 37–95.

"Angel Levine," *Commentary*, 20 (September 1955), 534–540.

"A Summer's Reading," *New Yorker*, 32 (September 22, 1956), 143–150.

"The Last Mohican," *Partisan Review*, 25 (Spring 1958), 175–196.

"Behold the Key," *Commentary*, 25 (May 1958), 416–427.

"The Maid's Shoes," *Partisan Review*, 26 (Winter 1959), 32–44.

"Thanks for Nothing," excerpt from *A New Life*, *Esquire*, 56 (August 1961), 101–112.

"A Long Ticket for Isaac," first published in John Kuehl, ed., *Creative Writing and Rewriting: Contemporary American Novelists at Work*. New York: Appleton, 1967, pp. 71–91.

"Still Life," *Partisan Review*, 29 (Winter 1962), 95–112.

"Suppose a Wedding," *New Statesman*, 65 (February 8, 1963), 198–200.

"The Jewbird," *Reporter*, 28 (April 11, 1963), 33–36.

"Life Is Better Than Death," *Esquire*, 59 (May 1963), 78–79.

"Naked Nude," *Playboy*, 10 (August 1963), 48–50.

"Black Is My Favorite Color," *Reporter*, 29 (July 18, 1963), 43–44.

"The Refugee," *Saturday Evening Post*, 236 (September 14, 1963), 38–39.

"Choice of Profession," *Commentary*, 36 (September 1963), 235–241.

"Take Pity," *The Magic Barrel*. New York: Farrar, Straus and Cudahy, 1958.

"A Pimp's Revenge," *Playboy,* 14 (February 1968), 68–70ff.
"Man in the Drawer," *Atlantic,* 221 (April 1968), 70–78ff.
"My Son the Murderer," *Esquire,* 70 (November 1968), 102–104.
"Pictures of Fidelman," *Atlantic,* 222 (December 1968), 63–70.
"An Exorcism," *Harper's,* 237 (December 1968), 76–89.
"Glass Blower of Venice," *Pictures of Fidelman.* New York: Straus and Giroux, 1969.
"God's Wrath," *Atlantic,* 229 (February 1972), 59–62.
"Talking Horse," *Atlantic,* 230 (August 1972), 27–34.
"The Letter," *Esquire,* 78 (August 1972), 136.
"The Silver Crown," *Playboy,* 19 (December 1972), 120–122ff.
"Notes from a Lady at a Dinner Party," *Harper's,* 246 (February 1973), 86–90.
"Rembrandt's Hat," *New Yorker,* 49 (March 17, 1973), 34–39.
"In Retirement," *Atlantic,* 231 (March 1973), 48–52.

Novels

The Natural. New York: Harcourt, Brace, 1952.
The Assistant. New York: Farrar, Straus & Cudahy, 1957.
A New Life. New York: Farrar, Straus & Cudahy, 1961.
The Fixer. New York: Farrar, Straus & Giroux, 1966.
Pictures of Fidelman: An Exhibition. Farrar, Straus & Giroux. 1969. (A picaresque novel.)
The Tenants. New York: Farrar, Straus & Giroux, 1971.

Collections of Short Stories

The Magic Barrel. New York: Farrar, Straus & Cudahy, 1958.
"The First Seven Years," "The Mourners," "The Girl of My Dreams," "Angel Levine," "Behold the Key," "Take Pity," "The Prison," "The Lady of the Lake," "A Summer's Reading," "The Bill," "The Last Mohican," "The Loan," "The Magic Barrel."
Idiots First. New York: Farrar, Straus, 1963.
"Idiots First," "Black Is My Favorite Color," "Still Life," "The Death of Me," "A Choice of Profession," "Life Is Better Than Death," "The Jewbird," "Naked Nude," "The Cost of Living," "The Maid's Shoes," "Suppose a Wedding," "The German Refugee."
Pictures of Fidelman: An Exhibition. New York: Farrar, Straus & Giroux, 1969.
"Last Mohican," "Still Life," "Naked Nude," "A Pimp's Revenge," "Pictures of the Artist" (originally published as "Pictures of Fidelman"), "Glass Blower of Venice."
Rembrandt's Hat. New York: Farrar, Straus & Giroux, 1973.
"The Silver Crown," "Man in the Drawer," "The Letter," "In Retirement," "Rembrandt's Hat," "Notes from a Lady at a Dinner Party," "My Son the Murderer," "Talking Horse."

Selected Bibliography

This bibliography consists of an alphabetical list of the more important biographical, critical, and scholarly studies of Bernard Malamud. Where more than one essay appears by the same author, the entries are listed in chronological order. We have omitted foreign criticism, unpublished theses or dissertations, transient reviews, and routine discussions in encyclopedias, handbooks, and histories of literature. Our bibliography covers materials through the fall of 1973. Essays and excerpts of books which appear in our earlier collection (*Bernard Malamud and the Critics*, N. Y., 1970) are noted by a single asterisk; those which appear in this present collection are noted by a double asterisk.

**Allen, John Alexander. "The Promised End: Bernard Malamud's *The Tenants*," *Hollins Critic*, 8:5 (1971), 1–15.

Allen, Walter. "War and Post War: American," in his *The Modern Novel in Britain and the United States* (New York: E. P. Dutton & Co., Inc., 1964), 330–332.

Alley, Alvin D. and Hugh Agee. "Existential Heroes: Frank Alpine and Rabbit Angstrom," *Ball State University Forum*, 9:1 (Winter 1968), 3–5.

*Alter, Robert. "Bernard Malamud: Jewishness as Metaphor," in his *After the Tradition: Essays on Modern Jewish Writing* (New York: E. P. Dutton & Co., Inc., 1969), pp. 116–130. Appeared earlier as "Malamud as Jewish Writer" in *Commentary*, 42:3 (September 1966), 71–76.

———. "Updike, Malamud, and the Fire This Time," *Commentary*, 54:4 (October 1972), 68–74.

**Astro, Richard. "In the Heart of the Valley: Bernard Malamud's *A New Life*." An original essay in Leslie A. and Joyce W. Field, eds., *Bernard Malamud: A Collection of Critical Essays* (Englewood Cliffs, New Jersey: Prentice-Hall, Inc., 1974), pp. 143–155.

Bailey, Anthony. "Insidious Patience," *Commonweal*, 66 (June 21, 1957), 307–308.

Barsness, John A. "*A New Life:* The Frontier Myth in Perspective," *Western American Literature*, 3 (Winter 1969), 297–302.

Baumbach, Jonathan. "The Economy of Love: The Novels of Bernard Malamud," *Kenyon Review*, 25 (Summer 1963), 438–457.

——. "All Men Are Jews: *The Assistant* by Bernard Malamud," in his *The Landscape of Nightmare: Studies in the Contemporary American Novel* (New York: New York University Press, 1965), pp. 101–122.

——. "Malamud's Heroes," *Commonweal*, 85 (October 1966), 97–98.

*Bellman, Samuel I. "Women, Children, and Idiots First: The Transformation Psychology of Bernard Malamud," *Critique*, 7:2 (Winter 1964–65), 123–138.

——. "Henry James' 'The Madonna of the Future' and Two Modern Parallels," *California English Journal*, 1:3 (1965), 47–53.

——. "Fathers and Sons in Jewish Fiction," *Congress Bi-Weekly*, 34:10 (May 22, 1967), 18–20.

*Bluefarb, Sam. "Bernard Malamud: The Scope of Caricature," *English Journal*, 53:5 (May 1964), 319–326, 335.

**——. "The Syncretism of Bernard Malamud." An original essay in Leslie A. and Joyce W. Field, eds., *Bernard Malamud: A Collection of Critical Essays* (Englewood Cliffs, New Jersey: Prentice-Hall, Inc., 1974), pp. 72–79.

Bryant, Jerry H. *The Open Decision—The Contemporary American Novel and Its Intellectual Background* (New York: Free Press, 1970), pp. 324–340.

Burrows, David J. "The American Past in Malamud's *A New Life*," in David J. Burrows, *et al.*, *Private Dealings: Eight Modern American Writers* (Stockholm: Almqvist & Wiksell, 1970), pp. 86–94.

Ducharme, Robert. "Structure and Content in Malamud's *Pictures of Fidelman*," *Connecticut Review*, 5:1 (1971), 26–36.

Dupee, F. W. "Malamud: The Uses and Abuses of Commitment," in his *The King of the Cats and Other Remarks on Writers and Writing* (New York: Farrar, Straus, & Giroux, 1965), pp. 156–163.

*Eigner, Edwin M. "Malamud's Use of the Quest Romance," *Genre*, 1:1 (January 1968), 55–74.

Elman, Richard J. "Malamud on Campus," *Con. ʾonweal*, 75.5 (October 27, 1961), 114–115.

Featherstone, Joseph. "Bernard Malamud," *Atlantic Monthly*, 219 (March 1967), 95–98.

Fiedler, Leslie A. "Malamud: The Commonplace as Absurd," in his *No! in Thunder* (Boston, Beacon Press, 1960), 101–110.

——. *Love and Death in the American Novel* (New York: Dell Publishing Co., 1966), pp. 492–493.

**Field, Leslie A. "Portrait of the Artist as *Schlemiel*." An original essay in Leslie A. and Joyce W. Field, eds., *Bernard Malamud: A Collection of Critical Essays* (Englewood Cliffs, New Jersey: Prentice-Hall, Inc., 1974), pp. 117–129.

—— and Joyce W., eds. *Bernard Malamud and the Critics* (New York: New York University Press, 1970).

**——. "An Interview with Bernard Malamud." An original essay in Leslie A. and Joyce W. Fields, eds., *Bernard Malamud: A Collection of*

Critical Essays (Englewood Cliffs, New Jersey: Prentice-Hall, Inc., 1974), pp. 8–17.

Fineman, Irving. "The Image of the Jew in our Fiction," *Tradition*, 8:4 (Winter 1966), 19–47.

Francis, H. E. "Bernard Malamud's Everyman," *Midstream*, 7:1 (Winter 1961), 93–97.

Frankel, Haskel. Interview with Bernard Malamud, *Saturday Review*, 49:37 (September 10, 1966), 39–40.

Freedman, William. "American Jewish Fiction: So What's the Big Deal?" *Chicago Review*, 19:1 (1966), 90–107.

**———. "From Bernard Malamud, With Discipline and With Love," in Warren French, ed., *The Fifties: Fiction, Poetry, Drama* (Deland, Fla.: Everett/Edwards, 1971), 133–143.

*Friedberg, Maurice. "History and Imagination: Two Views of the Beiliss Case," *Midstream*, 12:9 (November 1966), 72–76.

*Friedman, Alan Warren. "Bernard Malamud: The Hero as Schnook," *Southern Review*, 4:4 (October 1968), 927–944.

Glicksberg, Charles I. "A Jewish American Literature?" *Southwest Review*, 53:2 (Spring 1968), 196–205.

*Goldman, Mark. "Bernard Malamud's Comic Vision and the Theme of Identity," *Critique*, 7:2 (Winter 1964–65), 92–109.

Goodheart, Eugene. "Fantasy and Reality," *Midstream*, 7:4 (Autumn 1961), 102–105.

Goodman, Oscar B. "There Are Jews Everywhere," *Judaism*, 19:3 (Summer 1970), 283–294.

Graber, Ralph S. "Baseball in American Fiction," *English Journal*, 56:8 (November 1967), 1107–1114.

**Grebstein, Sheldon Norman. "Bernard Malamud and the Jewish Movement," in Irving Malin, ed., *Contemporary American-Jewish Literature: Critical Essays* (Bloomington, Ind.: Indiana University Press, 1973), pp. 175–212.

Greenfield, Josh. "Innocence and Punishment," *Book Week* (September 11, 1966), pp. 1, 10.

Greiff, Louis K. "Quest and Defeat in *The Natural*," *Thoth*, 8:1 (Winter 1967), 23–34.

Gunn, Giles B. "Bernard Malamud and the High Cost of Living," in Nathan A. Scott, ed., *Adversity and Grace: Studies in Recent American Literature* (Chicago: University of Chicago Press, 1968), pp. 59–85.

Guttman, Allen. *The Jewish Writer in America—Assimilation and the Crisis of Identity* (New York: Oxford University Press, 1971), pp. 112–120.

*Hassan, Ihab. "The Qualified Encounter: Three Novels by Buechner, Malamud, and Ellison," in his *Radical Innocence: Studies in the Contemporary American Novel* (Princeton, New Jersey: Princeton University Press, 1961; Harper & Row, 1966), pp. 161–168.

*Hays, Peter L. "The Complex Pattern of Redemption in *The Assistant*," *Centennial Review*, 13:2 (Spring 1969), 200–214.

Hicks, Granville. "Generation of the Fifties: Malamud, Gold, and Updike," in Nona Balakian and Charles Simmons, eds., *The Creative Present: Notes on Contemporary American Fiction* (New York: Doubleday & Co., 1963), pp. 217–237.

———. "One Man to Stand for Six Million," *Saturday Review*, 49:37 (September 10, 1966), 37–39.

———. *Literary Horizons: A Quarter Century of American Fiction* (New York: New York University Press, 1970), pp. 65–83.

Hill, John S. "Malamud's 'The Lady of the Lake'—A Lesson in Rejection," *The University Review-Kansas City*, 36 (Winter 1969), 149–150.

**Hoag Gerald. "Malamud's Trial: *The Fixer* and the Critics," *Western Humanities Review*, 24:1 (Winter 1970), 1–12.

Hollander, John. "To Find the Westward Path," *Partisan Review*, 29:1 (Winter 1962), 137–139.

*Hoyt, Charles Alva. "Bernard Malamud and the New Romanticism," in Harry T. Moore, ed., *Contemporary American Novelists* (Carbondale, Ill.: Southern Illinois University Press, 1964), pp. 65–79.

Hyman, Stanley E. "A New Life for a Good Man," *The New Leader*, 44:34 (October 2, 1961), 24–25. Reprinted in Richard Kostelanetz, ed., *On Contemporary Literature* (New York: Avon Books, 1964), pp. 442–446; and in Stanley E. Hyman, *Standards: A Chronicle of Books for Our Time* (New York: Horizon Press, 1966).

Kazin, Alfred. "Fantasist of the Ordinary," *Commentary*, 24:1 (July 1957), 89–92.

———. "Bernard Malamud: The Magic and the Dread," in his *Contemporaries* (Boston: Atlantic-Little, Brown & Co., 1962), pp. 202–207.

Kermode, Frank. "Bernard Malamud," *New Statesman*, 63 (March 30, 1962), 452–453.

*Klein, Marcus. "Bernard Malamud: The Sadness of Goodness," in his *After Alienation: American Novels in Mid-Century* (Cleveland: World Publishing Co., 1962), pp. 247–293.

Knopp, Josephine Z. "The Ways of Mentschlekhkayt: A Study of Morality in Some Fiction of Bernard Malamud and Philip Roth," *Tradition*, 13:3 (Winter 1973), 67–84.

Kort, Wesley Albert. *Shriven Selves: Religious Problems in Recent American Fiction* (Philadelphia: Fortress Press, 1972), pp. 90–115.

Kosofsky, Rita Nathalie. *Bernard Malamud: An Annotated Checklist* (Kent, Ohio: Kent State University Press, 1970).

Lamden, Lois S. "Malamud's Schemiels," in *A Modern Miscellany* (Carnegie Series in English, #11), pp. 31–42.

Leer, Norman. "Three American Novels and Contemporary Society: A Search for Commitment," *Wisconsin Studies in Contemporary Literature*, 3:3 (Fall 1962), 67–85.

―――. "The Double Theme in Malamud's Assistant: Dostoevsky with Irony," *Mosaic,* 4:3 (1971), 89–102.

Lefcowitz, Barbara F. "The *Hybris* of Neurosis: Malamud's *Pictures of Fidelman,*" *Literature and Psychology,* 20:3 (1970), 115–120.

Leibowitz, Herbert. "Malamud and the Anthropomorphic Business," *The New Republic,* 149:25 (December 21, 1963), 21–23.

Liptzin, Sol. *The Jew in American Literature* (New York: Block Publishing Co., 1966), pp. 226–228.

Ludwig, Jack. *Recent American Novelists,* University of Minnesota Pamphlets on American Writers, No. 22 (Minneapolis: University of Minnesota Press, 1962), pp. 39–41.

*Mandel, Ruth B. "Bernard Malamud's *The Assistant* and *A New Life:* Ironic Affirmation," *Critique,* 7:2 (Winter 1964–65), 110–121.

Marcus, Steven. "The Novel Again," *Partisan Review,* 29:2 (Spring 1962), 171–195.

May, Charles, E. "The Bread of Tears: Malamud's 'The Loan,' " *Studies in Short Fiction,* 7:4 (Fall (1970), 652–654.

Meeter, Glenn. *Bernard Malamud and Philip Roth: A Critical Essay* (Grand Rapids, Mich.: William B. Eerdmans Publishing Co., 1968).

*Mellard, James M. "Malamud's Novels: Four Versions of Pastoral," *Critique,* 9:2 (1967), 5–19.

―――. "Malamud's *The Assistant:* The City Novel as Pastoral," *Studies in Short Fiction,* 5:1 (Fall 1967), 1–11.

Miller, Theodore C. "The Minister and the Whore: An Examination of Bernard Malamud's *The Magic Barrel,*" *Studies in the Humanities,* 3:1 (October 1972), 43–44.

Mudrick, Marvin. "Who Killed Herzog? Or, Three American Novelists," *University of Denver Quarterly,* 1:1 (1966), 67–97. Reprinted as "Malamud, Bellow, and Roth" in his *On Culture and Literature* (New York: Horizon Press, 1970), pp. 200–230.

**Ozick, Cynthia. "Literary Blacks and Jews," *Midstream,* 18:6 (June/July 1972), 10–24.

Perrine, Laurence. "Malamud's 'Take Pity,' " *Studies in Short Fiction,* 2:1 (Fall 1964), 84–86.

Pinsker, Sanford. "Salinger, Malamud and Wallant: The Jewish Novelist's Quest," *The Reconstructionist,* 32 (November 25, 1966), 7–14.

―――. "The Achievement of Bernard Malamud," *Midwest Quarterly,* 10:4 (July 1969), 377–389.

―――. "A Note on Malamud's 'Take Pity,' " *Studies in Short Fiction,* 6:2 (Winter 1969), 212–213.

―――. "The 'Hassid' in Modern American Literature," *The Reconstructionist,* 30 (March 6, 1970), 7–15.

―――. "Christ as Revolutionary/Revolutionary as Christ: The Hero in Bernard Malamud's *The Fixer* and William Styron's *The Confessions of Nat Turner,*" *Barat Review,* 6 (1971), 29–37.

**———. "The Schlemiel as Moral Bungler—Bernard Malamud's Ironic Heroes," in his *The Schlemiel as Metaphor—Studies in the Yiddish and American Novel* (Carbondale, Ill.: Southern Illinois University Press, 1971), pp. 87–124.

Podhoretz, Norman. "Achilles in Left Field," *Commentary*, 15:3 (March 1953), 321–326.

———. "The New Nihilism in the American Novel," *Partisan Review*, 25:4 (Fall 1958), 589–590. Reprinted in his *Doings and Undoings: The Fifties and After in America* (New York: Farrar, Straus & Giroux, 1964), pp. 176–178.

Popkin, Henry. "Jewish Stories," *Kenyon Review*, 20:4 (Autumn 1958), 637–641.

Pradhan, S. V. "The Nature and Interpretation of Symbolism in Malamud's *The Assistant*," *Centennial Review*, 16 (Fall 1972), 394–407.

Pritchett, V. S. "A Pariah," *New York Review of Books*, 7:4 (September 22, 1966), 8, 10.

Raffel, Burton. "Bernard Malamud," *The Literary Review*, 13 (Winter 1969–70), 149–155.

Rahv, Philip. "Introduction," *A Malamud Reader* (New York: Farrar, Straus & Giroux, 1967), pp. vii–xiv.

Ratner, Marc L. "Style and Humanity in Malamud's Fiction," *Massachusetts Review*, 5:4 (1964), 663–683.

———. "The Humanism of Malamud's *The Fixer*," *Critique*, 9:2 (1967), 81–84.

Richey, C. W. " 'The Woman in the Dunes': A Note on Bernard Malamud's *The Tenants*," *Notes on Contemporary Literature*, 3 (January 1973), 4–5.

Richler, Mordecai. "Write, Boychick, Write," *New Statesman*, 73 (April 7, 1967), 473–474.

*Richman, Sidney. *Bernard Malamud* (New York: Twayne Publishers, Inc., 1966).

Roth, Philip. "Writing American Fiction," *Commentary*, 31 (March 1961), 223–233. Reprinted in Marcus Klein, ed., *The American Novel Since World War II* (Greenwich, Conn.: Fawcett Publications, 1969), pp. 142–158.

*Rovit, Earl H. "Bernard Malamud and the Jewish Literary Tradition," *Critique*, 3:2 (Winter–Spring 1960), 3–10.

Rupp, Richard H. "Bernard Malamud: A Party of One," in his *Celebration in Postwar American Fiction 1945–1967* (Coral Gables, Fla.: University of Miami Press, 1970), pp. 165–188.

Samuels, Charles Thomas. "The Career of Bernard Malamud," *New Republic*, 155:11 (September 1966), 19–21.

———. "The Fixer," in Gilbert A. Harrison, ed., *The Critic as Artist: Essays on Books 1920–1970* (New York: Liveright Publishing Corp., 1972), pp. 291–298.

Scholes, Robert. "Portrait of Artist as 'Escape-Goat,' " *Saturday Review*, 52 (May 10, 1969), 32–34.

*Schulz, Max F. "Bernard Malamud's Mythic Proletarians," in his *Radical Sophistication: Studies in Contemporary Jewish-American Novelists* (Athens, Ohio: Ohio University Press, 1969), pp. 56–68.

――――. "Malamud's *A New Life:* The New Wasteland of the Fifties," *Western Review* [Western New Mexico University], 6:1 (Spring 1969), 37–44.

*Shear, Walter. "Culture Conflict in *The Assistant,*" *Midwest Quarterly,* 7:4 (July 1966), 367–380.

Sheed, Wilfred. "Bernard Malamud: *Pictures of Fidelman,*" in his *The Morning After: Selected Essays and Reviews* (New York: Farrar, Straus & Giroux, 1971), pp. 59–61.

Shenker, Israel. "For Malamud It's Story," *The New York Times,* October 3, 1971, Sect. 7, pp. 20–22. Reprinted as "Bernard Malamud on Writing Fiction: an Interview by Israel Shenker," *Writer's Digest,* 52:7 (July 1972), 22–23.

Shulman, Robert. "Myth, Mr. Eliot, and the Comic Novel," *Modern Fiction Studies,* 12:4 (Winter 1966–67), 395–403.

*Siegel, Ben. "Victims in Motion: Bernard Malamud's Sad and Bitter Clowns," *Northwest Review,* 5:2 (Spring 1962), 69–80. Reprinted in Joseph J. Waldmeir, ed., *Recent American Fiction: Some Critical Views* (Boston: Houghton Mifflin Co., 1963), pp. 203–214.

Solotaroff, Theodore. "Philip Roth and the Jewish Novelists," *Chicago Review,* 13:4 (Winter 1959), 87–99. Reprinted in Irving Malin and Irwin Stark, eds., *Breakthrough: A Treasury of Contemporary American-Jewish Literature* (Philadelphia: The Jewish Publication Society of America, 1965), pp. 354–366.

*――――. "Bernard Malamud's Fiction: The Old Life and the New," *Commentary,* 33:3 (March 1962), 197–204. Reprinted in his *The Red Hot Vacuum and Other Pieces on the Writing of the Sixties* (New York: Atheneum, 1970), pp. 71–86.

Standley, Fred L. "Bernard Malamud: The Novel of Redemption," *Southern Humanities Review,* 5 (1971), 309–318.

Stanton, Robert. "Outrageous Fiction: *Crime and Punishment, The Assistant,* and *Native Son,*" *Pacific Coast Philology,* 4 (April 1969), 52–58.

Stevenson, David L. "The Activists," *Daedalus,* 92:2 (Spring 1963), 238–249.

Swados, Harvey. "The Emergence of an Artist," *Western Review,* 32 (Winter 1958), 149–151.

Tanner, Tony. "Bernard Malamud and the New Life," *Critical Quarterly,* 10 (Spring-Summer 1968), 151–168. Slightly revised and reprinted as "A New Life" in his *City of Words: American Fiction 1950–1970* (New York: Harper & Row, 1971), 322–343.

*Turner, Frederick W., III. "Myth Inside and Out: Malamud's *The Natural,*" *Novel,* 1:2 (Winter 1968), 133–139.

*Wasserman, Earl R. "*The Natural:* Malamud's World Ceres," *Centennial Review,* 9:4 (Fall 1965), 438–460.

Wechsler, Diane. "Analysis of 'The Prison' by Bernard Malamud," *English Journal,* 59:6 (September 1970), 782–784.

Wegelin, Christof. "The American Schlemiel Abroad: Malamud's Italian Stories and the End of American Innocence," *Twentieth Century Literature,* 19:2 (April 1973), 77–88.

Weinberg, Helen. "Minor American Novelists in the Activist Mode," in her *The New Novel in America: The Kafkan Mode in Contemporary Fiction* (Ithaca, New York: Cornell University Press, 1970), pp. 168–178.

Weiss, Samuel A. "Notes on Bernard Malamud," *Chicago Jewish Forum,* 21:2 (Winter 1962–63), 155–158.

————. "Passion and Purgation in Bernard Malamud," *University of Windsor Review,* 2:1 (Fall 1966), 93–99.

Wershba, Joseph. "Not Horror but 'Sadness,'" *New York Post* (September 14, 1958), p. M2.

White, Robert L. "The English Instructor as Hero: Two Novels by Roth and Malamud," *Forum* [Houston], 4 (Winter 1963), 16–22.

Widmer, Kingsley. "The American Road: The Contemporary Novel," *University of Kansas City Review,* 26:4 (June 1960), 309–317.

**Winegarten, Renee. "Malamud's Head," *Midstream,* 19:8 (October 1973), 76–79.

Wisse, Ruth R. *The Schlemiel as Modern Hero* (Chicago: University of Chicago Press, 1971), pp. 110–118.